agnes quill

an anthology of mystery

Published by SLG Publishing
PO Box 26427
San Jose, CA 95159-6427

President & Publisher: **Dan Vado**
Editor-in-chief: **Jennifer de Guzman**
Production Assistant: **Eleanor Lawson**

Cover illustration *by* **Jason Ho**
Cover and book design *by* **Erin E. Houlihan**
Production thanks: **John Green**

www.slavelabor.com
www.yaytime.com
www.agnesquill.com

Printed in Canada

Second Printing: 2007

ISBN: 1-59362-052-7
ISBN-13: 978-1-59362-052-3

AGNES QUILL

an anthology of mystery

all transcripts written by DAVE ROMAN

INTRODUCTION

The Data Analysis Keep is a community of scholars dedicated to the advancement of all things scientific, mystical, and existential. Through the activity of our field members, The Keep has collected a substantial wealth of information concerning supernatural phenomena in the city of Legerdemain, as well as profiles on many of the citizens who inhabit it.

The book you hold in your hands is a compilation of exploits focusing on the detective, Agnes Quill, who has kindly granted us permission to archive several of her cases, in the form of illustrated stories. Based on first-hand accounts, they have been interpreted by artisans with experience on the unique subject matter relating to her work. Also included as reference are excerpts from Agnes Quill's journal entries and a working file of our ongoing records.

We hope this and further collections with help to advance our understanding of the spirit realm that surrounds us.

"the" MUMMIFIED HEIRLOOM"

&

"the" DIVIDED MAN"

WRITTEN *by* **DAVE ROMAN**
ILLUSTRATED *by* **JASON HO**
LETTERED *by* **JOHN GREEN**

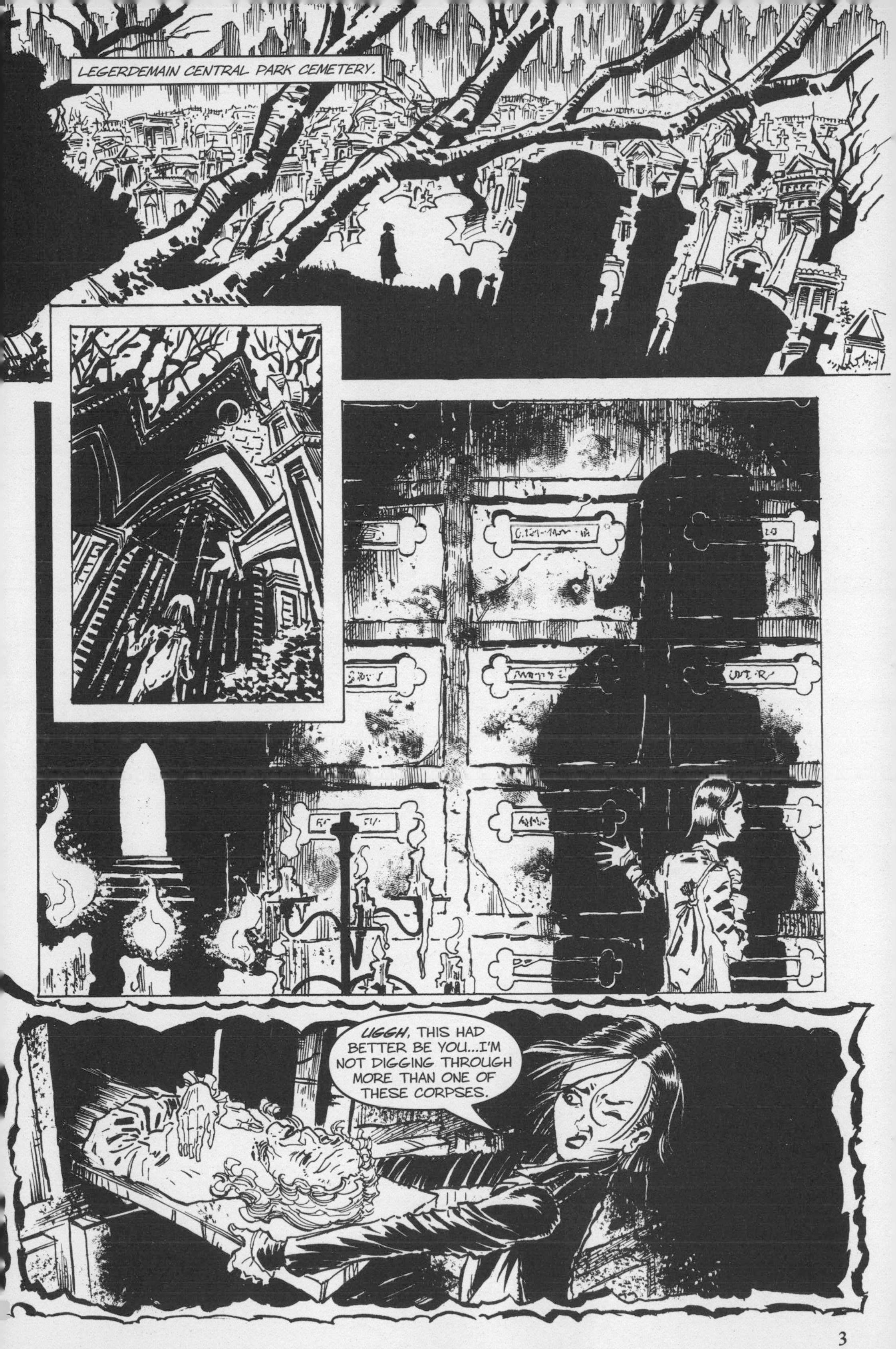
LEGERDEMAIN CENTRAL PARK CEMETERY.
UGGH, THIS HAD BETTER BE YOU...I'M NOT DIGGING THROUGH MORE THAN ONE OF THESE CORPSES.

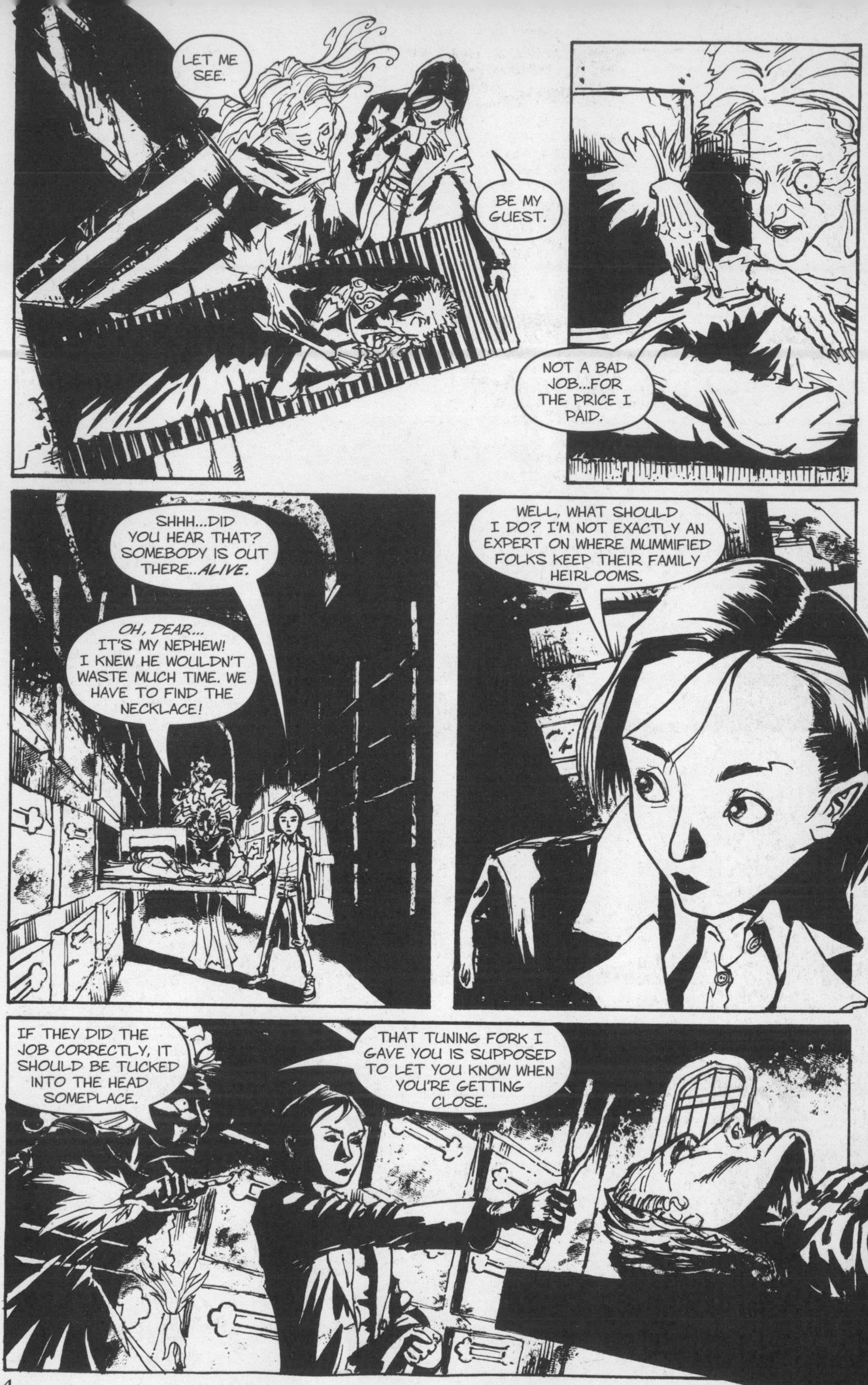
LET ME SEE.
BE MY GUEST.
NOT A BAD JOB...FOR THE PRICE I PAID.
SHHH...DID YOU HEAR THAT? SOMEBODY IS OUT THERE...*ALIVE.*
OH, DEAR... IT'S MY NEPHEW! I KNEW HE WOULDN'T WASTE MUCH TIME. WE HAVE TO FIND THE NECKLACE!
WELL, WHAT SHOULD I DO? I'M NOT EXACTLY AN EXPERT ON WHERE MUMMIFIED FOLKS KEEP THEIR FAMILY HEIRLOOMS.
IF THEY DID THE JOB CORRECTLY, IT SHOULD BE TUCKED INTO THE HEAD SOMEPLACE.
THAT TUNING FORK I GAVE YOU IS SUPPOSED TO LET YOU KNOW WHEN YOU'RE GETTING CLOSE.

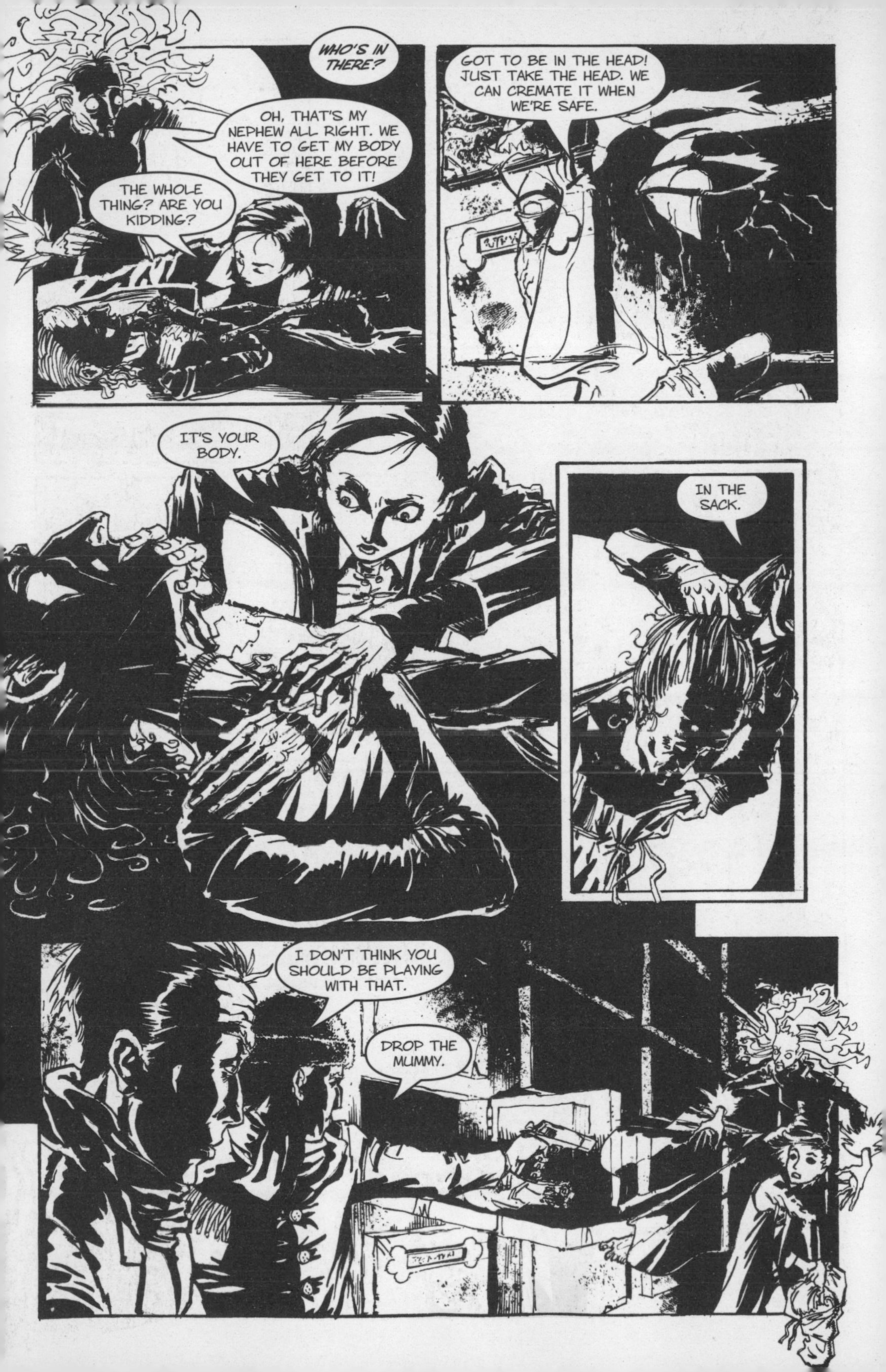
WHO'S IN THERE?
OH, THAT'S MY NEPHEW ALL RIGHT. WE HAVE TO GET MY BODY OUT OF HERE BEFORE THEY GET TO IT!
THE WHOLE THING? ARE YOU KIDDING?
GOT TO BE IN THE HEAD! JUST TAKE THE HEAD. WE CAN CREMATE IT WHEN WE'RE SAFE.
IT'S YOUR BODY.
IN THE SACK.
I DON'T THINK YOU SHOULD BE PLAYING WITH THAT.
DROP THE MUMMY.

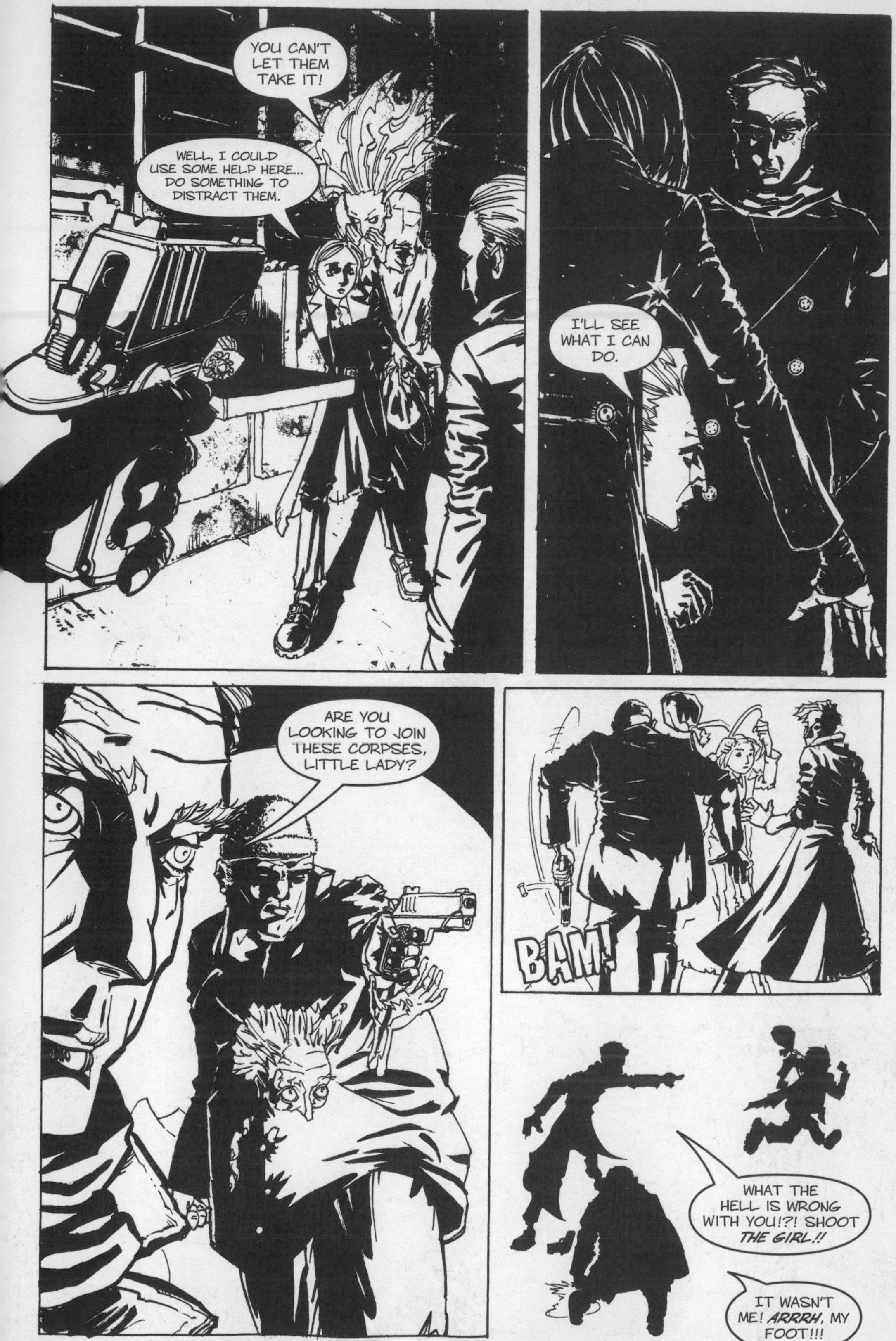
YOU CAN'T LET THEM TAKE IT!
WELL, I COULD USE SOME HELP HERE... DO SOMETHING TO DISTRACT THEM.
I'LL SEE WHAT I CAN DO.
ARE YOU LOOKING TO JOIN THESE CORPSES, LITTLE LADY?
BAM!
WHAT THE HELL IS WRONG WITH YOU!?! SHOOT THE GIRL!!
IT WASN'T ME! ARRRH, MY FOOT!!!

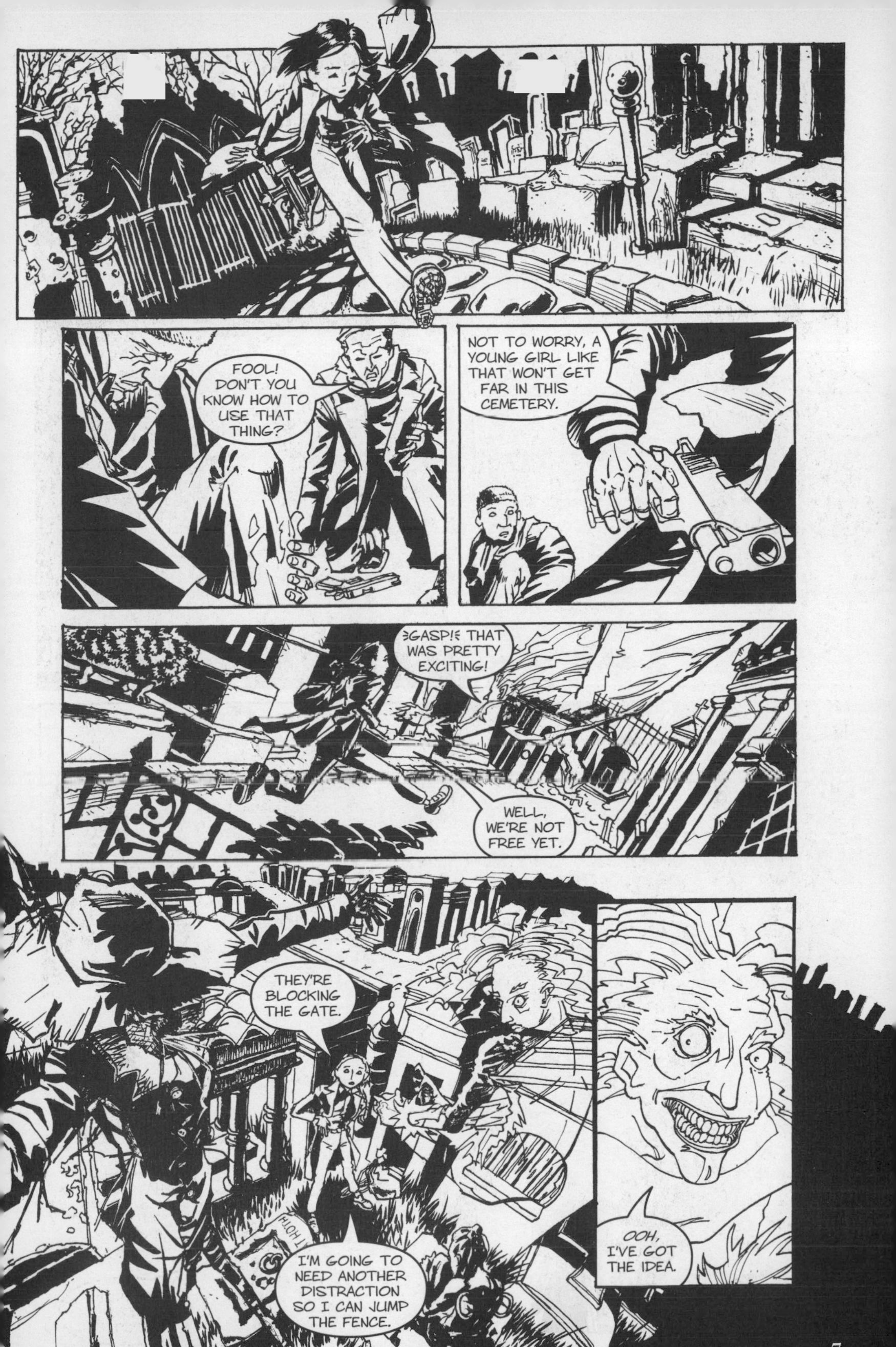
FOOL! DON'T YOU KNOW HOW TO USE THAT THING?
NOT TO WORRY, A YOUNG GIRL LIKE THAT WON'T GET FAR IN THIS CEMETERY.
GASP! THAT WAS PRETTY EXCITING!
WELL, WE'RE NOT FREE YET.
THEY'RE BLOCKING THE GATE.
I'M GOING TO NEED ANOTHER DISTRACTION SO I CAN JUMP THE FENCE.
OOH, I'VE GOT THE IDEA.

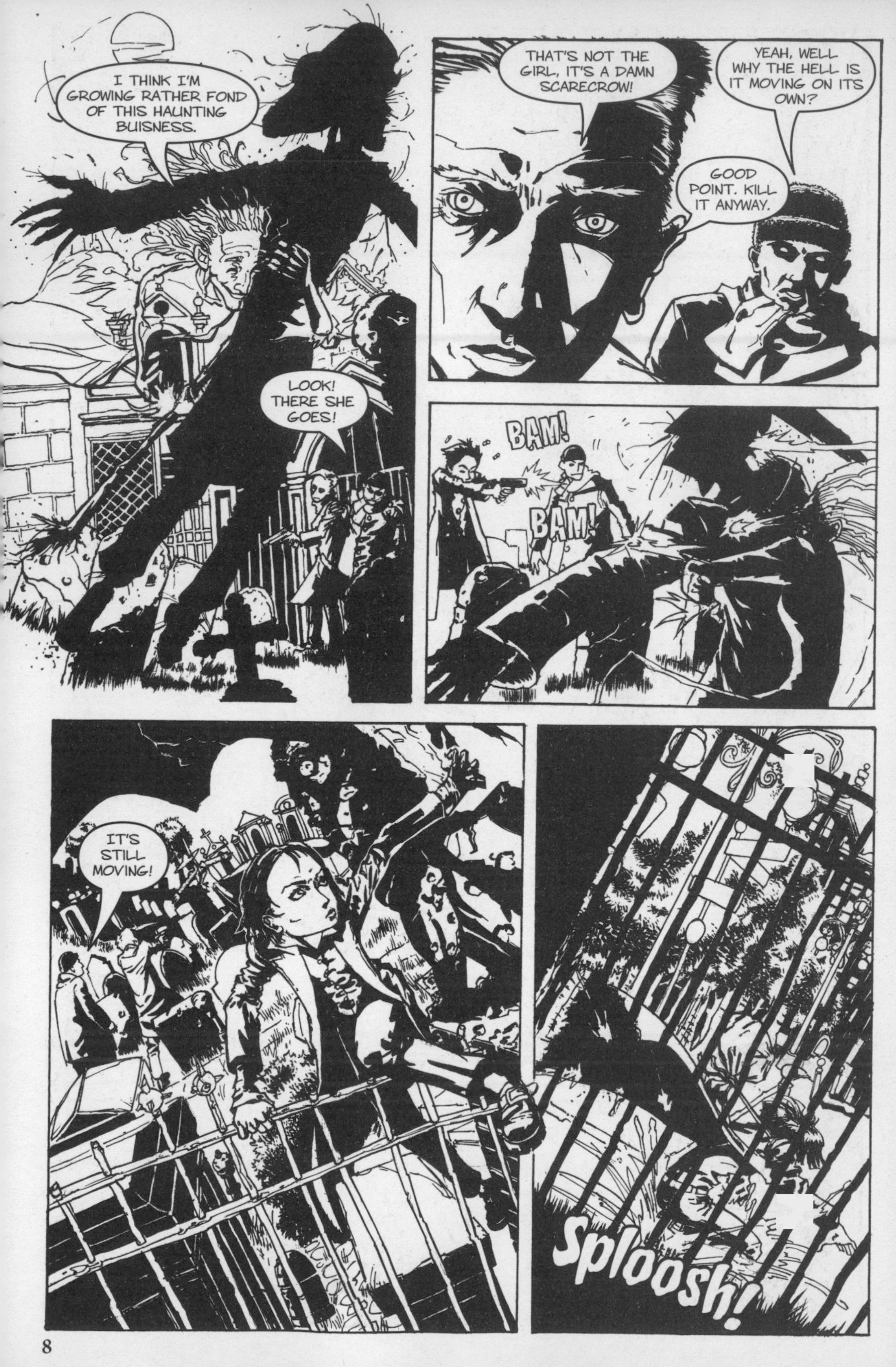
I THINK I'M GROWING RATHER FOND OF THIS HAUNTING BUISNESS.
LOOK! THERE SHE GOES!
THAT'S NOT THE GIRL, IT'S A DAMN SCARECROW!
YEAH, WELL WHY THE HELL IS IT MOVING ON ITS OWN?
GOOD POINT. KILL IT ANYWAY.
BAM!
BAM!
IT'S STILL MOVING!
Sploosh!

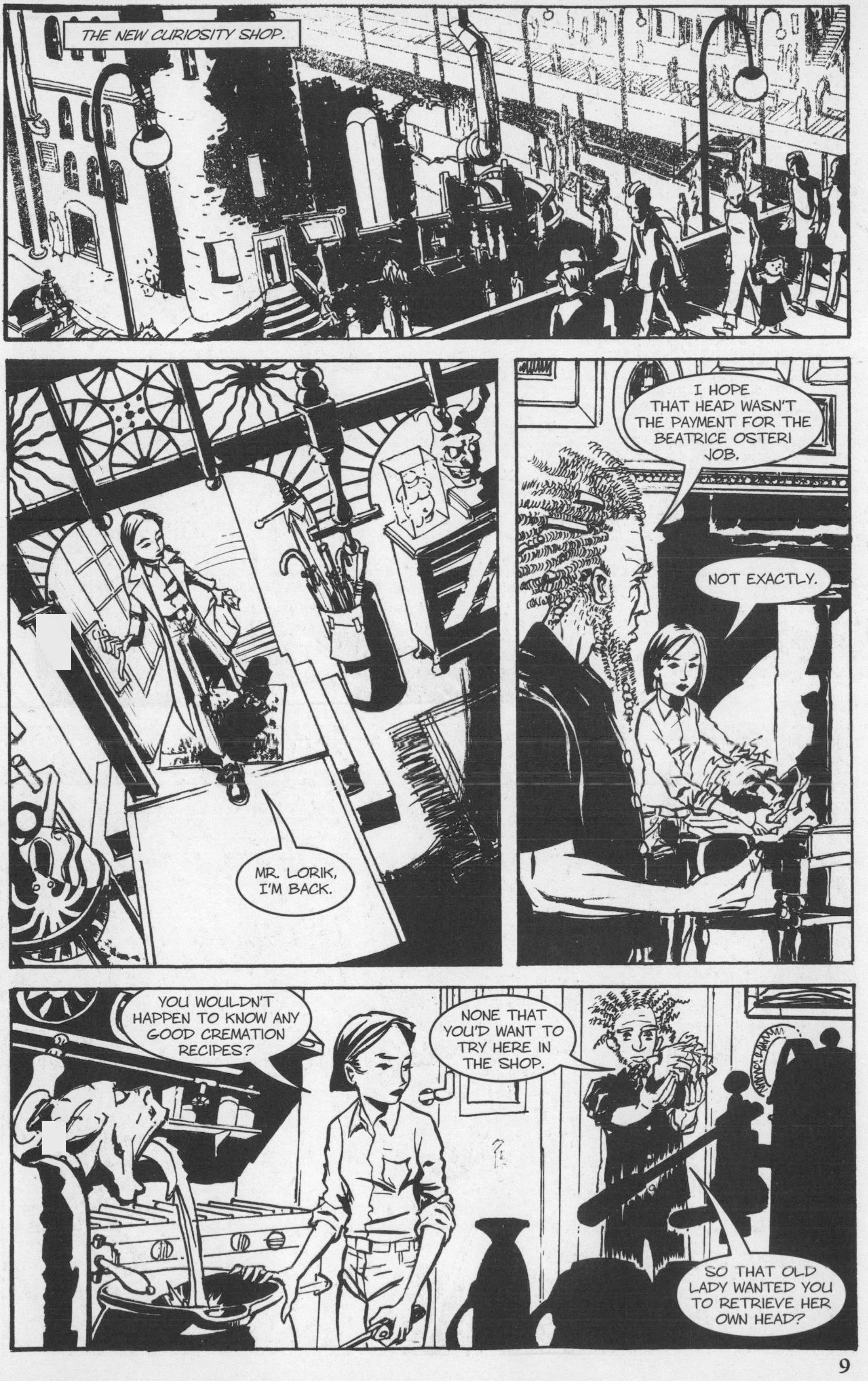
THE NEW CURIOSITY SHOP.
MR. LORIK, I'M BACK.
I HOPE THAT HEAD WASN'T THE PAYMENT FOR THE BEATRICE OSTERI JOB.
NOT EXACTLY.
YOU WOULDN'T HAPPEN TO KNOW ANY GOOD CREMATION RECIPES?
NONE THAT YOU'D WANT TO TRY HERE IN THE SHOP.
SO THAT OLD LADY WANTED YOU TO RETRIEVE HER OWN HEAD?

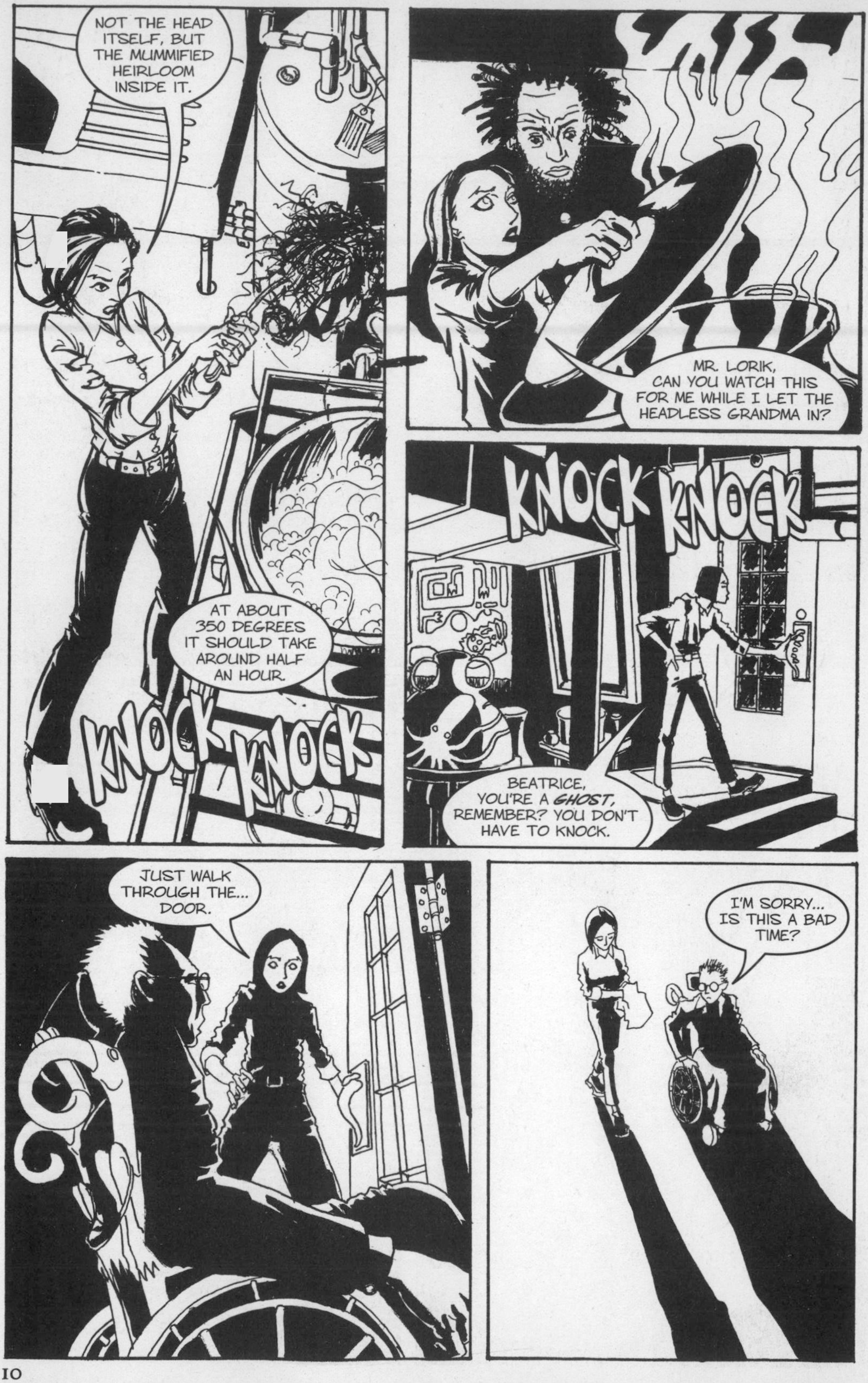
NOT THE HEAD ITSELF, BUT THE MUMMIFIED HEIRLOOM INSIDE IT.
MR. LORIK, CAN YOU WATCH THIS FOR ME WHILE I LET THE HEADLESS GRANDMA IN?
AT ABOUT 350 DEGREES IT SHOULD TAKE AROUND HALF AN HOUR.
KNOCK KNOCK
KNOCK KNOCK
BEATRICE, YOU'RE A *GHOST*, REMEMBER? YOU DON'T HAVE TO KNOCK.
JUST WALK THROUGH THE... DOOR.
I'M SORRY... IS THIS A BAD TIME?

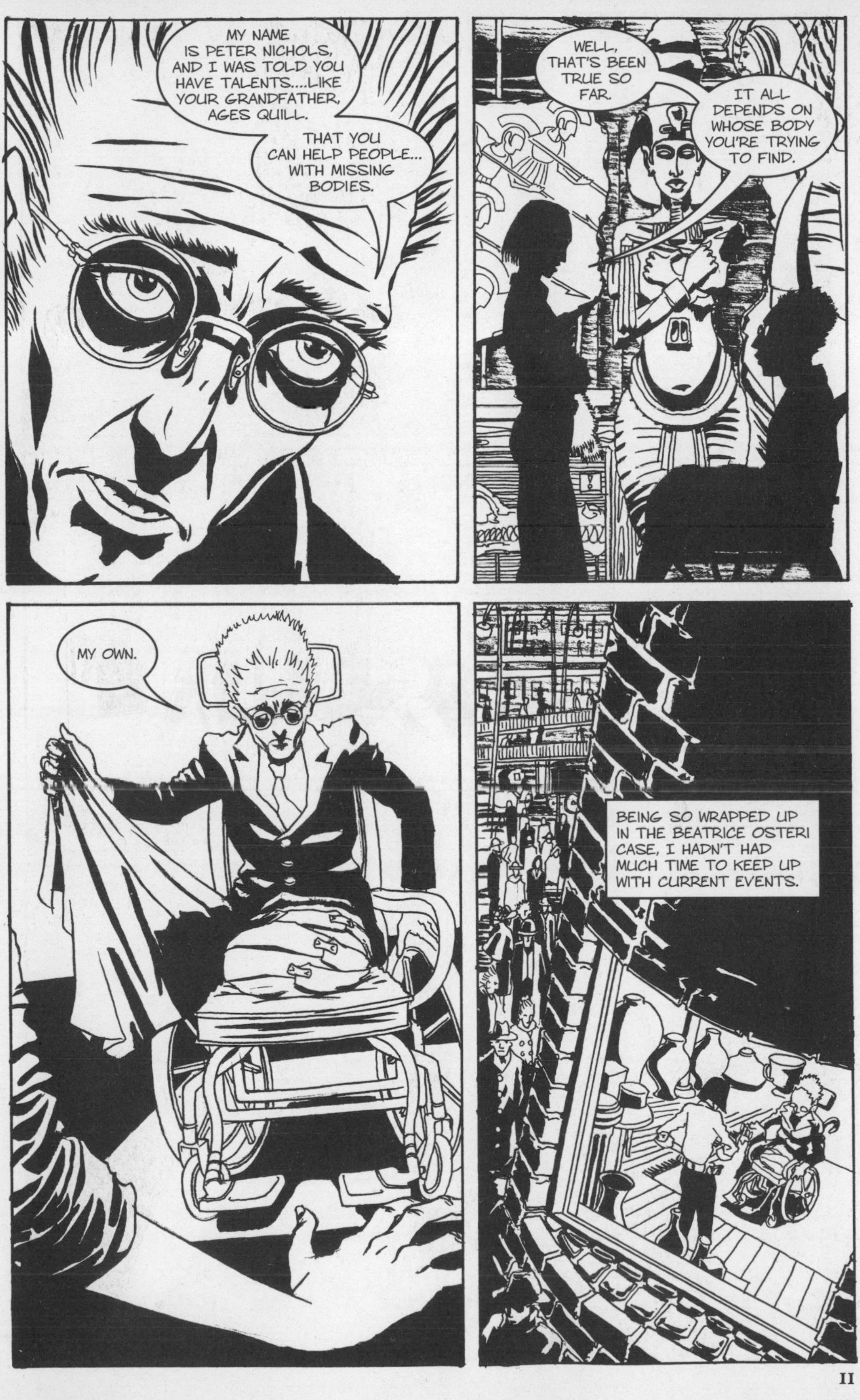
MY NAME IS PETER NICHOLS, AND I WAS TOLD YOU HAVE TALENTS....LIKE YOUR GRANDFATHER, AGES QUILL.
THAT YOU CAN HELP PEOPLE... WITH MISSING BODIES.
WELL, THAT'S BEEN TRUE SO FAR.
IT ALL DEPENDS ON WHOSE BODY YOU'RE TRYING TO FIND.
MY OWN.
BEING SO WRAPPED UP IN THE BEATRICE OSTERI CASE, I HADN'T HAD MUCH TIME TO KEEP UP WITH CURRENT EVENTS.

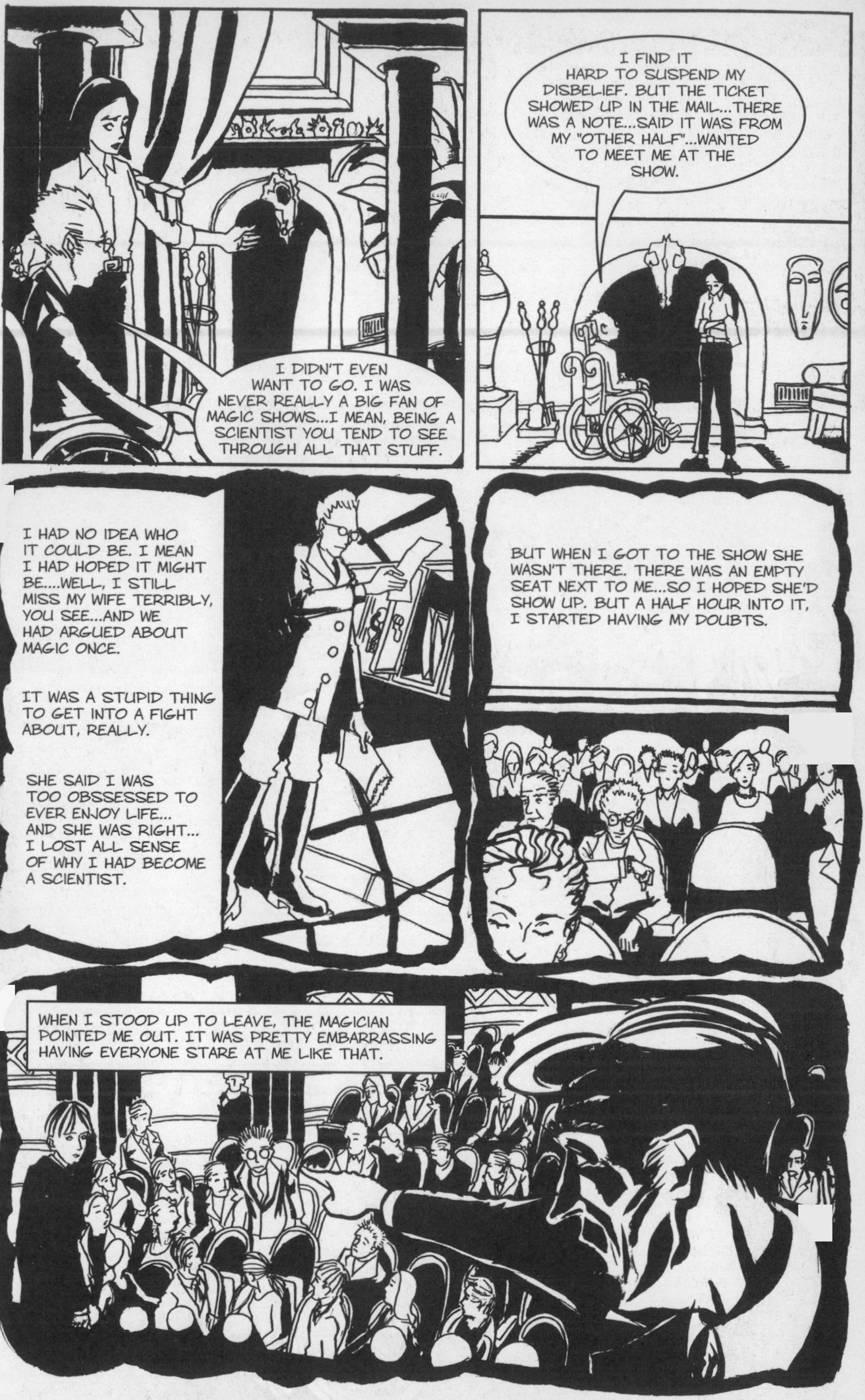
I DIDN'T EVEN WANT TO GO. I WAS NEVER REALLY A BIG FAN OF MAGIC SHOWS...I MEAN, BEING A SCIENTIST YOU TEND TO SEE THROUGH ALL THAT STUFF.
I FIND IT HARD TO SUSPEND MY DISBELIEF. BUT THE TICKET SHOWED UP IN THE MAIL...THERE WAS A NOTE...SAID IT WAS FROM MY "OTHER HALF"...WANTED TO MEET ME AT THE SHOW.
I HAD NO IDEA WHO IT COULD BE. I MEAN I HAD HOPED IT MIGHT BE....WELL, I STILL MISS MY WIFE TERRIBLY, YOU SEE...AND WE HAD ARGUED ABOUT MAGIC ONCE.
IT WAS A STUPID THING TO GET INTO A FIGHT ABOUT, REALLY.
SHE SAID I WAS TOO OBSSESSED TO EVER ENJOY LIFE... AND SHE WAS RIGHT... I LOST ALL SENSE OF WHY I HAD BECOME A SCIENTIST.
BUT WHEN I GOT TO THE SHOW SHE WASN'T THERE. THERE WAS AN EMPTY SEAT NEXT TO ME...SO I HOPED SHE'D SHOW UP. BUT A HALF HOUR INTO IT, I STARTED HAVING MY DOUBTS.
WHEN I STOOD UP TO LEAVE, THE MAGICIAN POINTED ME OUT. IT WAS PRETTY EMBARRASSING HAVING EVERYONE STARE AT ME LIKE THAT.

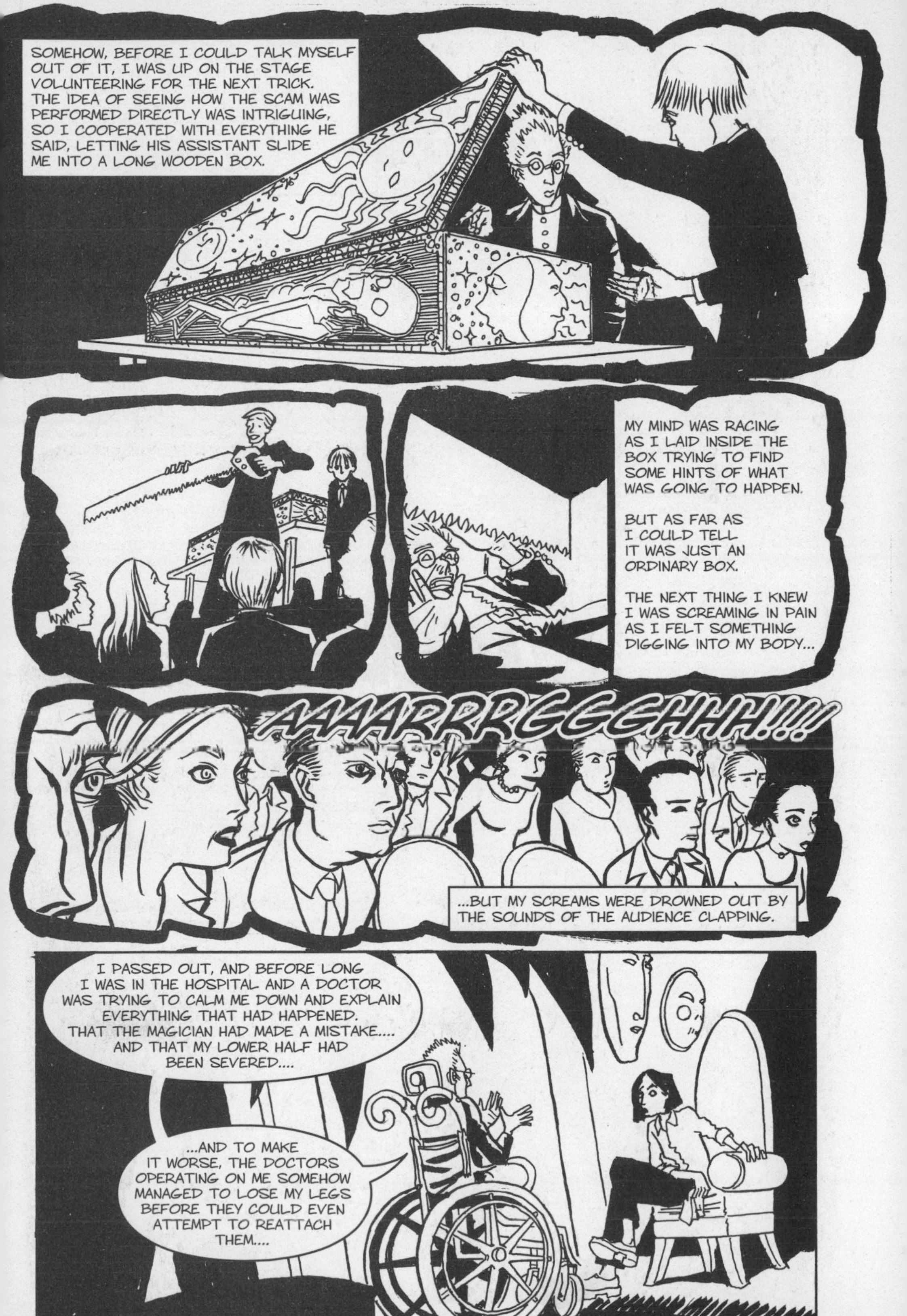
SOMEHOW, BEFORE I COULD TALK MYSELF OUT OF IT, I WAS UP ON THE STAGE VOLUNTEERING FOR THE NEXT TRICK. THE IDEA OF SEEING HOW THE SCAM WAS PERFORMED DIRECTLY WAS INTRIGUING, SO I COOPERATED WITH EVERYTHING HE SAID, LETTING HIS ASSISTANT SLIDE ME INTO A LONG WOODEN BOX.
MY MIND WAS RACING AS I LAID INSIDE THE BOX TRYING TO FIND SOME HINTS OF WHAT WAS GOING TO HAPPEN.
BUT AS FAR AS I COULD TELL IT WAS JUST AN ORDINARY BOX.
THE NEXT THING I KNEW I WAS SCREAMING IN PAIN AS I FELT SOMETHING DIGGING INTO MY BODY...
AAAARRRGGGGHHH!!!
...BUT MY SCREAMS WERE DROWNED OUT BY THE SOUNDS OF THE AUDIENCE CLAPPING.
I PASSED OUT, AND BEFORE LONG I WAS IN THE HOSPITAL AND A DOCTOR WAS TRYING TO CALM ME DOWN AND EXPLAIN EVERYTHING THAT HAD HAPPENED. THAT THE MAGICIAN HAD MADE A MISTAKE.... AND THAT MY LOWER HALF HAD BEEN SEVERED....
...AND TO MAKE IT WORSE, THE DOCTORS OPERATING ON ME SOMEHOW MANAGED TO LOSE MY LEGS BEFORE THEY COULD EVEN ATTEMPT TO REATTACH THEM....

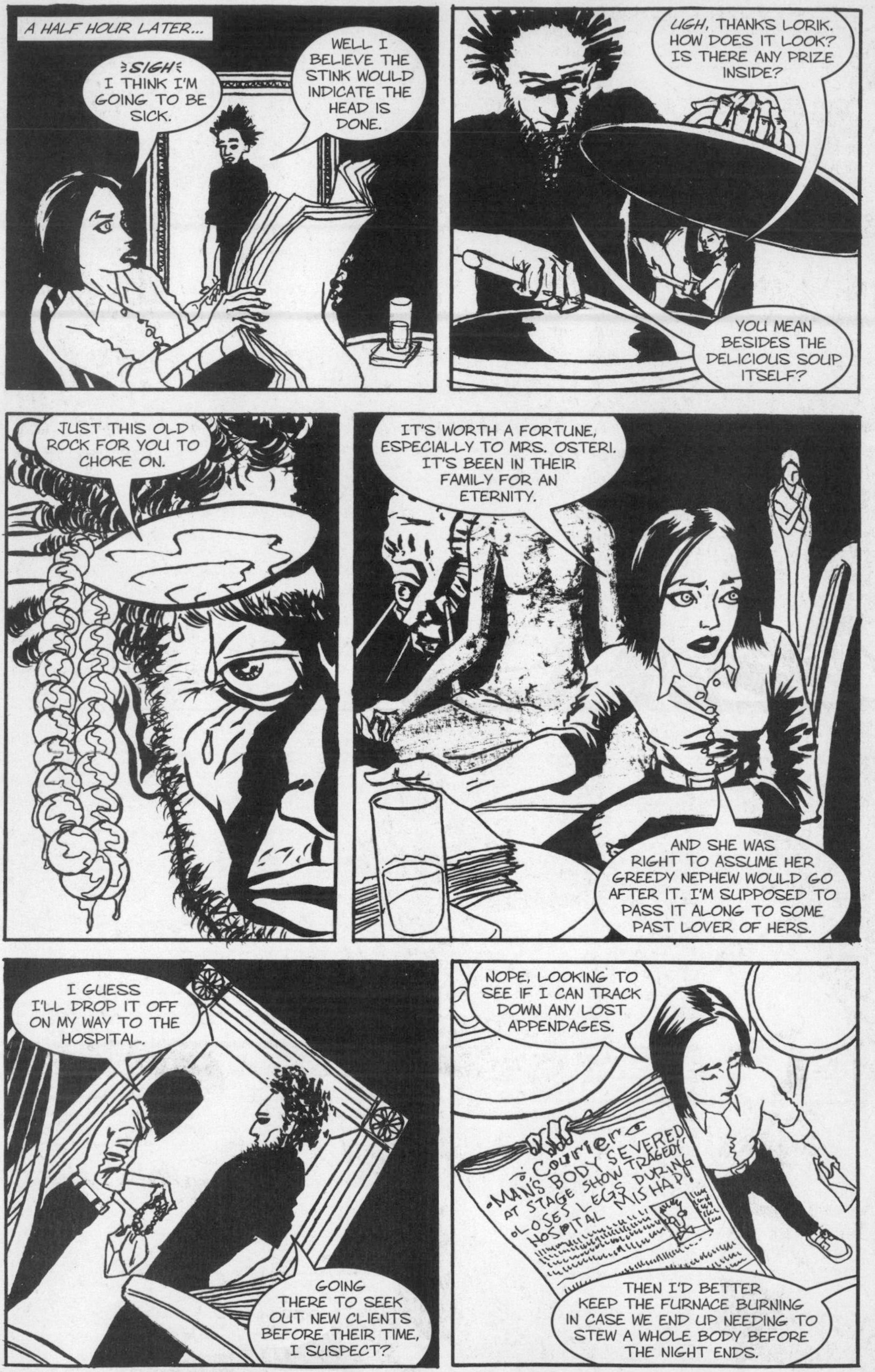
A HALF HOUR LATER...
SIGH
I THINK I'M GOING TO BE SICK.
WELL I BELIEVE THE STINK WOULD INDICATE THE HEAD IS DONE.
UGH, THANKS LORIK. HOW DOES IT LOOK? IS THERE ANY PRIZE INSIDE?
YOU MEAN BESIDES THE DELICIOUS SOUP ITSELF?
JUST THIS OLD ROCK FOR YOU TO CHOKE ON.
IT'S WORTH A FORTUNE, ESPECIALLY TO MRS. OSTERI. IT'S BEEN IN THEIR FAMILY FOR AN ETERNITY.
AND SHE WAS RIGHT TO ASSUME HER GREEDY NEPHEW WOULD GO AFTER IT. I'M SUPPOSED TO PASS IT ALONG TO SOME PAST LOVER OF HERS.
I GUESS I'LL DROP IT OFF ON MY WAY TO THE HOSPITAL.
GOING THERE TO SEEK OUT NEW CLIENTS BEFORE THEIR TIME, I SUSPECT?
NOPE, LOOKING TO SEE IF I CAN TRACK DOWN ANY LOST APPENDAGES.
Courier
MAN'S BODY SEVERED AT STAGE SHOW TRAGEDY
LOSES LEGS DURING HOSPITAL MISHAP!
THEN I'D BETTER KEEP THE FURNACE BURNING IN CASE WE END UP NEEDING TO STEW A WHOLE BODY BEFORE THE NIGHT ENDS.

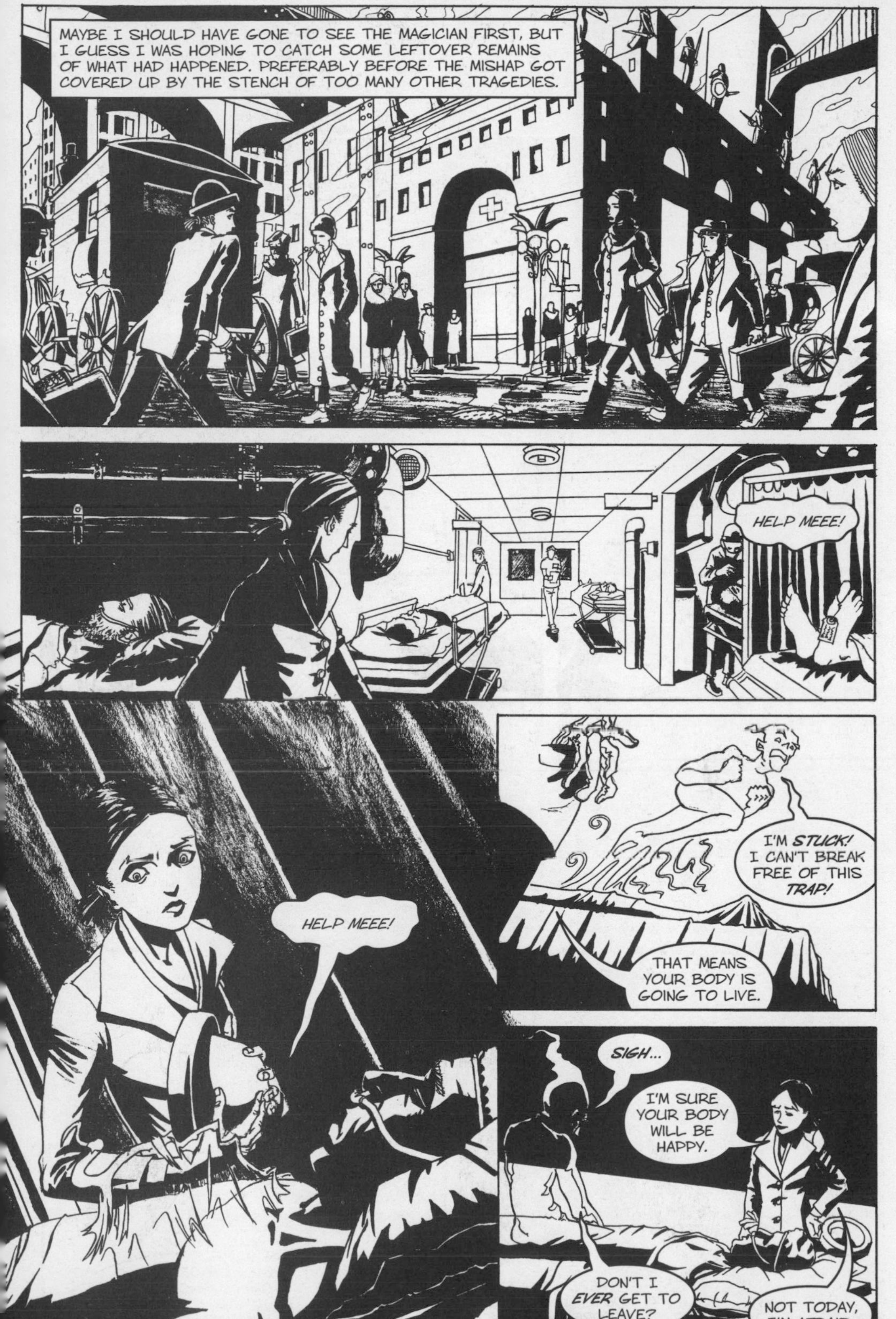
MAYBE I SHOULD HAVE GONE TO SEE THE MAGICIAN FIRST, BUT I GUESS I WAS HOPING TO CATCH SOME LEFTOVER REMAINS OF WHAT HAD HAPPENED. PREFERABLY BEFORE THE MISHAP GOT COVERED UP BY THE STENCH OF TOO MANY OTHER TRAGEDIES.
HELP MEEE!
HELP MEEE!
I'M STUCK! I CAN'T BREAK FREE OF THIS TRAP!
THAT MEANS YOUR BODY IS GOING TO LIVE.
SIGH...
I'M SURE YOUR BODY WILL BE HAPPY.
DON'T I EVER GET TO LEAVE?
NOT TODAY, I'M AFRAID.

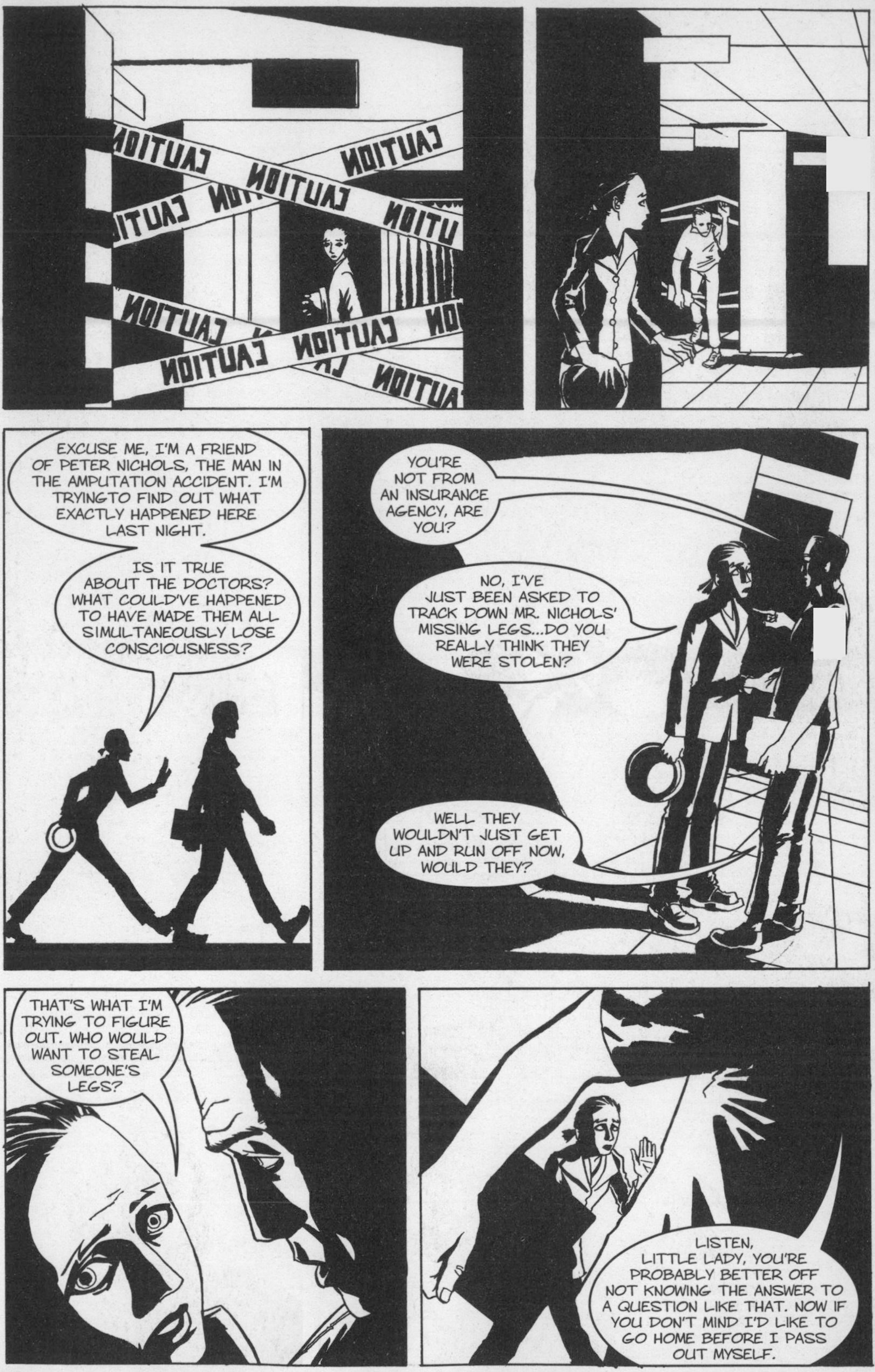
EXCUSE ME, I'M A FRIEND OF PETER NICHOLS, THE MAN IN THE AMPUTATION ACCIDENT. I'M TRYINGTO FIND OUT WHAT EXACTLY HAPPENED HERE LAST NIGHT.
IS IT TRUE ABOUT THE DOCTORS? WHAT COULD'VE HAPPENED TO HAVE MADE THEM ALL SIMULTANEOUSLY LOSE CONSCIOUSNESS?
YOU'RE NOT FROM AN INSURANCE AGENCY, ARE YOU?
NO, I'VE JUST BEEN ASKED TO TRACK DOWN MR. NICHOLS' MISSING LEGS...DO YOU REALLY THINK THEY WERE STOLEN?
WELL THEY WOULDN'T JUST GET UP AND RUN OFF NOW, WOULD THEY?
THAT'S WHAT I'M TRYING TO FIGURE OUT. WHO WOULD WANT TO STEAL SOMEONE'S LEGS?
LISTEN, LITTLE LADY, YOU'RE PROBABLY BETTER OFF NOT KNOWING THE ANSWER TO A QUESTION LIKE THAT. NOW IF YOU DON'T MIND I'D LIKE TO GO HOME BEFORE I PASS OUT MYSELF.

YOU SAID YOU WERE A FRIEND OF PETER'S?

UM...YEAH, SORT OF. ARE YOU LOOKING FOR HIM?

I CAME AS SOON AS I HEARD SOMETHING HAD HAPPENED.

YOU'RE THE FIRST PERSON HERE WHO WILL EVEN TALK TO ME....

EVERYONE'S SO BUSY AROUND HERE... DO YOU KNOW IF HE'S OKAY?

WELL, NOT EXACTLY. HE LOST HIS LEGS IN AN ACCIDENT. HE HIRED ME TO HELP FIND OUT WHAT HAPPENED TO HIS LEGS.

THAT'S JUST LIKE PETER. ALWAYS OBSSESSED ABOUT HIS STUPID LEGS. THE WAY THE DOCTORS WERE REACTING I THOUGHT MAYBE SOMETHING SERIOUS HAD HAPPENED.

NEVER BEING ABLE TO WALK AGAIN ISN'T SERIOUS?

PETER HAS *ALWAYS* BEEN PARALYZED...HE JUST CAN'T LEARN TO ACCEPT IT.

HE JUST KEEPS GETTING WORSE AND WORSE. QUITTING HIS JOB, HIS RESEARCH. GIVING ALL HIS MONEY TO THOSE VOODOO CON ARTISTS. HE'S TOO BUSY TRYING TO BECOME SOMEONE HE'S NOT THAT HE'S FORGOTTEN WHY I MARRIED HIM IN THE FIRST PLACE.

VOODOO? BUT I THOUGHT HE DIDN'T BELIEVE IN MAGIC--

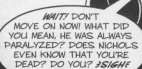

WAIT! DON'T MOVE ON NOW! WHAT DID YOU MEAN, HE WAS ALWAYS PARALYZED? DOES NICHOLS EVEN KNOW THAT YOU'RE DEAD? DO YOU? ₹SIGH₹

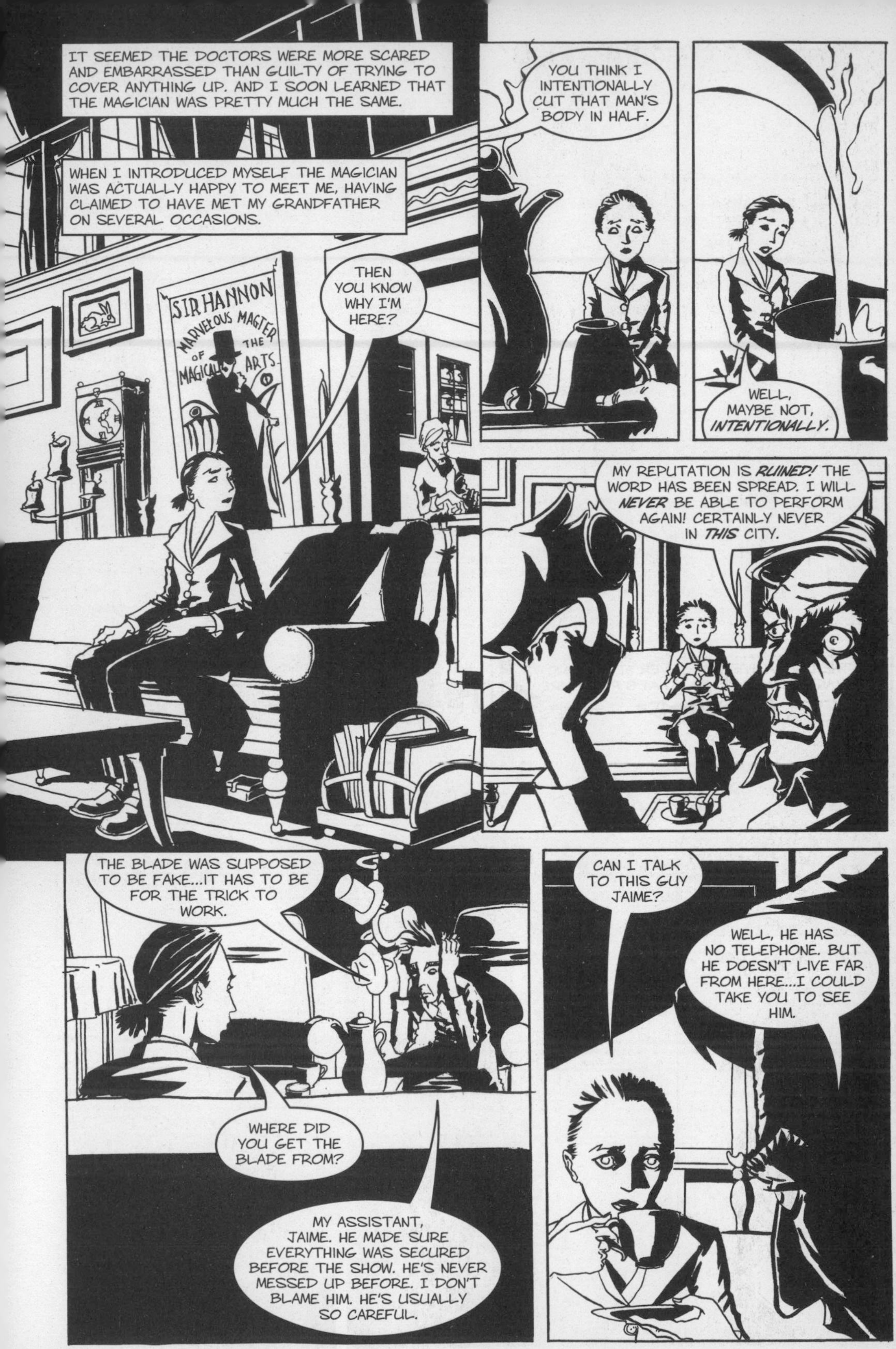
IT SEEMED THE DOCTORS WERE MORE SCARED AND EMBARRASSED THAN GUILTY OF TRYING TO COVER ANYTHING UP. AND I SOON LEARNED THAT THE MAGICIAN WAS PRETTY MUCH THE SAME.
WHEN I INTRODUCED MYSELF THE MAGICIAN WAS ACTUALLY HAPPY TO MEET ME, HAVING CLAIMED TO HAVE MET MY GRANDFATHER ON SEVERAL OCCASIONS.
SIR HANNON
MARVELOUS MAGTER OF THE MAGICAL ARTS
THEN YOU KNOW WHY I'M HERE?
YOU THINK I INTENTIONALLY CUT THAT MAN'S BODY IN HALF.
WELL, MAYBE NOT, *INTENTIONALLY.*
MY REPUTATION IS *RUINED!* THE WORD HAS BEEN SPREAD. I WILL *NEVER* BE ABLE TO PERFORM AGAIN! CERTAINLY NEVER IN *THIS* CITY.
THE BLADE WAS SUPPOSED TO BE FAKE...IT HAS TO BE FOR THE TRICK TO WORK.
WHERE DID YOU GET THE BLADE FROM?
MY ASSISTANT, JAIME. HE MADE SURE EVERYTHING WAS SECURED BEFORE THE SHOW. HE'S NEVER MESSED UP BEFORE. I DON'T BLAME HIM. HE'S USUALLY SO CAREFUL.
CAN I TALK TO THIS GUY JAIME?
WELL, HE HAS NO TELEPHONE. BUT HE DOESN'T LIVE FAR FROM HERE...I COULD TAKE YOU TO SEE HIM.

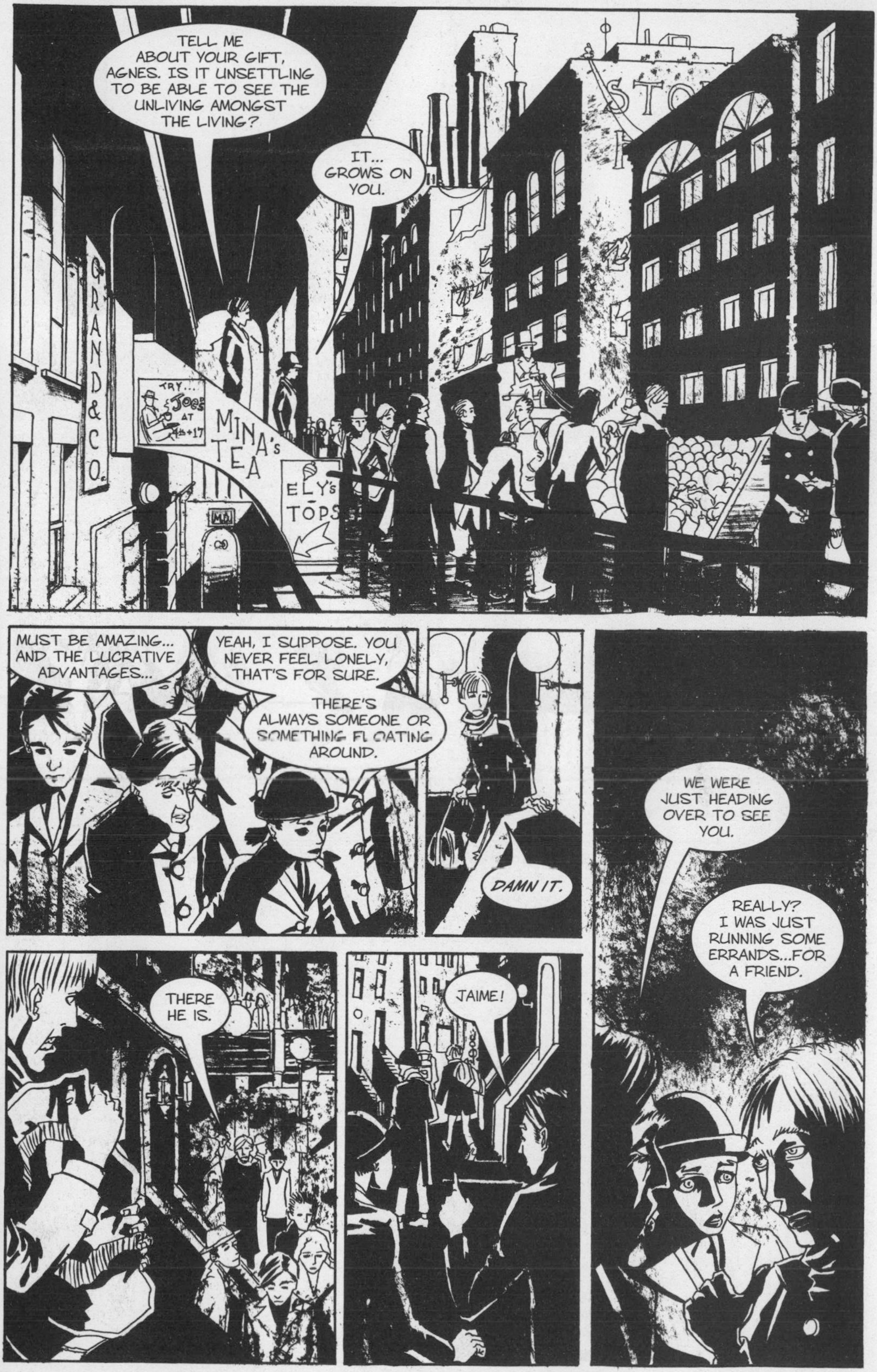
TELL ME ABOUT YOUR GIFT, AGNES. IS IT UNSETTLING TO BE ABLE TO SEE THE UNLIVING AMONGST THE LIVING?
IT... GROWS ON YOU.
GRAND & CO.
TRY... JOE'S AT 4th+17
MINA'S TEA
ELY'S TOPS
MUST BE AMAZING... AND THE LUCRATIVE ADVANTAGES...
YEAH, I SUPPOSE. YOU NEVER FEEL LONELY, THAT'S FOR SURE.
THERE'S ALWAYS SOMEONE OR SOMETHING FLOATING AROUND.
DAMN IT.
WE WERE JUST HEADING OVER TO SEE YOU.
REALLY? I WAS JUST RUNNING SOME ERRANDS...FOR A FRIEND.
THERE HE IS.
JAIME!

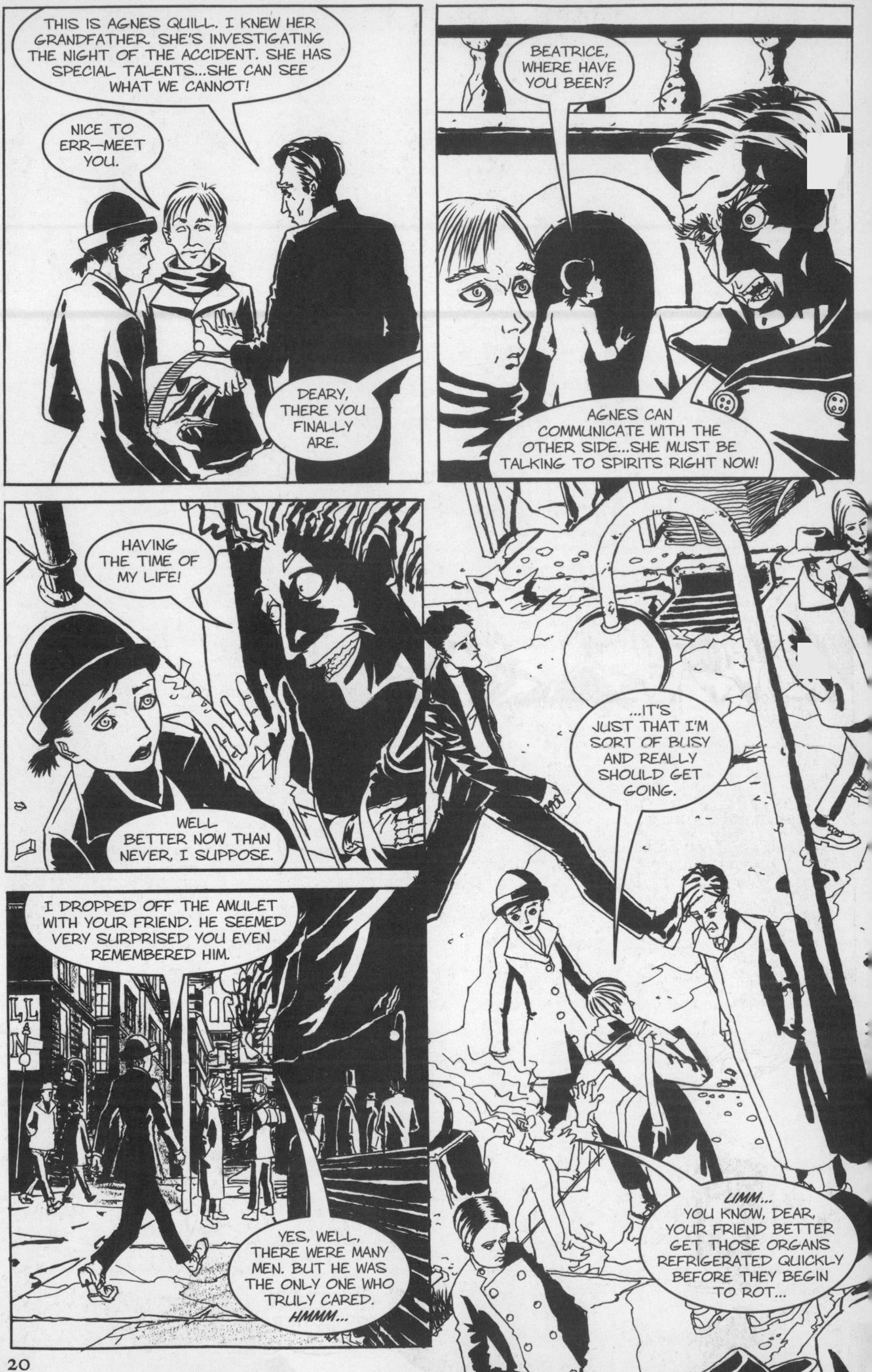
THIS IS AGNES QUILL. I KNEW HER GRANDFATHER. SHE'S INVESTIGATING THE NIGHT OF THE ACCIDENT. SHE HAS SPECIAL TALENTS...SHE CAN SEE WHAT WE CANNOT!
NICE TO ERR—MEET YOU.
DEARY, THERE YOU FINALLY ARE.
BEATRICE, WHERE HAVE YOU BEEN?
AGNES CAN COMMUNICATE WITH THE OTHER SIDE...SHE MUST BE TALKING TO SPIRITS RIGHT NOW!
HAVING THE TIME OF MY LIFE!
WELL BETTER NOW THAN NEVER, I SUPPOSE.
...IT'S JUST THAT I'M SORT OF BUSY AND REALLY SHOULD GET GOING.
I DROPPED OFF THE AMULET WITH YOUR FRIEND. HE SEEMED VERY SURPRISED YOU EVEN REMEMBERED HIM.
YES, WELL, THERE WERE MANY MEN. BUT HE WAS THE ONLY ONE WHO TRULY CARED. HMMM...
UMM... YOU KNOW, DEAR, YOUR FRIEND BETTER GET THOSE ORGANS REFRIGERATED QUICKLY BEFORE THEY BEGIN TO ROT...

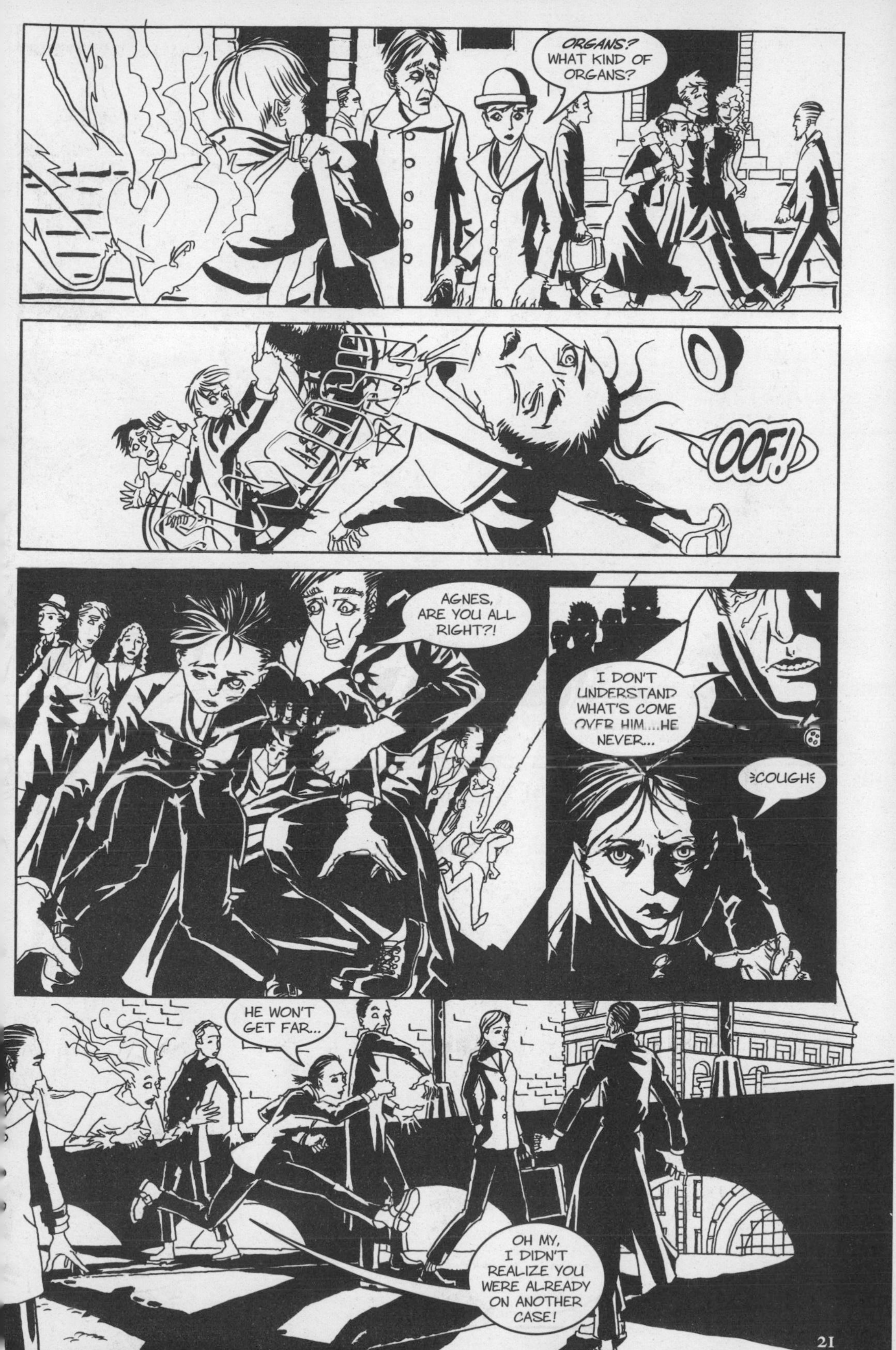
ORGANS? WHAT KIND OF ORGANS?
OOF!
AGNES, ARE YOU ALL RIGHT?!
I DON'T UNDERSTAND WHAT'S COME OVER HIM....HE NEVER...
COUGH
HE WON'T GET FAR...
OH MY, I DIDN'T REALIZE YOU WERE ALREADY ON ANOTHER CASE!

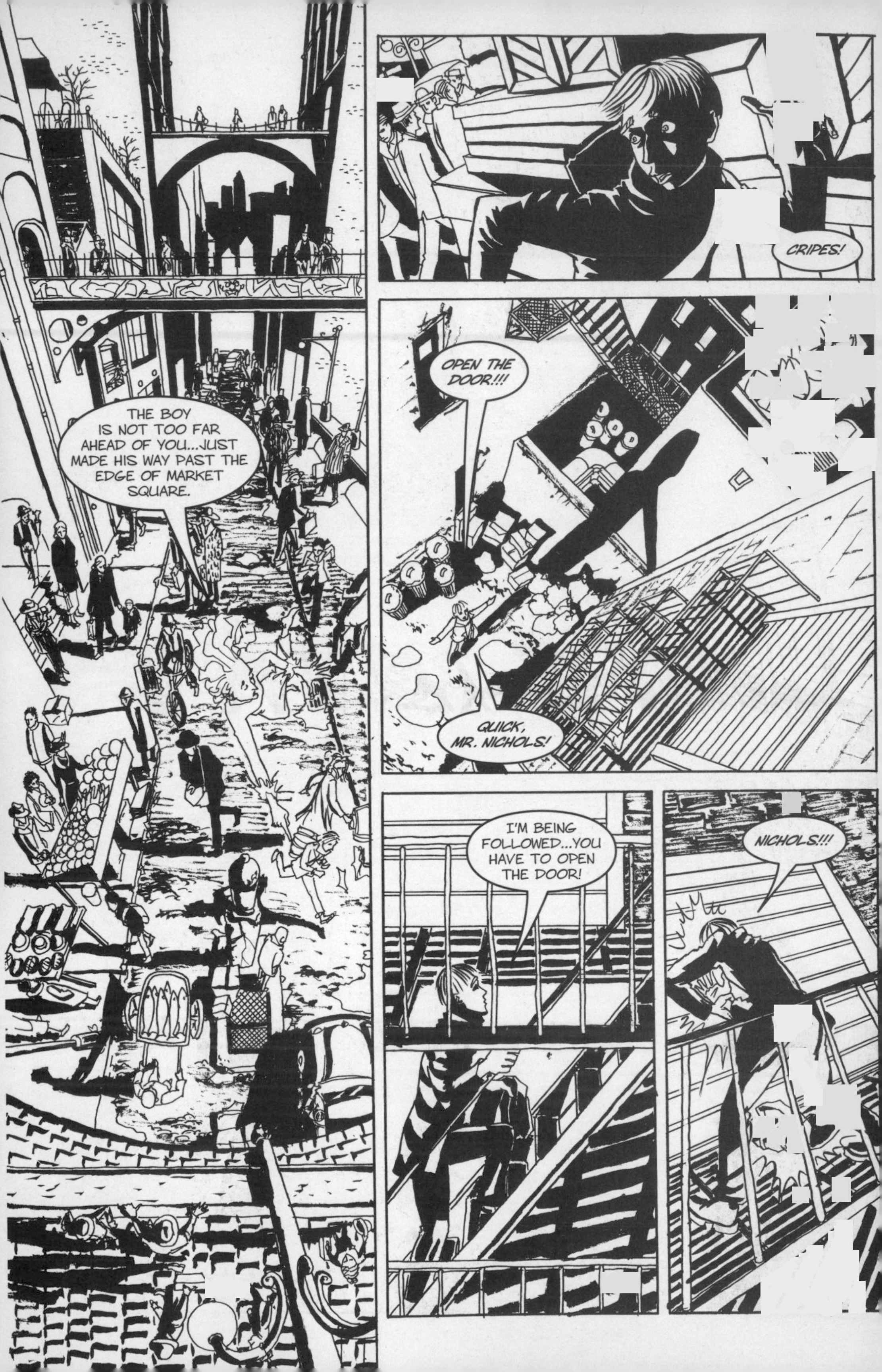
THE BOY IS NOT TOO FAR AHEAD OF YOU...JUST MADE HIS WAY PAST THE EDGE OF MARKET SQUARE.
CRIPES!
OPEN THE DOOR!!!
QUICK, MR. NICHOLS!
I'M BEING FOLLOWED...YOU HAVE TO OPEN THE DOOR!
NICHOLS!!!

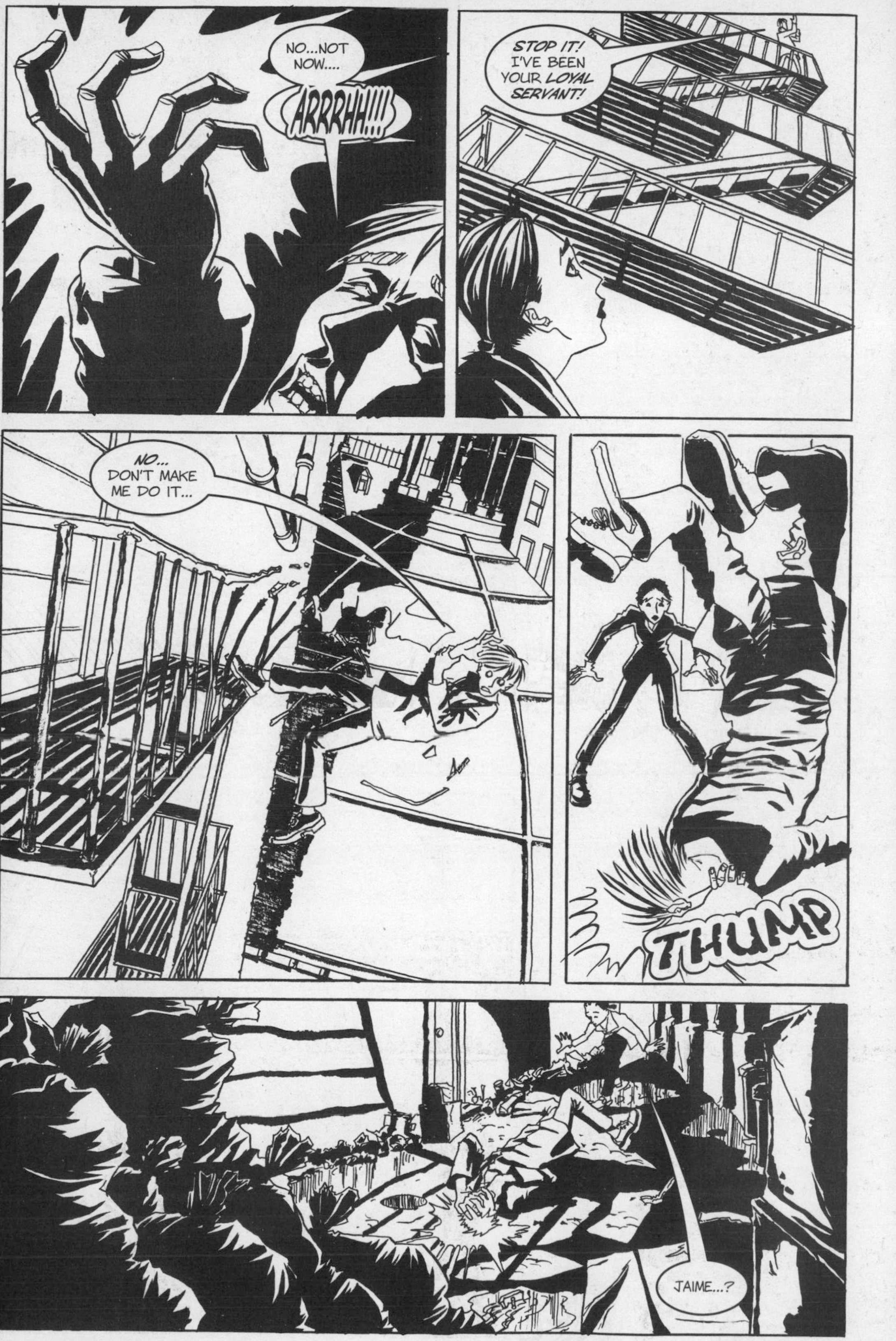
NO...NOT NOW....
ARRRHH!!!
STOP IT! I'VE BEEN YOUR LOYAL SERVANT!
NO... DON'T MAKE ME DO IT...
THUMP
JAIME...?

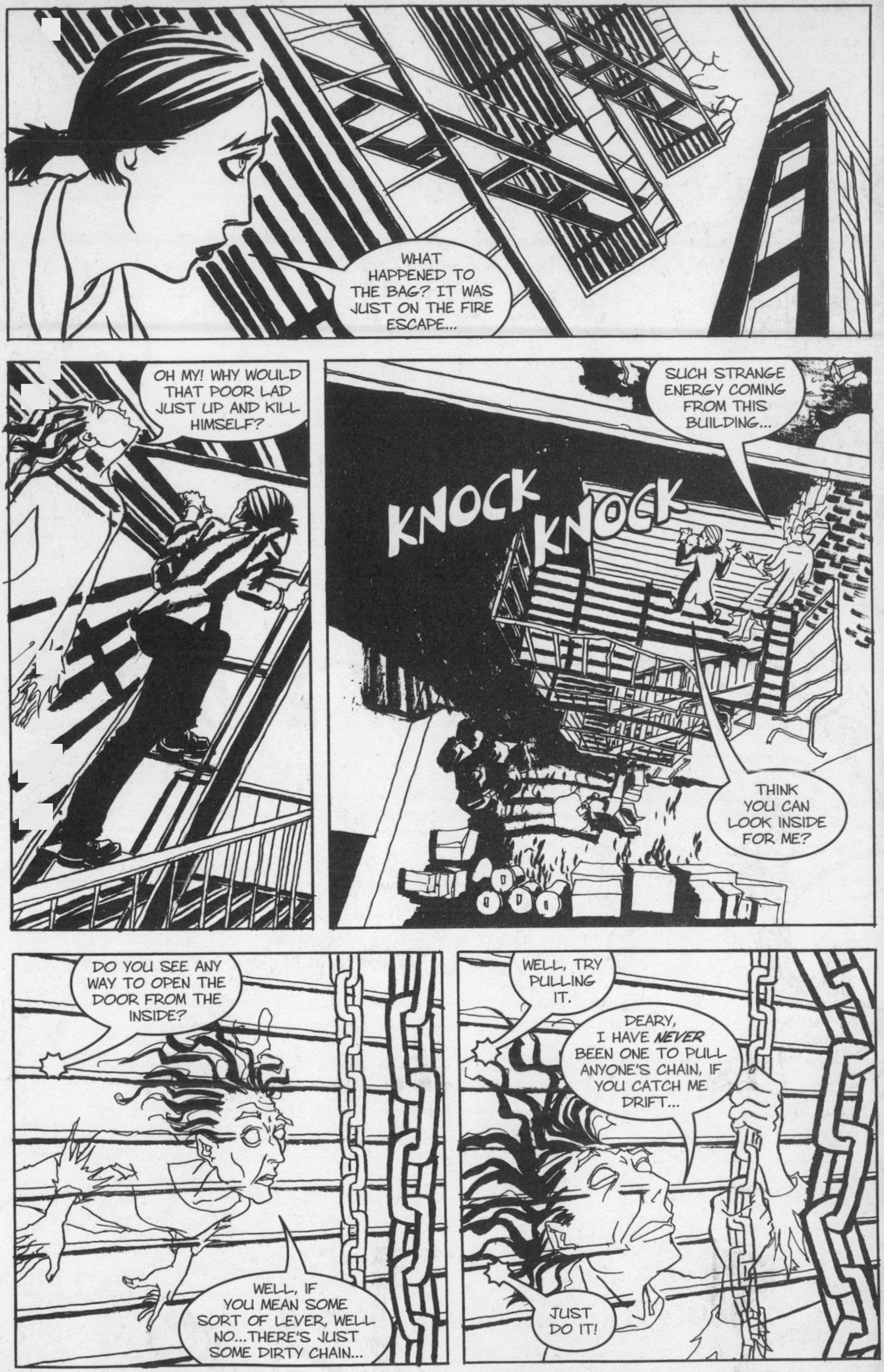
WHAT HAPPENED TO THE BAG? IT WAS JUST ON THE FIRE ESCAPE...
OH MY! WHY WOULD THAT POOR LAD JUST UP AND KILL HIMSELF?
SUCH STRANGE ENERGY COMING FROM THIS BUILDING...
KNOCK
KNOCK
THINK YOU CAN LOOK INSIDE FOR ME?
DO YOU SEE ANY WAY TO OPEN THE DOOR FROM THE INSIDE?
WELL, IF YOU MEAN SOME SORT OF LEVER, WELL NO...THERE'S JUST SOME DIRTY CHAIN...
WELL, TRY PULLING IT.
DEARY, I HAVE *NEVER* BEEN ONE TO PULL ANYONE'S CHAIN, IF YOU CATCH ME DRIFT...
JUST DO IT!

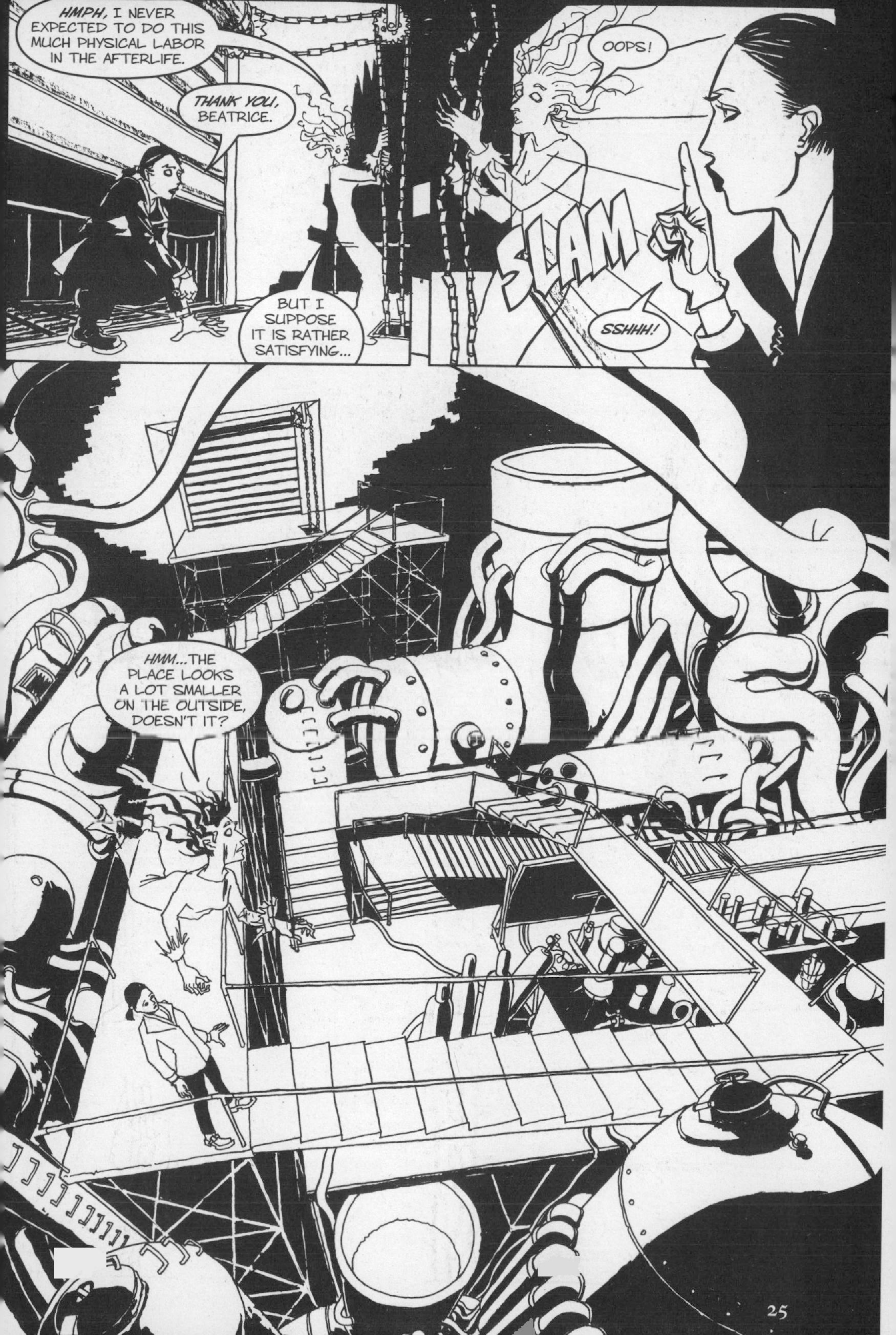
HMPH, I NEVER EXPECTED TO DO THIS MUCH PHYSICAL LABOR IN THE AFTERLIFE.
THANK YOU, BEATRICE.
BUT I SUPPOSE IT IS RATHER SATISFYING...
OOPS!
SLAM
SSHHH!
HMM... THE PLACE LOOKS A LOT SMALLER ON THE OUTSIDE, DOESN'T IT?

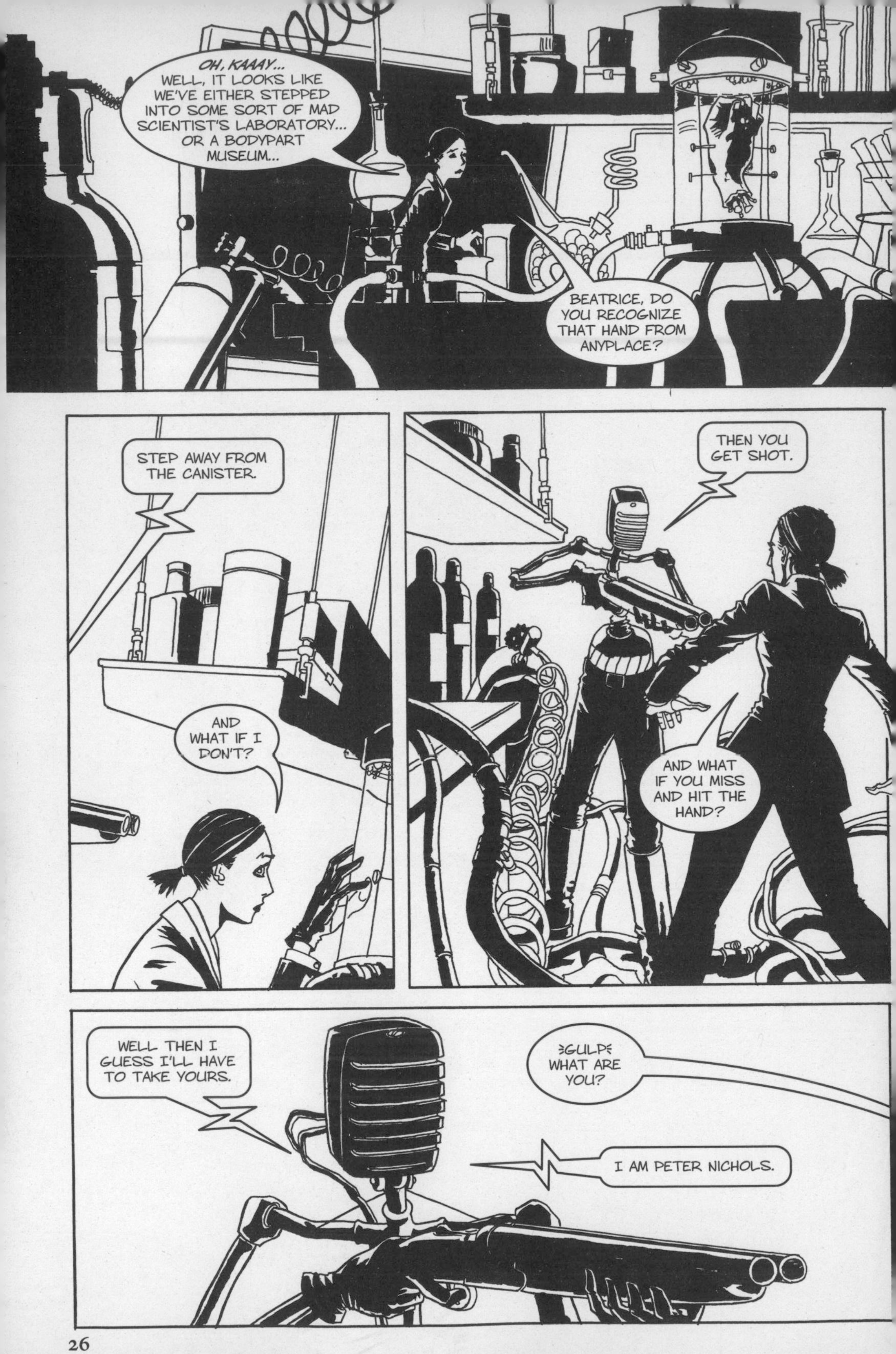
OH, KAAAY... WELL, IT LOOKS LIKE WE'VE EITHER STEPPED INTO SOME SORT OF MAD SCIENTIST'S LABORATORY... OR A BODYPART MUSEUM...
BEATRICE, DO YOU RECOGNIZE THAT HAND FROM ANYPLACE?
STEP AWAY FROM THE CANISTER.
AND WHAT IF I DON'T?
THEN YOU GET SHOT.
AND WHAT IF YOU MISS AND HIT THE HAND?
WELL THEN I GUESS I'LL HAVE TO TAKE YOURS.
GULP WHAT ARE YOU?
I AM PETER NICHOLS.

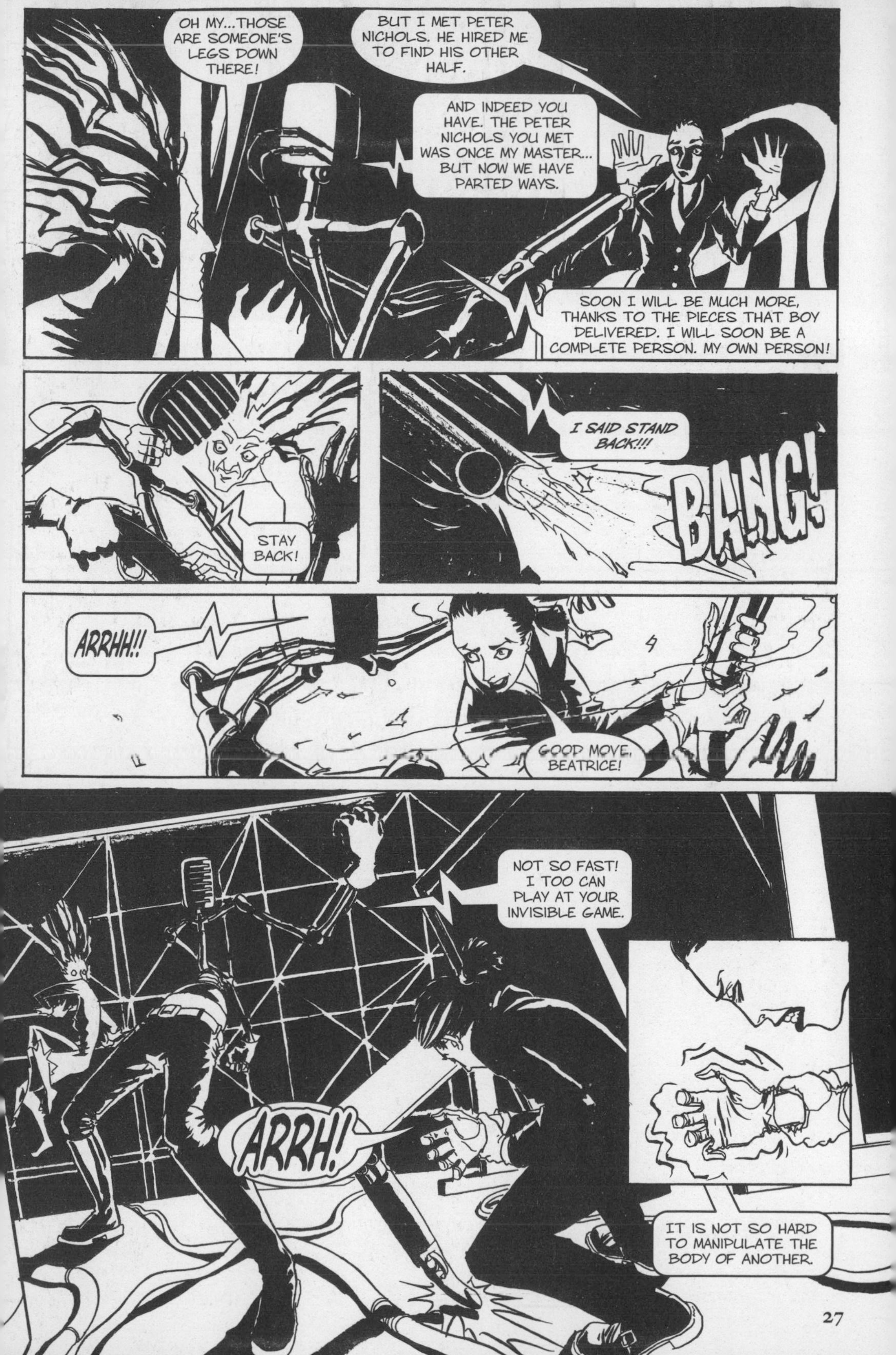
OH MY...THOSE ARE SOMEONE'S LEGS DOWN THERE!
BUT I MET PETER NICHOLS. HE HIRED ME TO FIND HIS OTHER HALF.
AND INDEED YOU HAVE. THE PETER NICHOLS YOU MET WAS ONCE MY MASTER... BUT NOW WE HAVE PARTED WAYS.
SOON I WILL BE MUCH MORE, THANKS TO THE PIECES THAT BOY DELIVERED. I WILL SOON BE A COMPLETE PERSON. MY OWN PERSON!
STAY BACK!
I SAID STAND BACK!!!
BANG!
ARRHH!!
GOOD MOVE, BEATRICE!
NOT SO FAST! I TOO CAN PLAY AT YOUR INVISIBLE GAME.
ARRH!
IT IS NOT SO HARD TO MANIPULATE THE BODY OF ANOTHER.

ARRGHH. THIS IS HOW YOU KILLED JAIME... CONTROLLING HIS BODY AGAINST HIM...

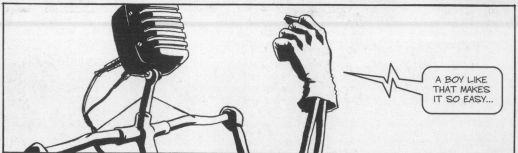

A BOY LIKE THAT MAKES IT SO EASY...

BUT I'VE HAD MUCH PRACTICE, YOU SEE...

I CAN FEEL SOMETHING...

I FEEL IT IN MY LEGS...IF I CONCENTRATE...IF I FOCUS THE ENERGY...

THE PROCEDURE WORKED THEN?

YEARS OF TEACHING ME TO WALK...BUT I LEARNED SO MUCH MORE. I LEARNED WHAT IT IS TO CONTROL SOMETHING...SOME*ONE*.

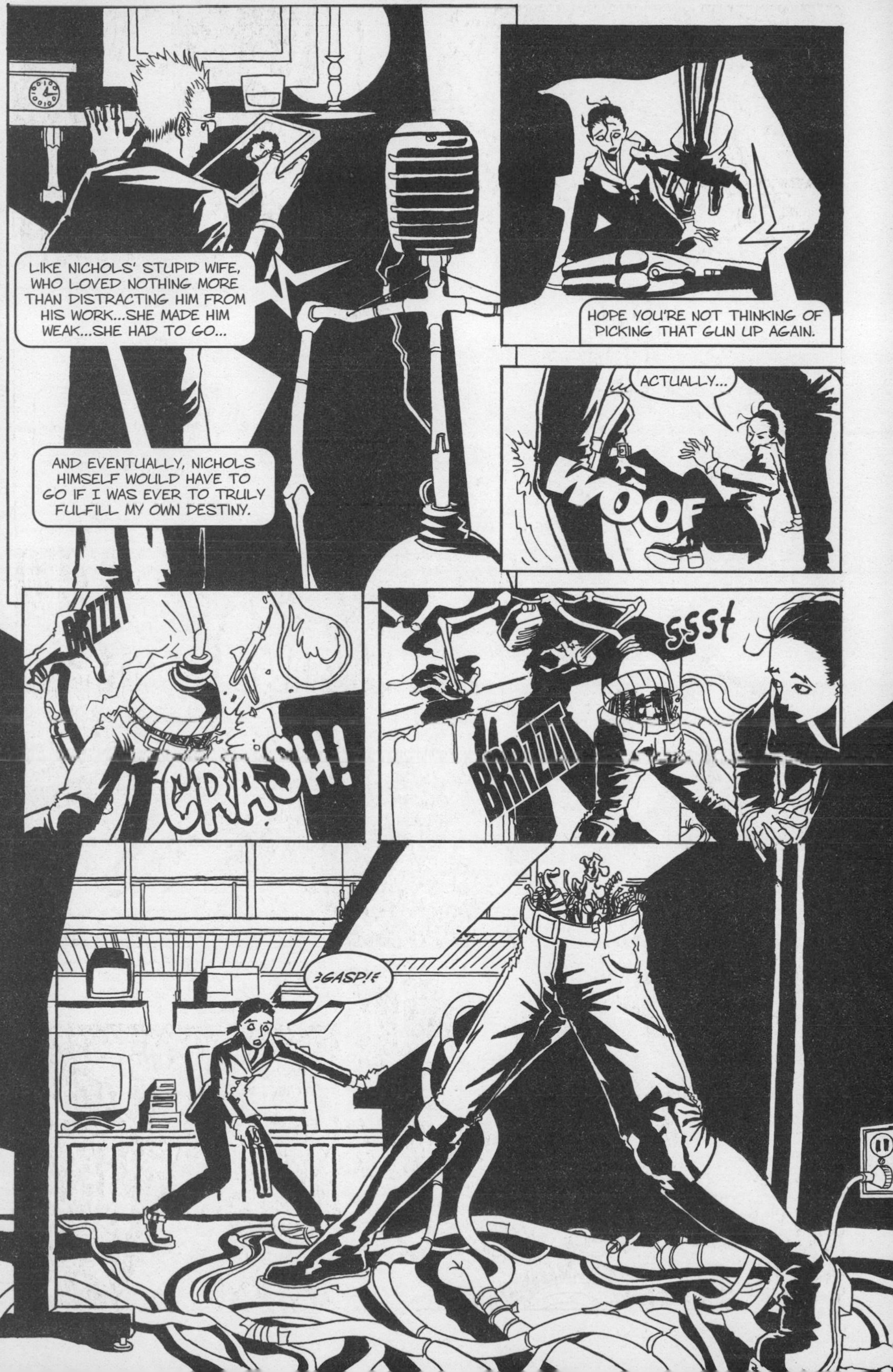
LIKE NICHOLS' STUPID WIFE, WHO LOVED NOTHING MORE THAN DISTRACTING HIM FROM HIS WORK...SHE MADE HIM WEAK...SHE HAD TO GO...
AND EVENTUALLY, NICHOLS HIMSELF WOULD HAVE TO GO IF I WAS EVER TO TRULY FULFILL MY OWN DESTINY.
HOPE YOU'RE NOT THINKING OF PICKING THAT GUN UP AGAIN.
ACTUALLY...
WOOF
BRZZZT
CRASH!
SSST
BRRZZT
GASP!

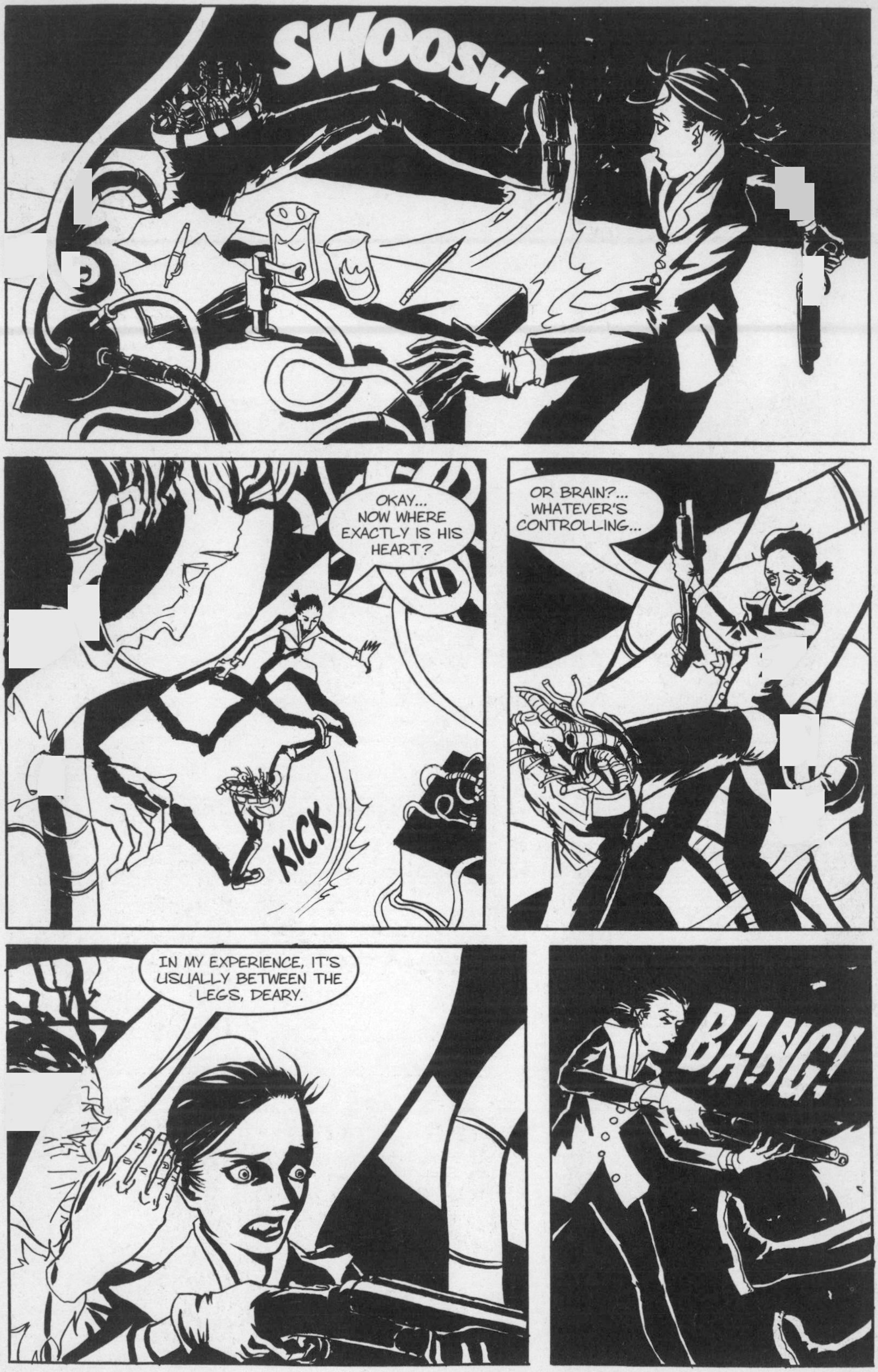
SWOOSH
OKAY... NOW WHERE EXACTLY IS HIS HEART?
KICK
OR BRAIN?... WHATEVER'S CONTROLLING...
IN MY EXPERIENCE, IT'S USUALLY BETWEEN THE LEGS, DEARY.
BANG!

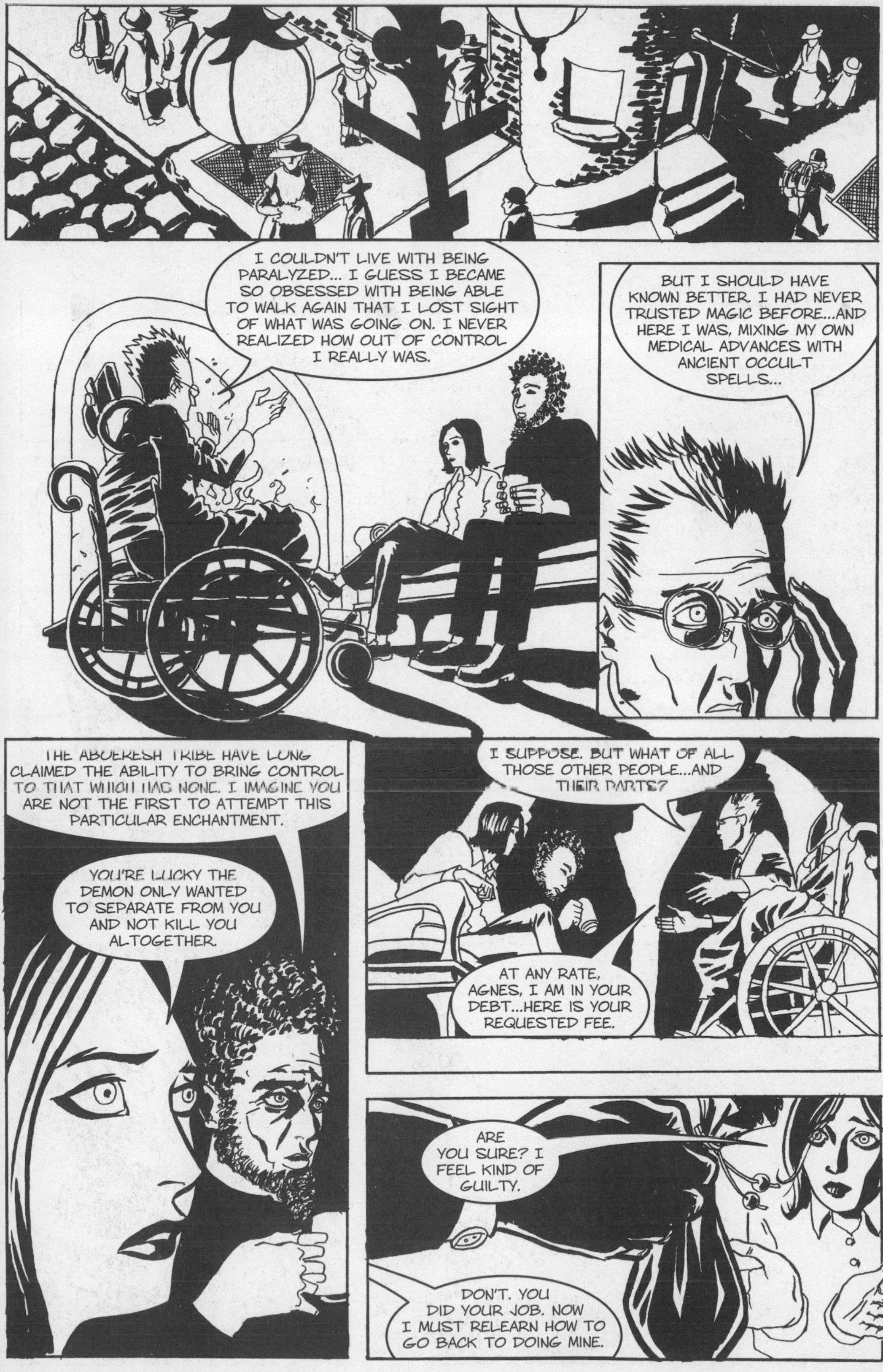
I COULDN'T LIVE WITH BEING PARALYZED... I GUESS I BECAME SO OBSESSED WITH BEING ABLE TO WALK AGAIN THAT I LOST SIGHT OF WHAT WAS GOING ON. I NEVER REALIZED HOW OUT OF CONTROL I REALLY WAS.
BUT I SHOULD HAVE KNOWN BETTER. I HAD NEVER TRUSTED MAGIC BEFORE...AND HERE I WAS, MIXING MY OWN MEDICAL ADVANCES WITH ANCIENT OCCULT SPELLS...
THE ABUERESH TRIBE HAVE LONG CLAIMED THE ABILITY TO BRING CONTROL TO THAT WHICH HAS NONE. I IMAGINE YOU ARE NOT THE FIRST TO ATTEMPT THIS PARTICULAR ENCHANTMENT.
YOU'RE LUCKY THE DEMON ONLY WANTED TO SEPARATE FROM YOU AND NOT KILL YOU ALTOGETHER.
I SUPPOSE. BUT WHAT OF ALL THOSE OTHER PEOPLE...AND THEIR PARTS?
AT ANY RATE, AGNES, I AM IN YOUR DEBT...HERE IS YOUR REQUESTED FEE.
ARE YOU SURE? I FEEL KIND OF GUILTY.
DON'T. YOU DID YOUR JOB. NOW I MUST RELEARN HOW TO GO BACK TO DOING MINE.

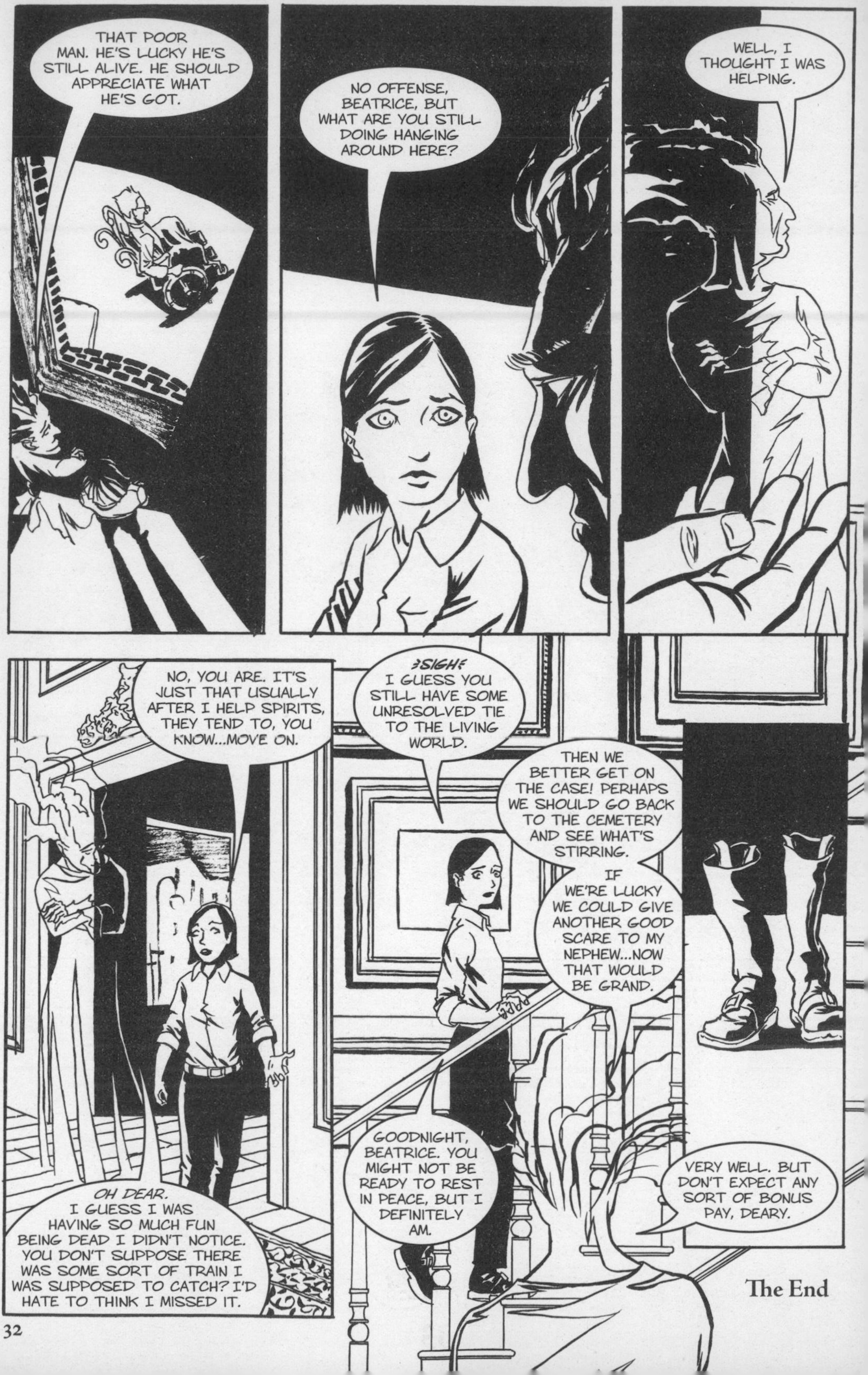
THAT POOR MAN. HE'S LUCKY HE'S STILL ALIVE. HE SHOULD APPRECIATE WHAT HE'S GOT.
NO OFFENSE, BEATRICE, BUT WHAT ARE YOU STILL DOING HANGING AROUND HERE?
WELL, I THOUGHT I WAS HELPING.
NO, YOU ARE. IT'S JUST THAT USUALLY AFTER I HELP SPIRITS, THEY TEND TO, YOU KNOW...MOVE ON.
OH DEAR.
I GUESS I WAS HAVING SO MUCH FUN BEING DEAD I DIDN'T NOTICE. YOU DON'T SUPPOSE THERE WAS SOME SORT OF TRAIN I WAS SUPPOSED TO CATCH? I'D HATE TO THINK I MISSED IT.
SIGH
I GUESS YOU STILL HAVE SOME UNRESOLVED TIE TO THE LIVING WORLD.
THEN WE BETTER GET ON THE CASE! PERHAPS WE SHOULD GO BACK TO THE CEMETERY AND SEE WHAT'S STIRRING.
IF WE'RE LUCKY WE COULD GIVE ANOTHER GOOD SCARE TO MY NEPHEW...NOW THAT WOULD BE GRAND.
GOODNIGHT, BEATRICE. YOU MIGHT NOT BE READY TO REST IN PEACE, BUT I DEFINITELY AM.
VERY WELL. BUT DON'T EXPECT ANY SORT OF BONUS PAY, DEARY.
The End

CHAPTER 2

"LOST
and
FOUND"

WRITTEN *by* **DAVE ROMAN**
ILLUSTRATED *and* LETTERED
by **RAINA TELGEMEIER**

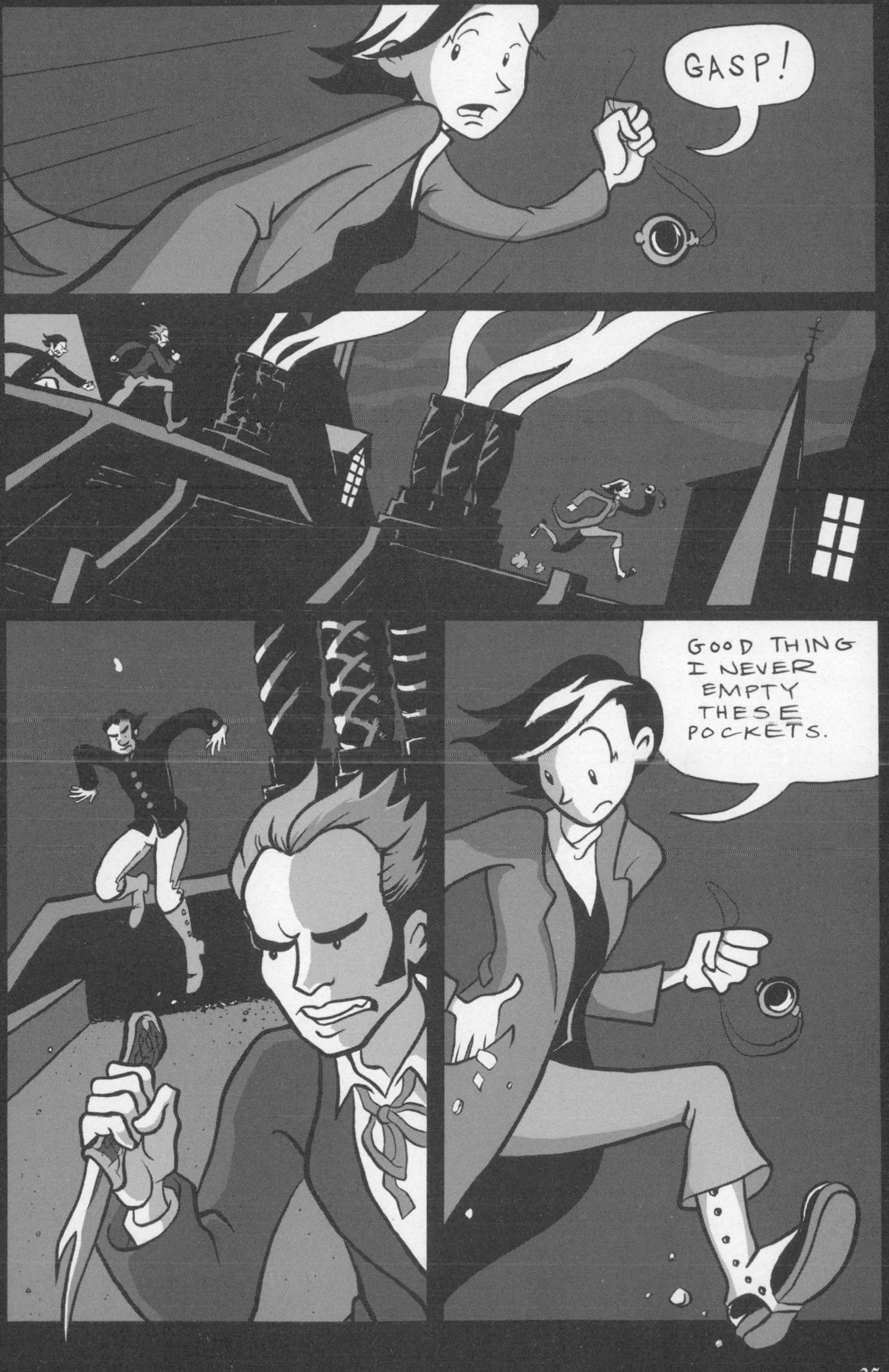
GASP!
GOOD THING I NEVER EMPTY THESE POCKETS.

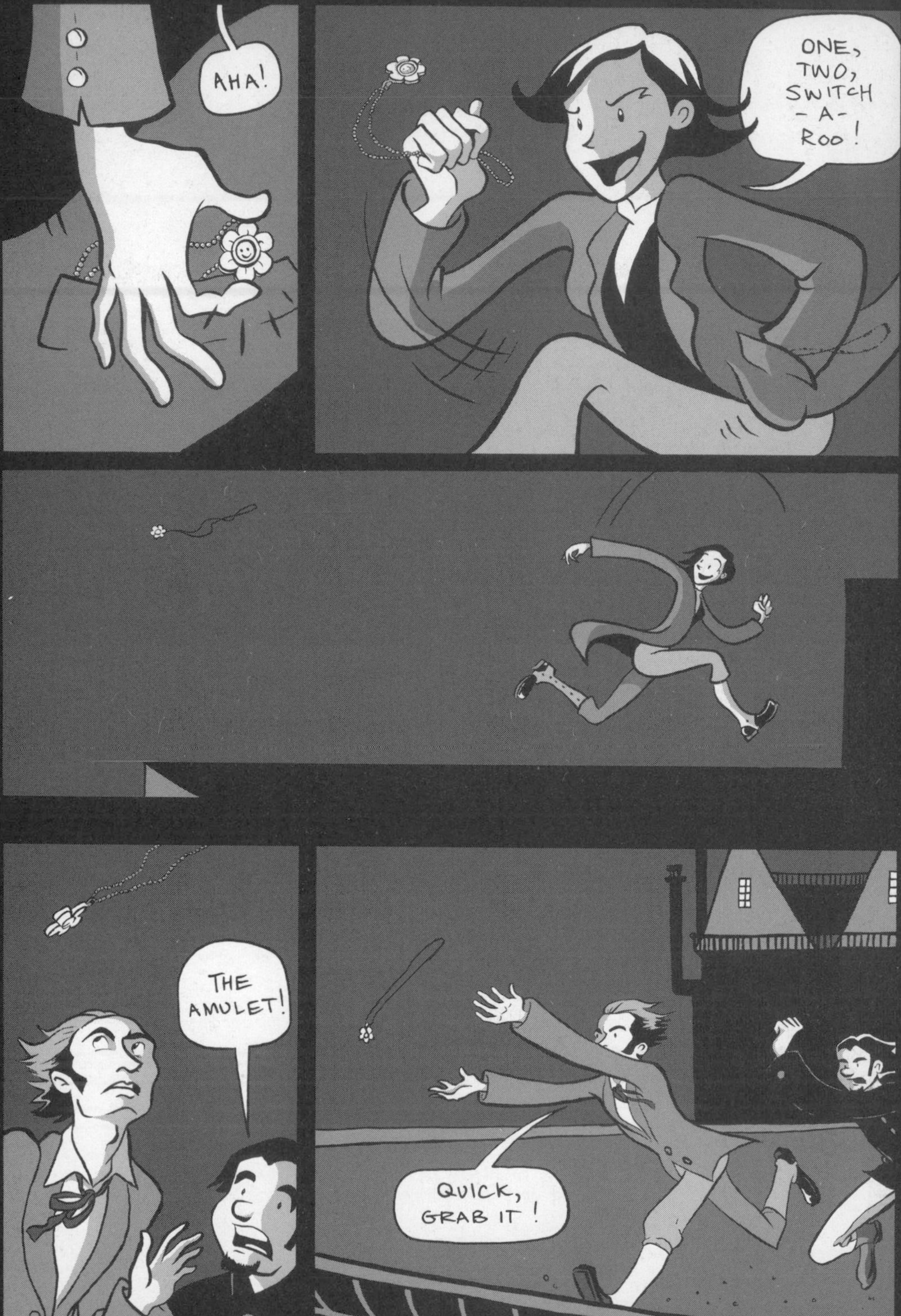
AHA!
ONE, TWO, SWITCH -A- ROO!
THE AMULET!
QUICK, GRAB IT!

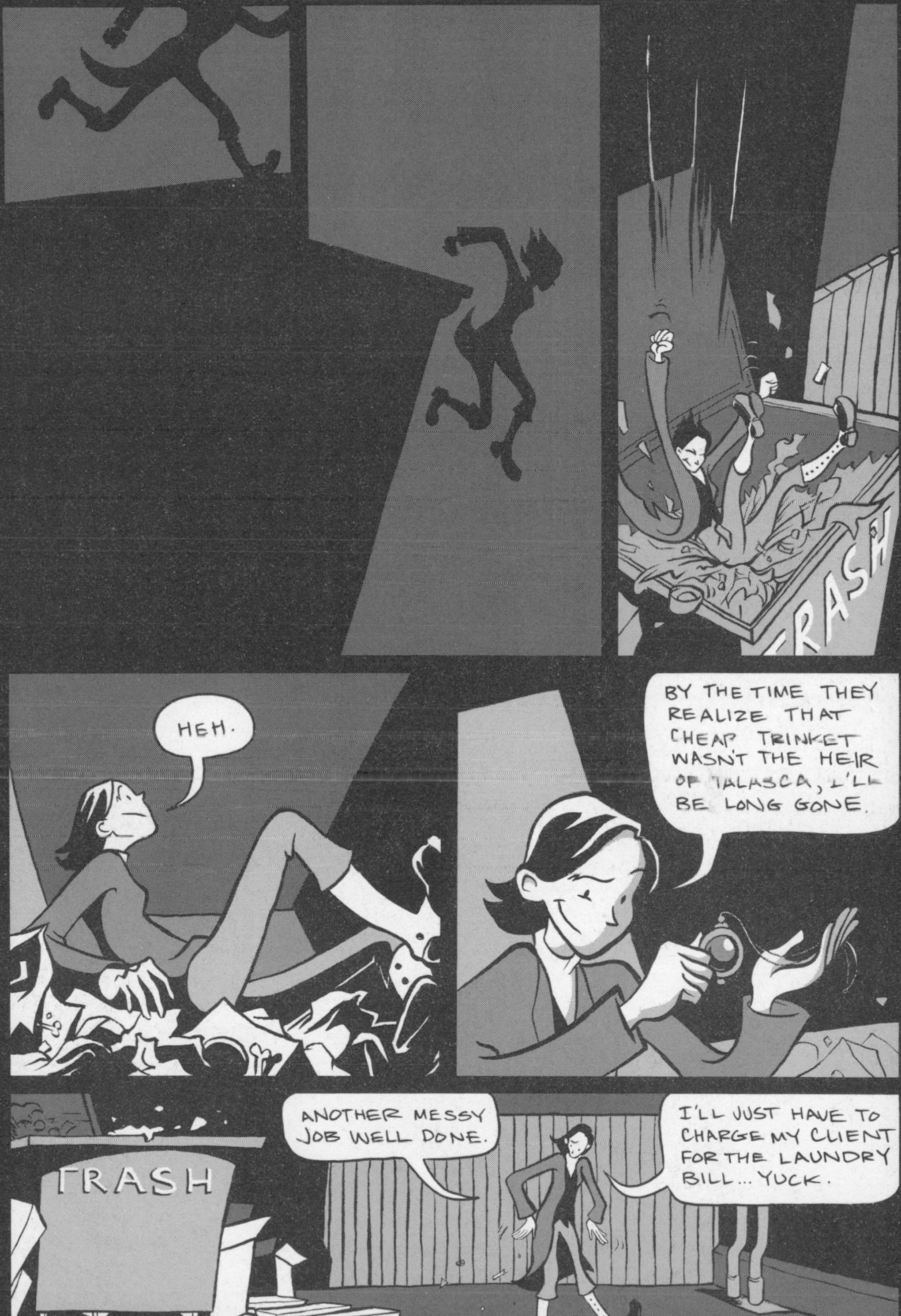
HEH.
BY THE TIME THEY REALIZE THAT CHEAP TRINKET WASN'T THE HEIR OF TALASCA, I'LL BE LONG GONE.
TRASH
ANOTHER MESSY JOB WELL DONE.
I'LL JUST HAVE TO CHARGE MY CLIENT FOR THE LAUNDRY BILL... YUCK.

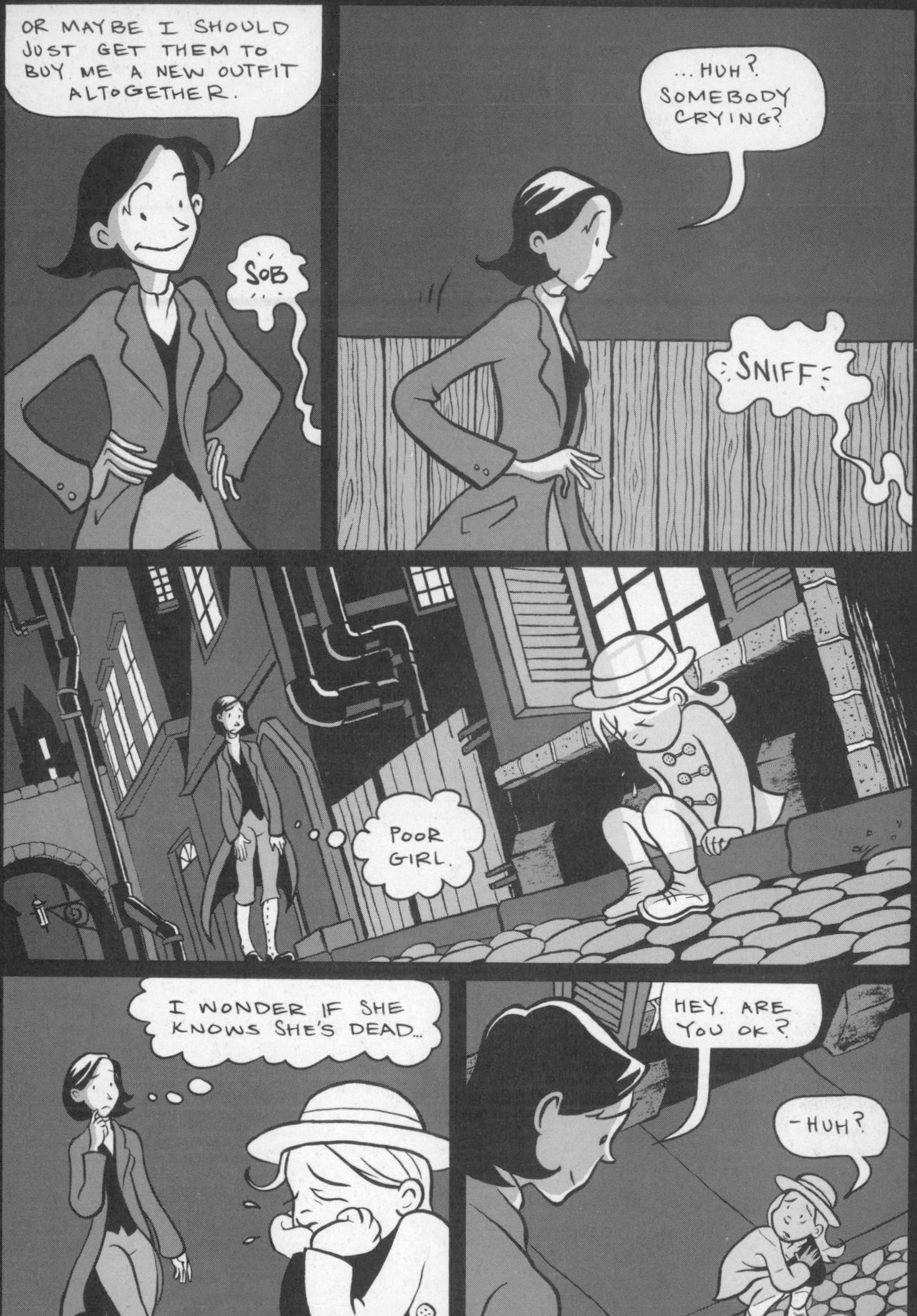
OR MAYBE I SHOULD JUST GET THEM TO BUY ME A NEW OUTFIT ALTOGETHER.
SOB
...HUH? SOMEBODY CRYING?
SNIFF
POOR GIRL.
I WONDER IF SHE KNOWS SHE'S DEAD...
HEY. ARE YOU OK?
-HUH?

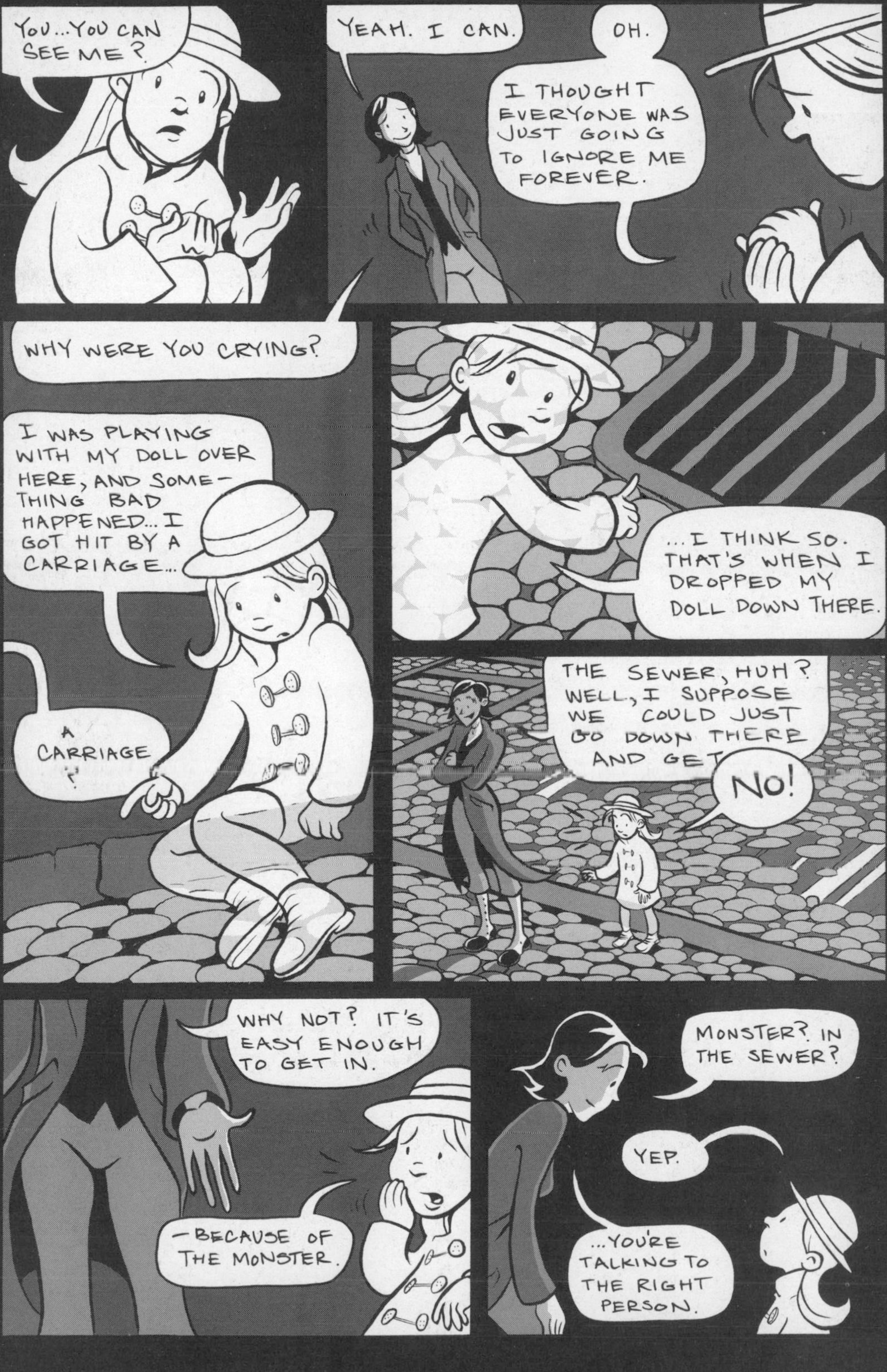

YOU...YOU CAN SEE ME?
YEAH. I CAN.
OH.
I THOUGHT EVERYONE WAS JUST GOING TO IGNORE ME FOREVER.
WHY WERE YOU CRYING?
I WAS PLAYING WITH MY DOLL OVER HERE, AND SOME-THING BAD HAPPENED... I GOT HIT BY A CARRIAGE...
A CARRIAGE?
...I THINK SO. THAT'S WHEN I DROPPED MY DOLL DOWN THERE.
THE SEWER, HUH? WELL, I SUPPOSE WE COULD JUST GO DOWN THERE AND GET
No!
WHY NOT? IT'S EASY ENOUGH TO GET IN.
—BECAUSE OF THE MONSTER.
MONSTER? IN THE SEWER?
YEP.
...YOU'RE TALKING TO THE RIGHT PERSON.

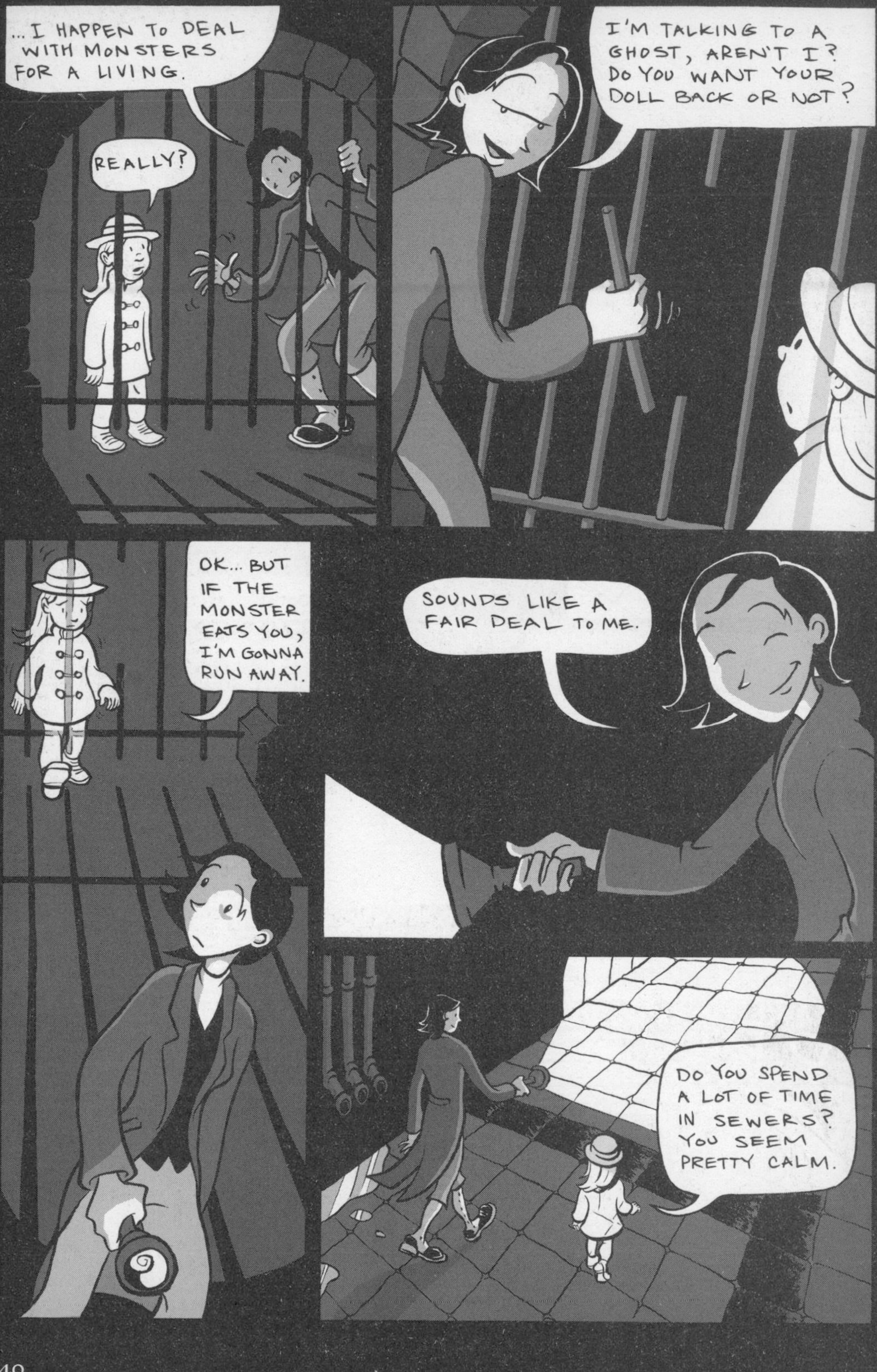
...I HAPPEN TO DEAL WITH MONSTERS FOR A LIVING.
REALLY?
I'M TALKING TO A GHOST, AREN'T I? DO YOU WANT YOUR DOLL BACK OR NOT?
OK... BUT IF THE MONSTER EATS YOU, I'M GONNA RUN AWAY.
SOUNDS LIKE A FAIR DEAL TO ME.
DO YOU SPEND A LOT OF TIME IN SEWERS? YOU SEEM PRETTY CALM.

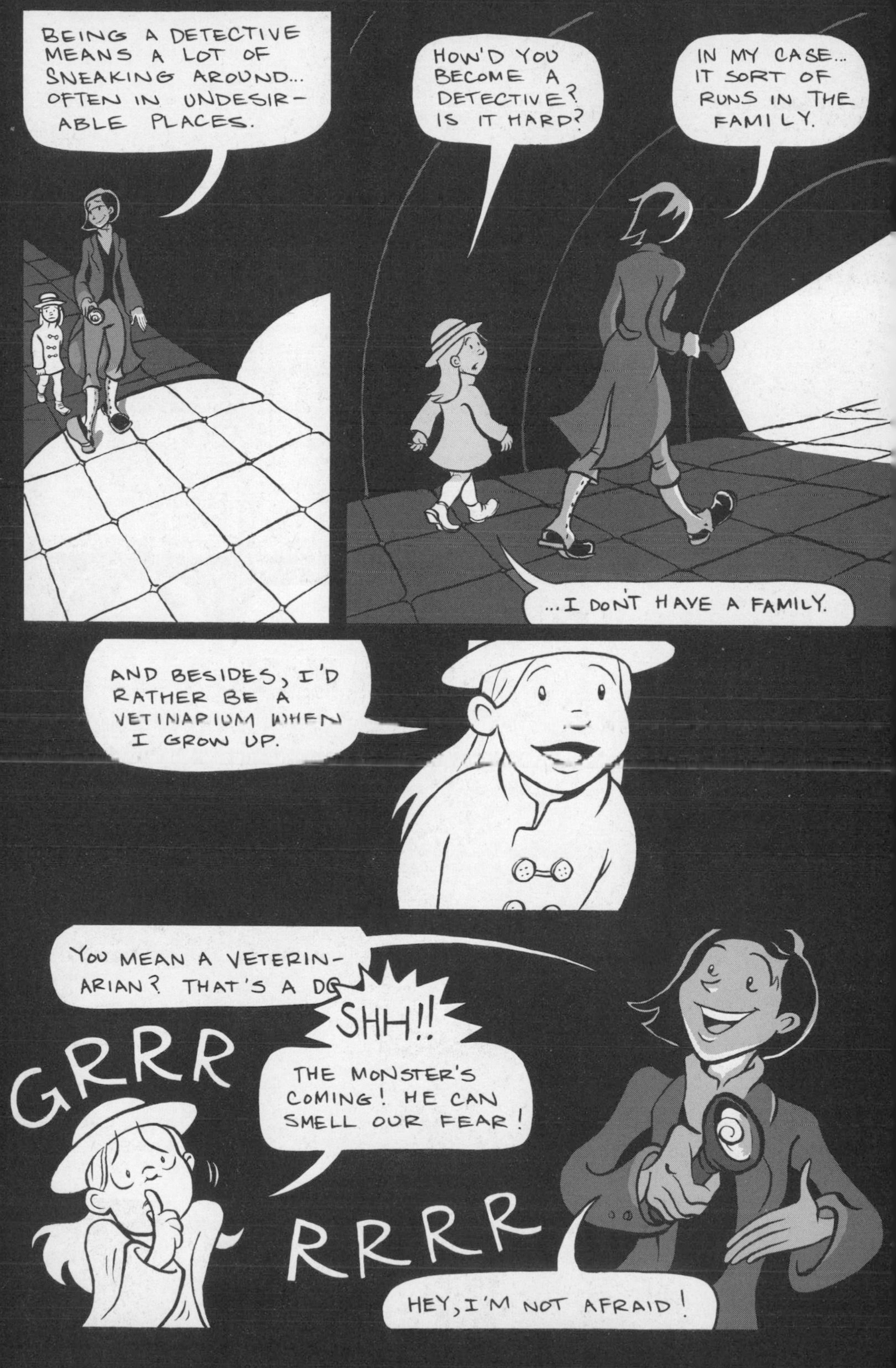
BEING A DETECTIVE MEANS A LOT OF SNEAKING AROUND... OFTEN IN UNDESIR-ABLE PLACES.
HOW'D YOU BECOME A DETECTIVE? IS IT HARD?
IN MY CASE... IT SORT OF RUNS IN THE FAMILY.
...I DON'T HAVE A FAMILY.
AND BESIDES, I'D RATHER BE A VETINARIUM WHEN I GROW UP.
YOU MEAN A VETERIN-ARIAN? THAT'S A DO
SHH!!
GRRR
THE MONSTER'S COMING! HE CAN SMELL OUR FEAR!
RRRR
HEY, I'M NOT AFRAID!

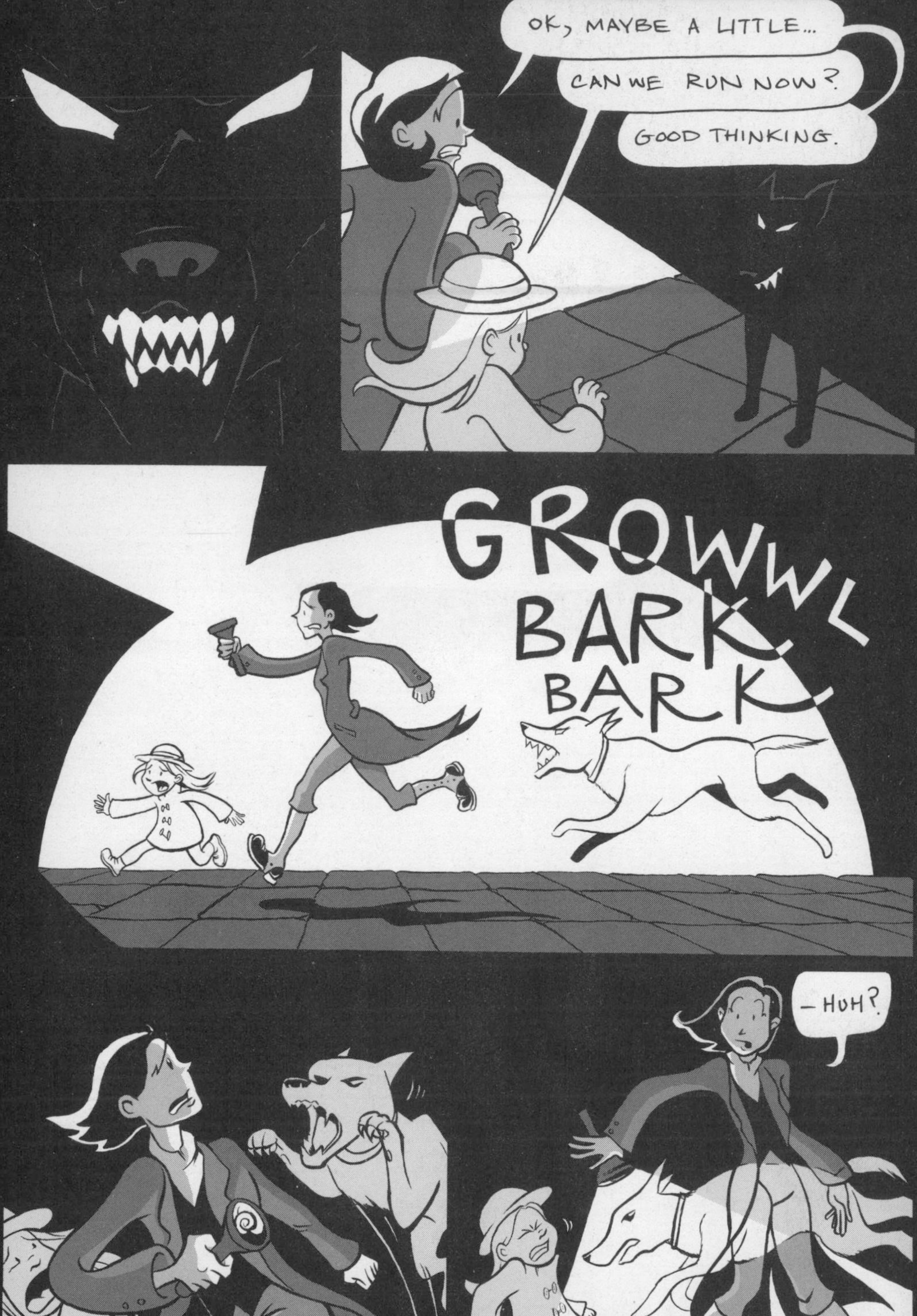
OK, MAYBE A LITTLE...
CAN WE RUN NOW?
GOOD THINKING.
GROWWL
BARK
BARK
—HUH?

HA HA!

SLURP

IT'S LICKING ME!

HE MUST BE A GHOST DOG.

THEY'RE A GOOD MATCH FOR EACH OTHER.

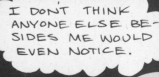

I THINK HE WANTS ME TO LIVE DOWN HERE WITH HIM.

DO YOU THINK IT'S OK?

OF COURSE.

HA HA!

I DON'T THINK ANYONE ELSE BE- SIDES ME WOULD EVEN NOTICE.

END

CHAPTER 3

"ZOMBIE LOVE TRAP"

&

"BURIED HOMES *and* GARDENS"

WRITTEN *by* **DAVE ROMAN**
ILLUSTRATED *by* **JEFF ZORNOW**
LETTERED *by* **JOHN GREEN**

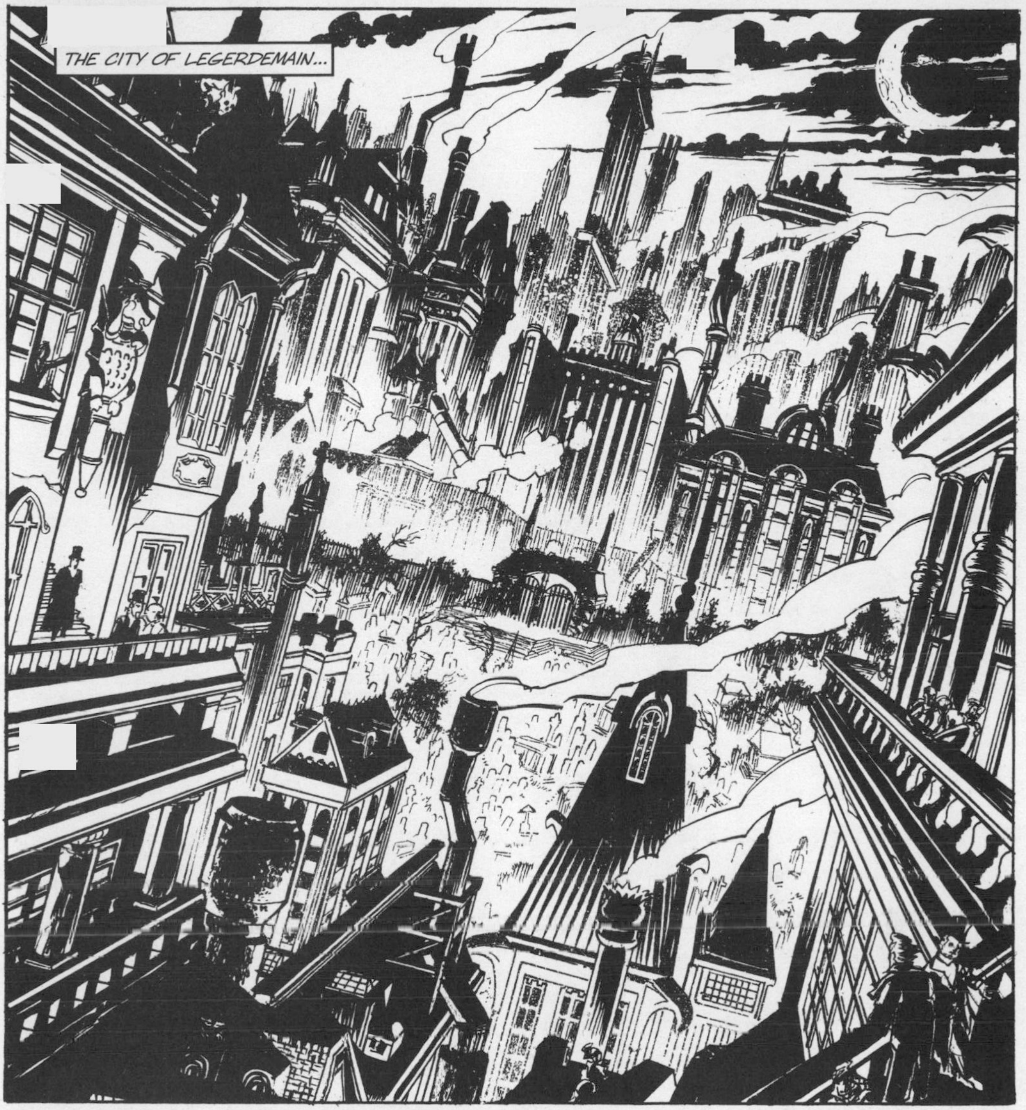
THE CITY OF LEGERDEMAIN...

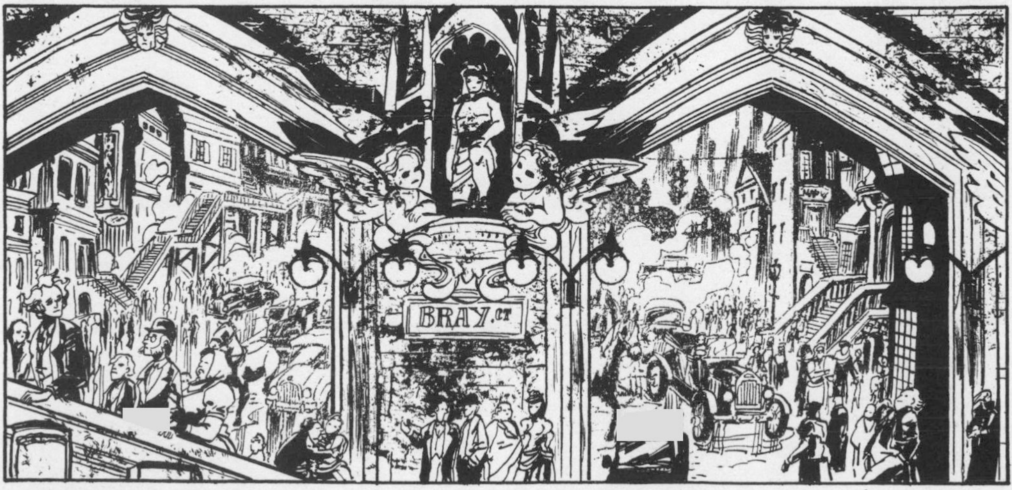
BRAY CT

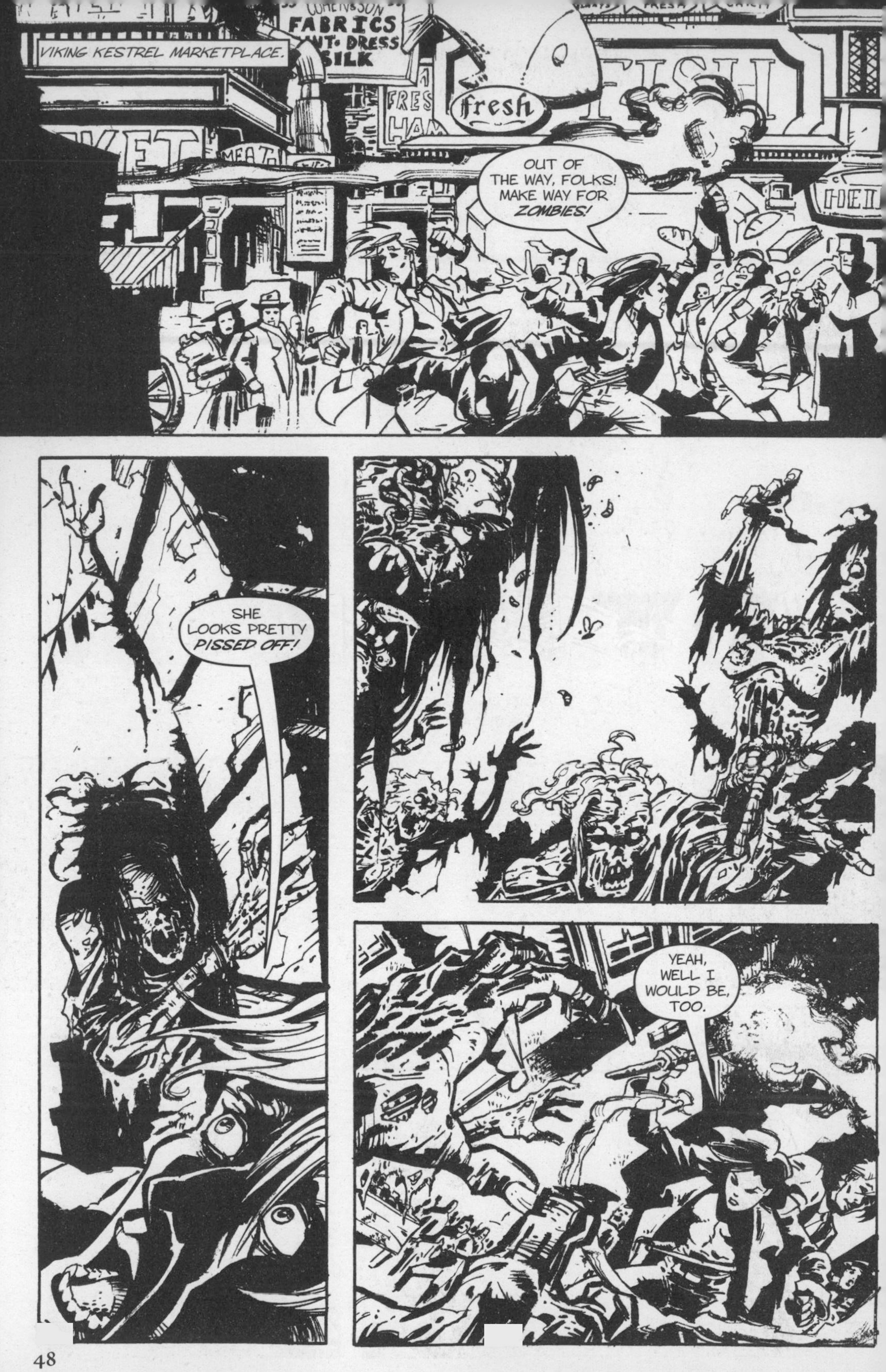
VIKING KESTREL MARKETPLACE.
COHEN & SON
FABRICS
SILK
fresh
OUT OF THE WAY, FOLKS! MAKE WAY FOR ZOMBIES!
SHE LOOKS PRETTY PISSED OFF!
YEAH, WELL I WOULD BE, TOO.

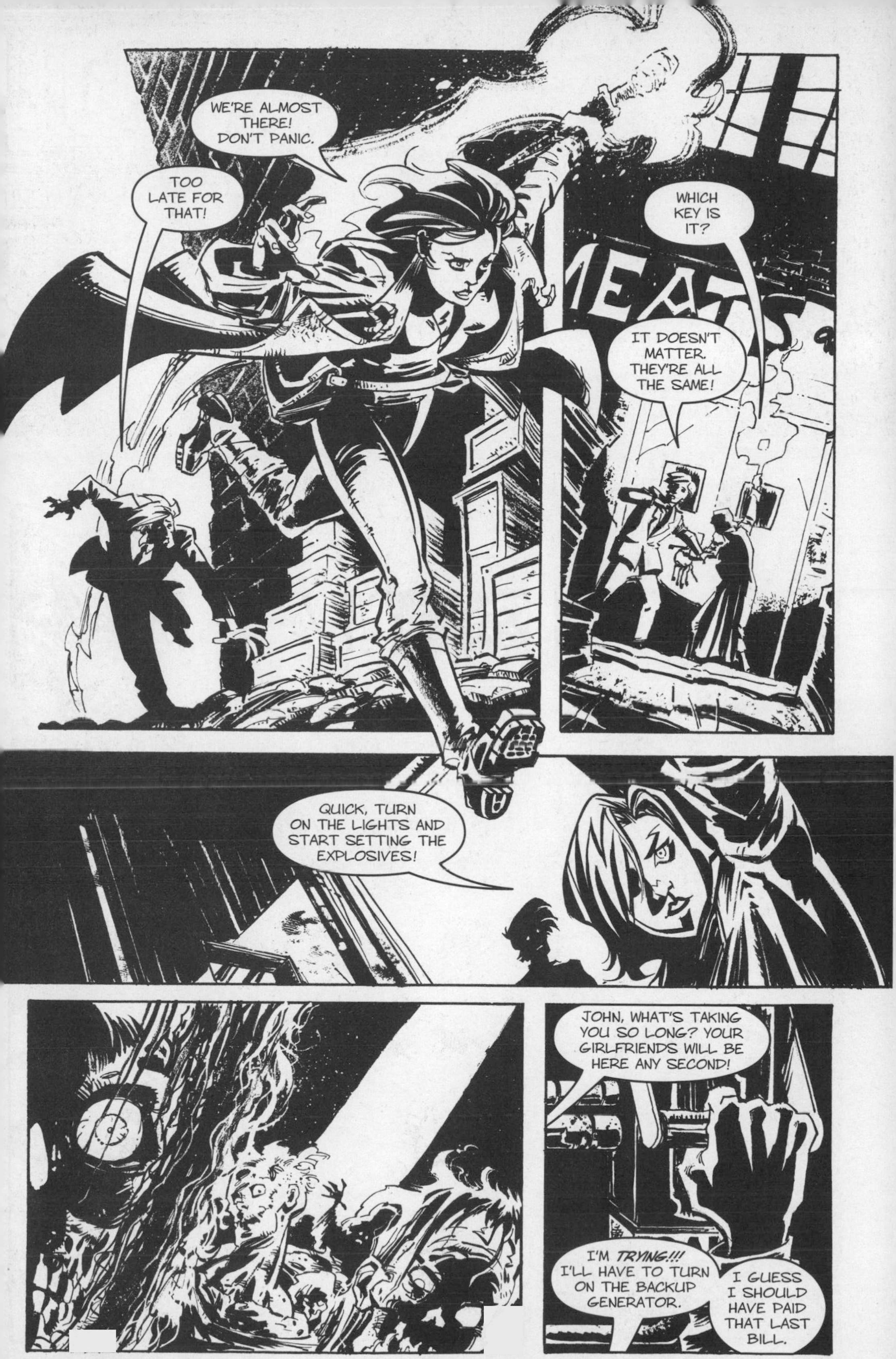
WE'RE ALMOST THERE! DON'T PANIC.
TOO LATE FOR THAT!
WHICH KEY IS IT?
IT DOESN'T MATTER. THEY'RE ALL THE SAME!
QUICK, TURN ON THE LIGHTS AND START SETTING THE EXPLOSIVES!
JOHN, WHAT'S TAKING YOU SO LONG? YOUR GIRLFRIENDS WILL BE HERE ANY SECOND!
I'M *TRYING!!!* I'LL HAVE TO TURN ON THE BACKUP GENERATOR.
I GUESS I SHOULD HAVE PAID THAT LAST BILL.

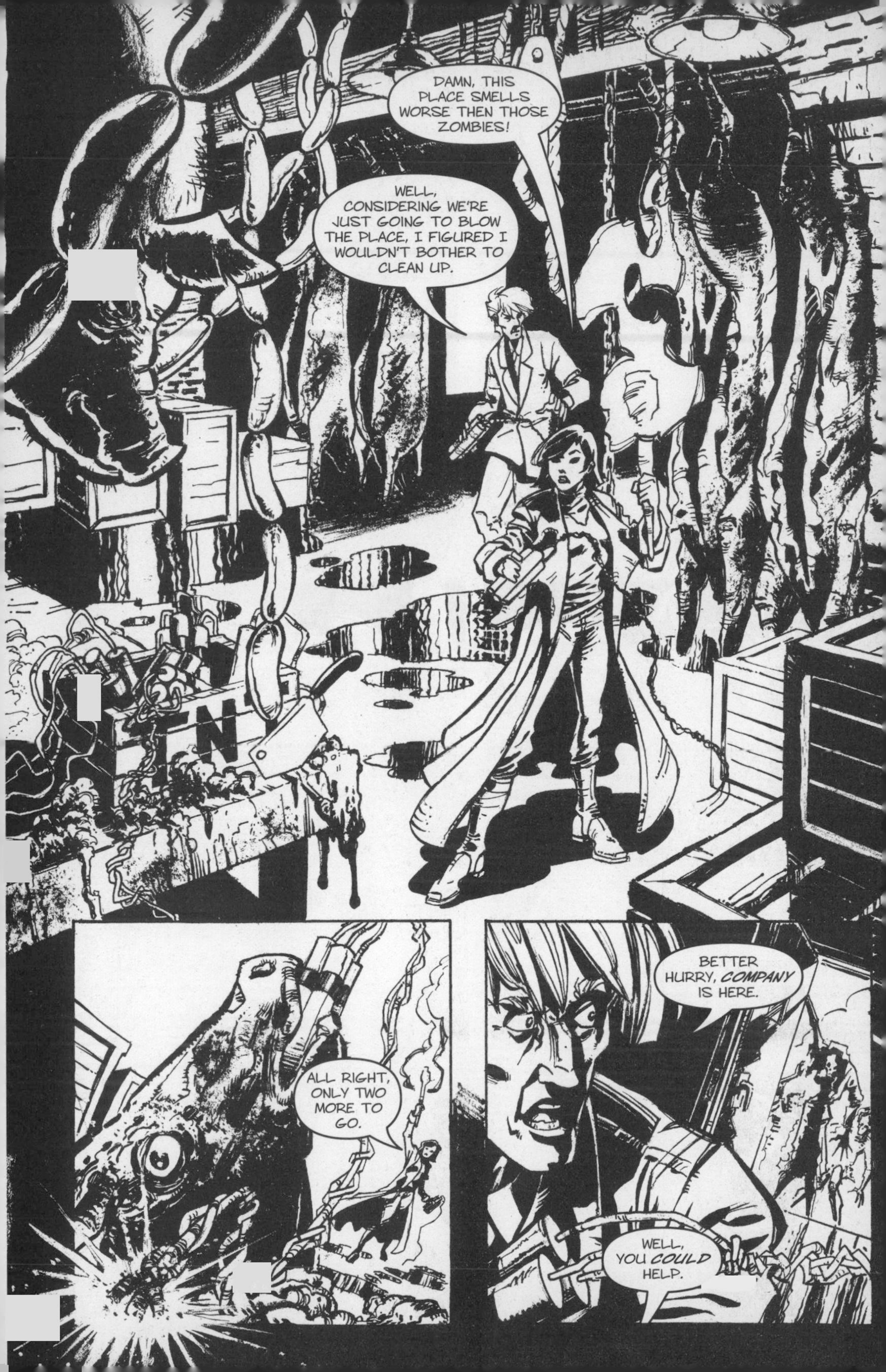
DAMN, THIS PLACE SMELLS WORSE THEN THOSE ZOMBIES!
WELL, CONSIDERING WE'RE JUST GOING TO BLOW THE PLACE, I FIGURED I WOULDN'T BOTHER TO CLEAN UP.
ALL RIGHT, ONLY TWO MORE TO GO.
BETTER HURRY, COMPANY IS HERE.
WELL, YOU COULD HELP.

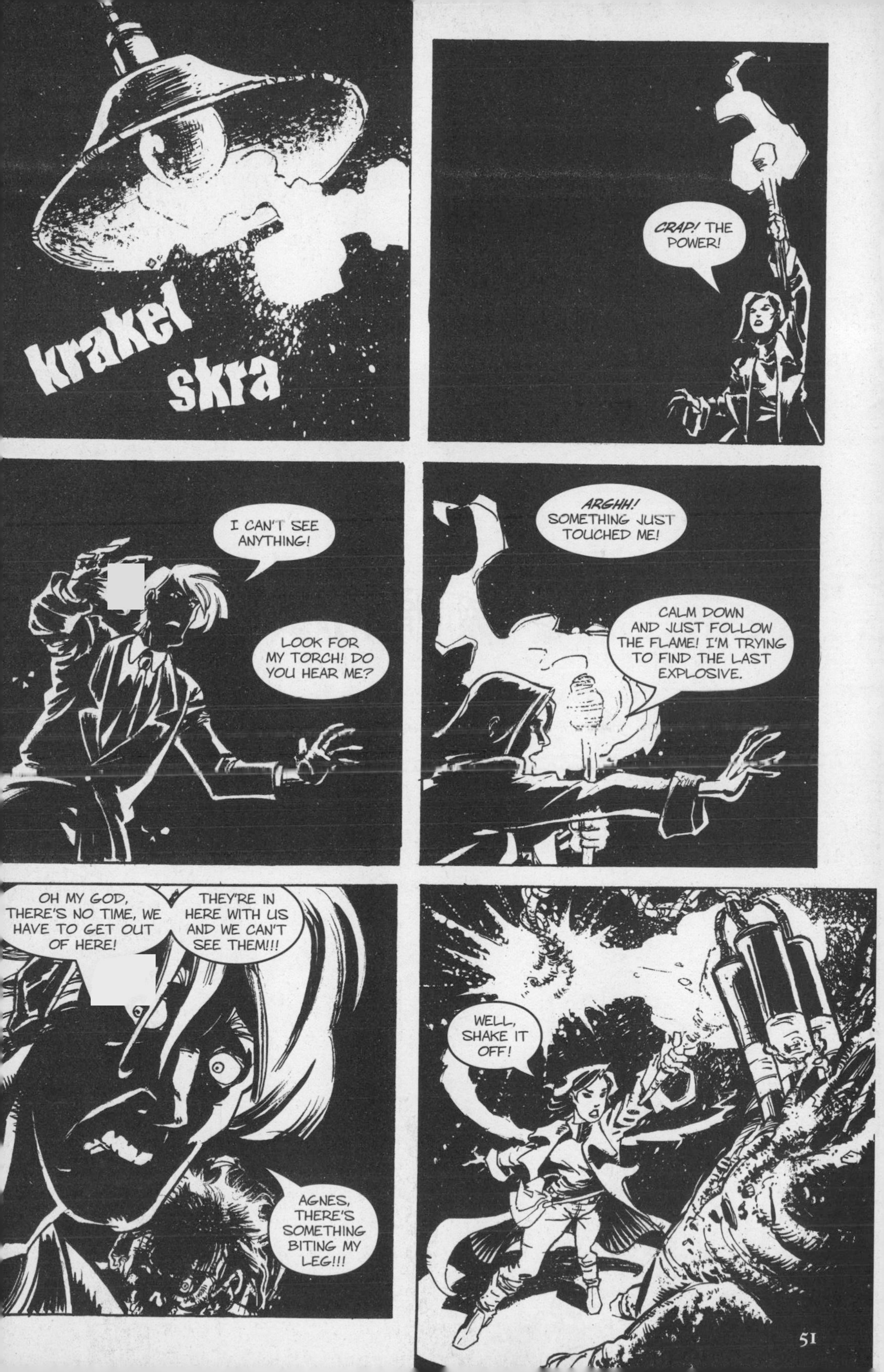
krakel
skra
CRAP! THE POWER!
I CAN'T SEE ANYTHING!
LOOK FOR MY TORCH! DO YOU HEAR ME?
ARGHH! SOMETHING JUST TOUCHED ME!
CALM DOWN AND JUST FOLLOW THE FLAME! I'M TRYING TO FIND THE LAST EXPLOSIVE.
OH MY GOD, THERE'S NO TIME, WE HAVE TO GET OUT OF HERE!
THEY'RE IN HERE WITH US AND WE CAN'T SEE THEM!!!
AGNES, THERE'S SOMETHING BITING MY LEG!!!
WELL, SHAKE IT OFF!

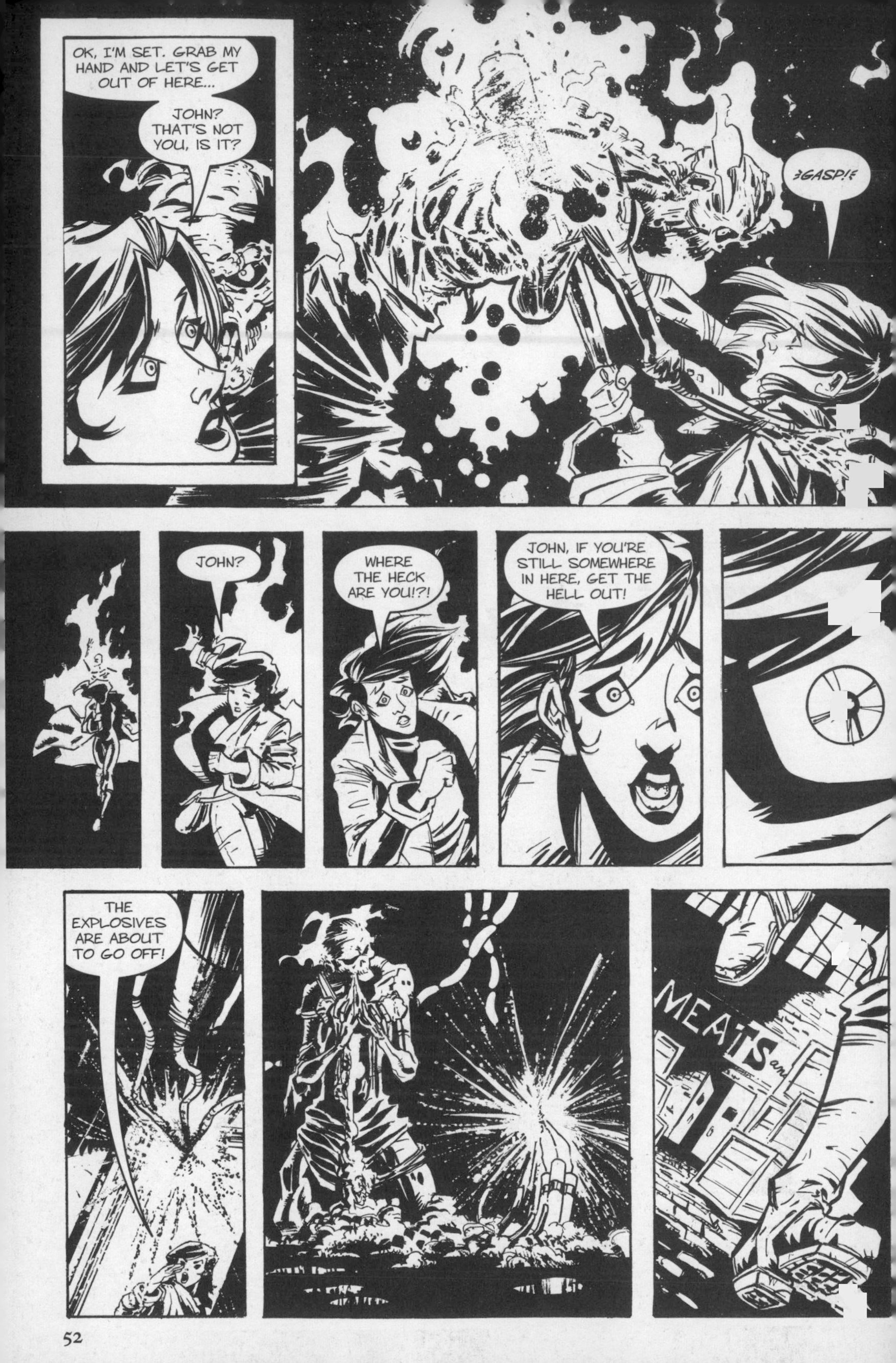
OK, I'M SET. GRAB MY HAND AND LET'S GET OUT OF HERE...
JOHN? THAT'S NOT YOU, IS IT?
GASP!
JOHN?
WHERE THE HECK ARE YOU!?!
JOHN, IF YOU'RE STILL SOMEWHERE IN HERE, GET THE HELL OUT!
THE EXPLOSIVES ARE ABOUT TO GO OFF!
MEATS

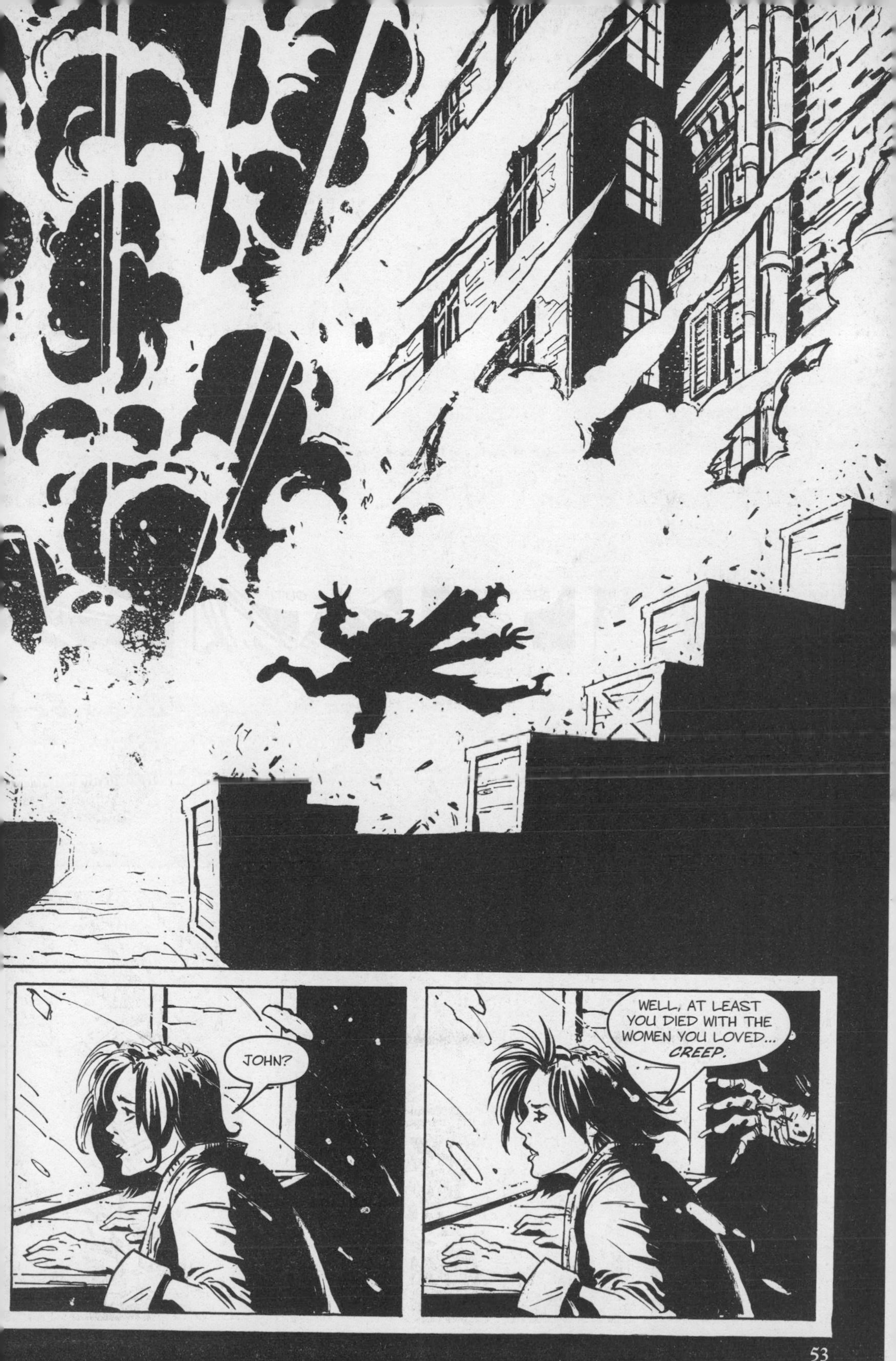
JOHN?
WELL, AT LEAST YOU DIED WITH THE WOMEN YOU LOVED... CREEP.

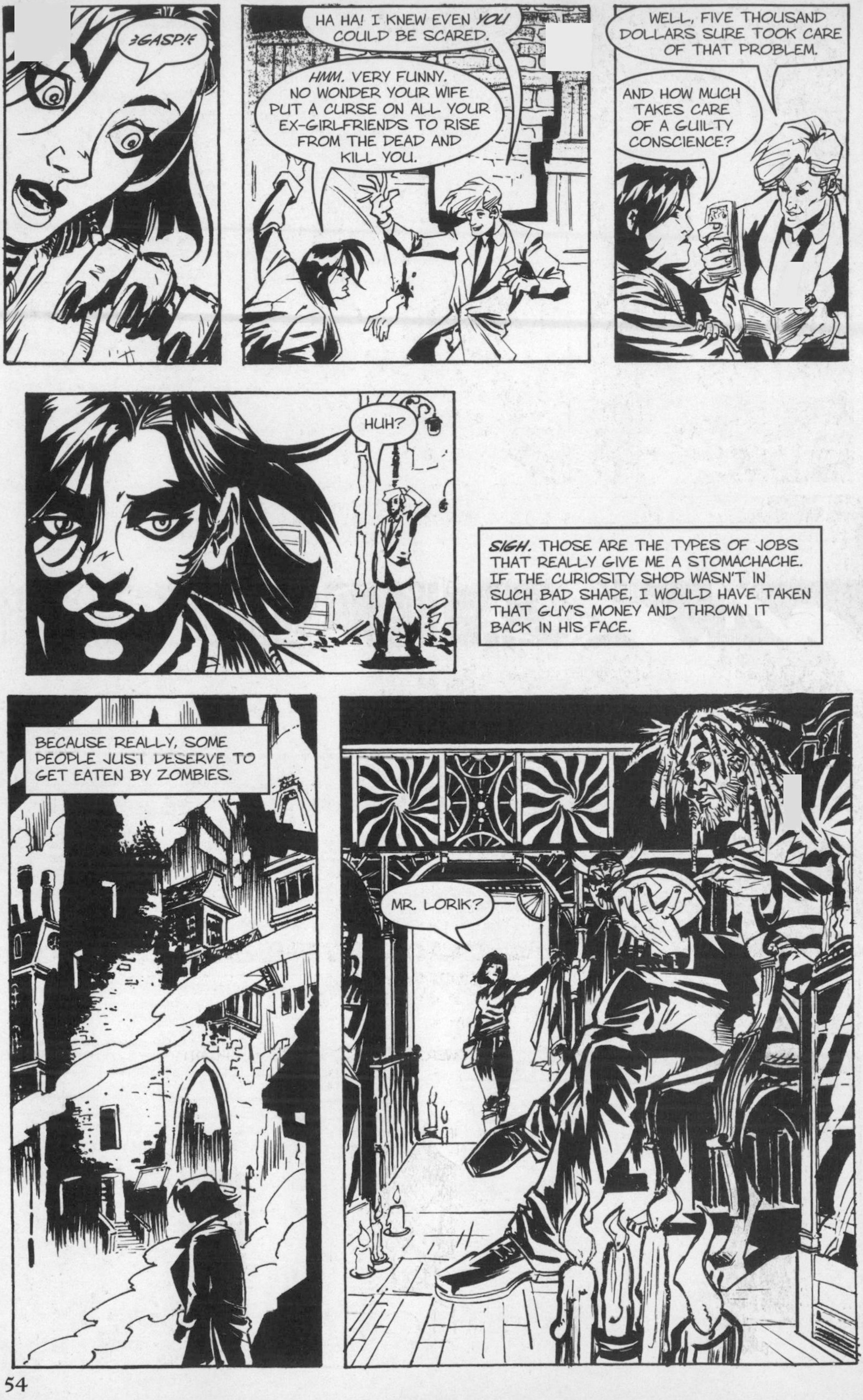
GASP!
HA HA! I KNEW EVEN YOU COULD BE SCARED.
HMM. VERY FUNNY. NO WONDER YOUR WIFE PUT A CURSE ON ALL YOUR EX-GIRLFRIENDS TO RISE FROM THE DEAD AND KILL YOU.
WELL, FIVE THOUSAND DOLLARS SURE TOOK CARE OF THAT PROBLEM.
AND HOW MUCH TAKES CARE OF A GUILTY CONSCIENCE?
HUH?
SIGH. THOSE ARE THE TYPES OF JOBS THAT REALLY GIVE ME A STOMACHACHE. IF THE CURIOSITY SHOP WASN'T IN SUCH BAD SHAPE, I WOULD HAVE TAKEN THAT GUY'S MONEY AND THROWN IT BACK IN HIS FACE.
BECAUSE REALLY, SOME PEOPLE JUST DESERVE TO GET EATEN BY ZOMBIES.
MR. LORIK?

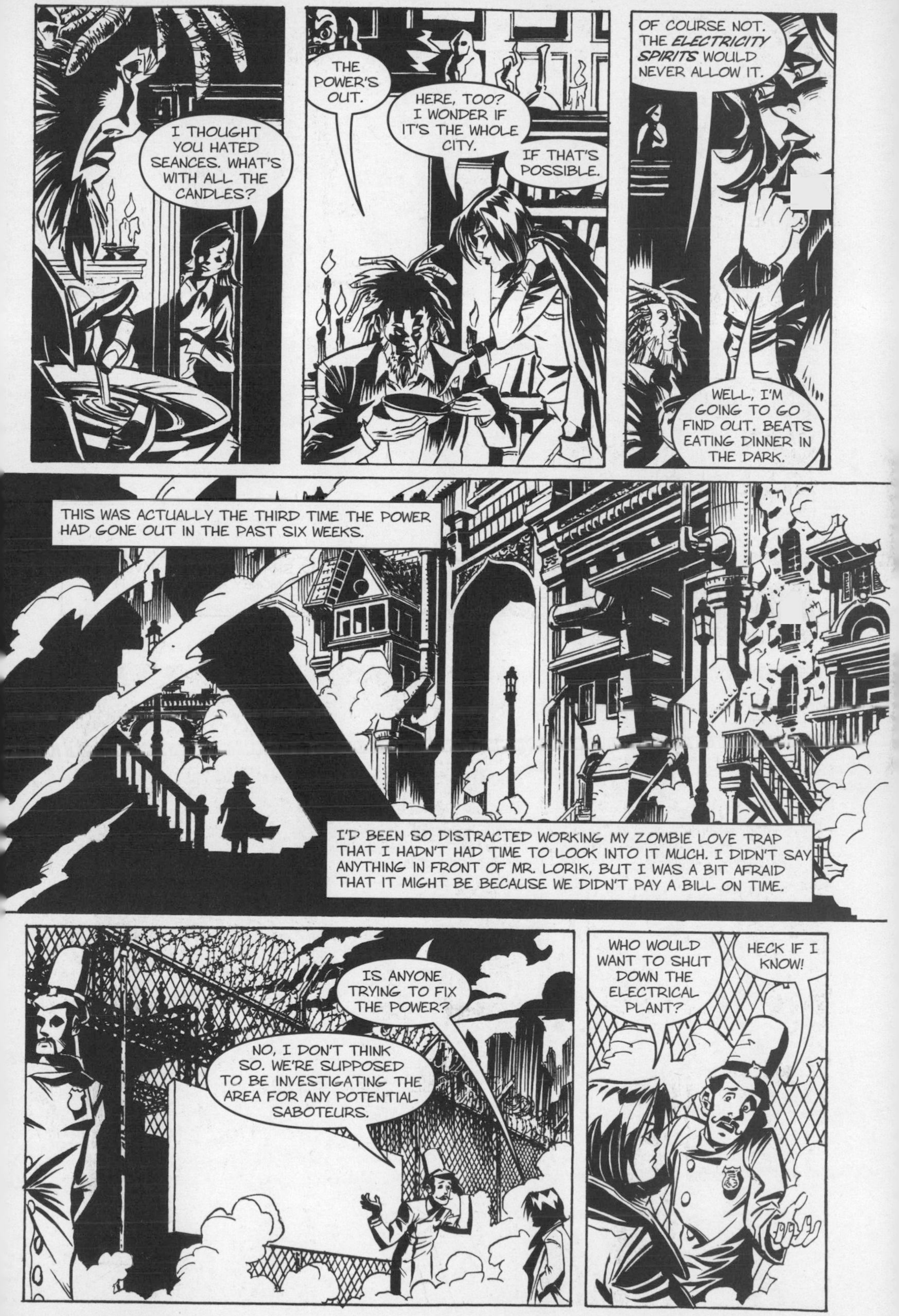
I THOUGHT YOU HATED SEANCES. WHAT'S WITH ALL THE CANDLES?
THE POWER'S OUT.
HERE, TOO? I WONDER IF IT'S THE WHOLE CITY.
IF THAT'S POSSIBLE.
OF COURSE NOT. THE *ELECTRICITY SPIRITS* WOULD NEVER ALLOW IT.
WELL, I'M GOING TO GO FIND OUT. BEATS EATING DINNER IN THE DARK.
THIS WAS ACTUALLY THE THIRD TIME THE POWER HAD GONE OUT IN THE PAST SIX WEEKS.
I'D BEEN SO DISTRACTED WORKING MY ZOMBIE LOVE TRAP THAT I HADN'T HAD TIME TO LOOK INTO IT MUCH. I DIDN'T SAY ANYTHING IN FRONT OF MR. LORIK, BUT I WAS A BIT AFRAID THAT IT MIGHT BE BECAUSE WE DIDN'T PAY A BILL ON TIME.
IS ANYONE TRYING TO FIX THE POWER?
NO, I DON'T THINK SO. WE'RE SUPPOSED TO BE INVESTIGATING THE AREA FOR ANY POTENTIAL SABOTEURS.
WHO WOULD WANT TO SHUT DOWN THE ELECTRICAL PLANT?
HECK IF I KNOW!

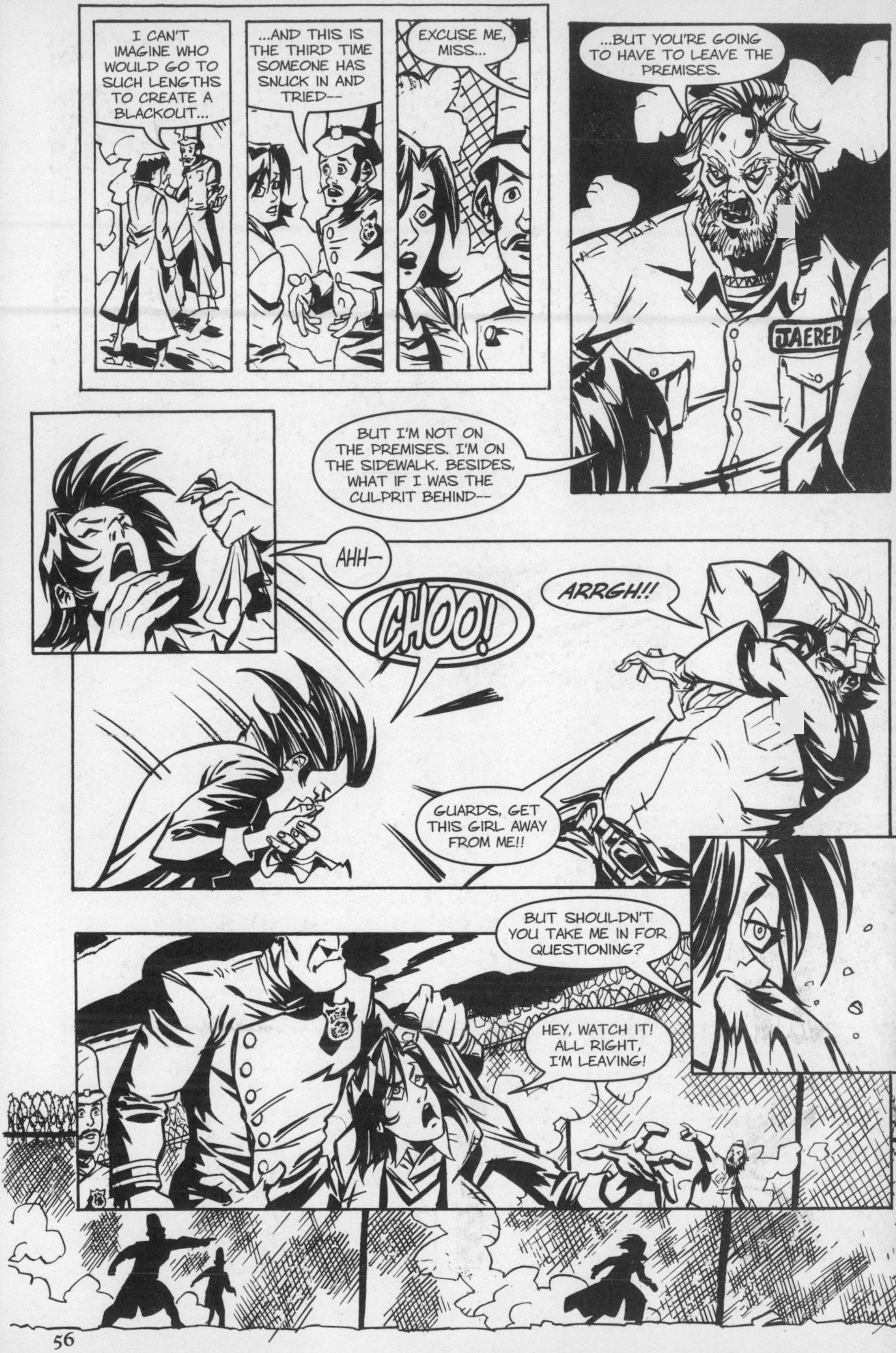
I CAN'T IMAGINE WHO WOULD GO TO SUCH LENGTHS TO CREATE A BLACKOUT...
...AND THIS IS THE THIRD TIME SOMEONE HAS SNUCK IN AND TRIED--
EXCUSE ME, MISS...
...BUT YOU'RE GOING TO HAVE TO LEAVE THE PREMISES.
JAERED
BUT I'M NOT ON THE PREMISES. I'M ON THE SIDEWALK. BESIDES, WHAT IF I WAS THE CULPRIT BEHIND--
AHH-
CHOO!
ARRGH!!
GUARDS, GET THIS GIRL AWAY FROM ME!!
BUT SHOULDN'T YOU TAKE ME IN FOR QUESTIONING?
HEY, WATCH IT! ALL RIGHT, I'M LEAVING!

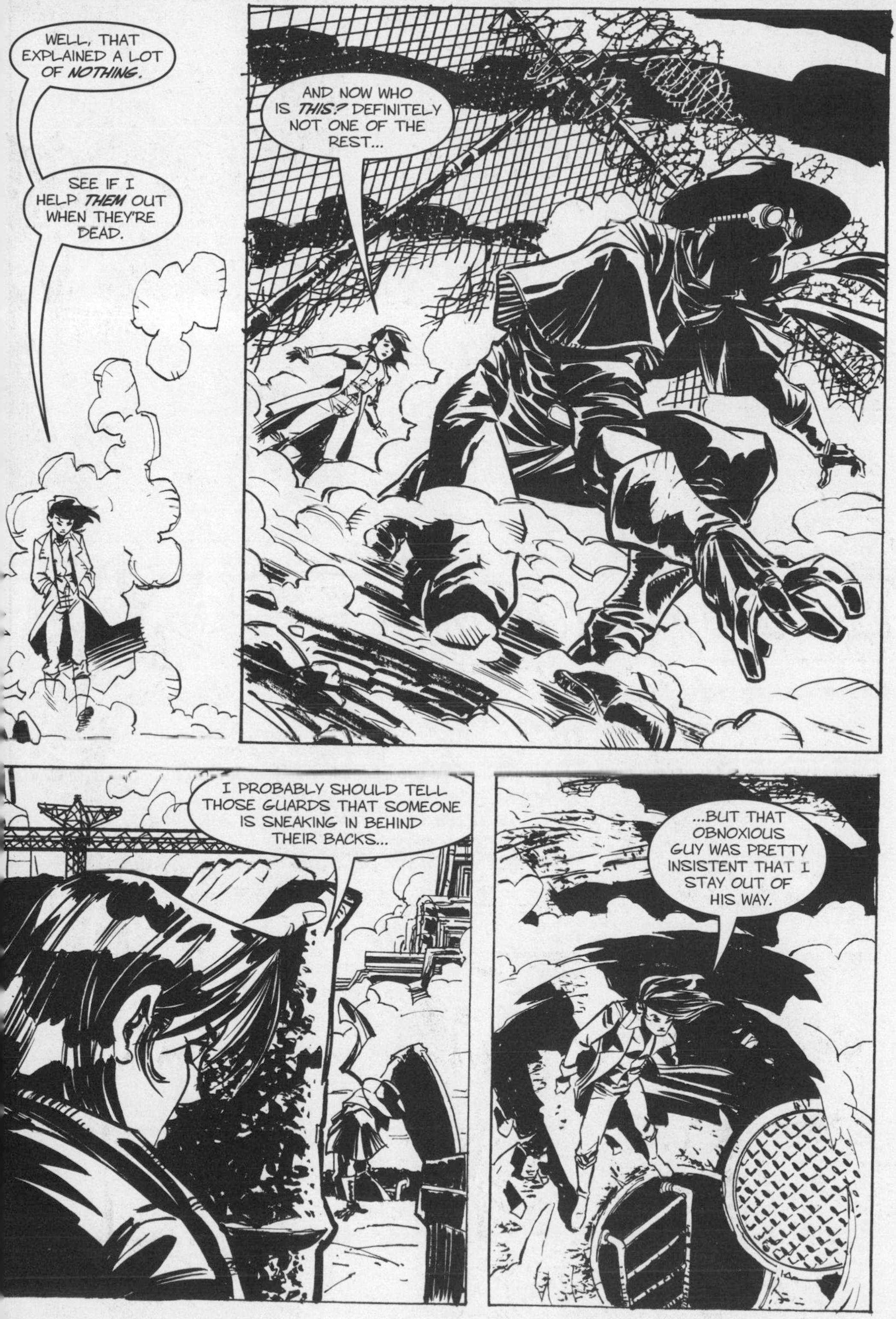
WELL, THAT EXPLAINED A LOT OF NOTHING.
SEE IF I HELP THEM OUT WHEN THEY'RE DEAD.
AND NOW WHO IS THIS? DEFINITELY NOT ONE OF THE REST...
I PROBABLY SHOULD TELL THOSE GUARDS THAT SOMEONE IS SNEAKING IN BEHIND THEIR BACKS...
...BUT THAT OBNOXIOUS GUY WAS PRETTY INSISTENT THAT I STAY OUT OF HIS WAY.

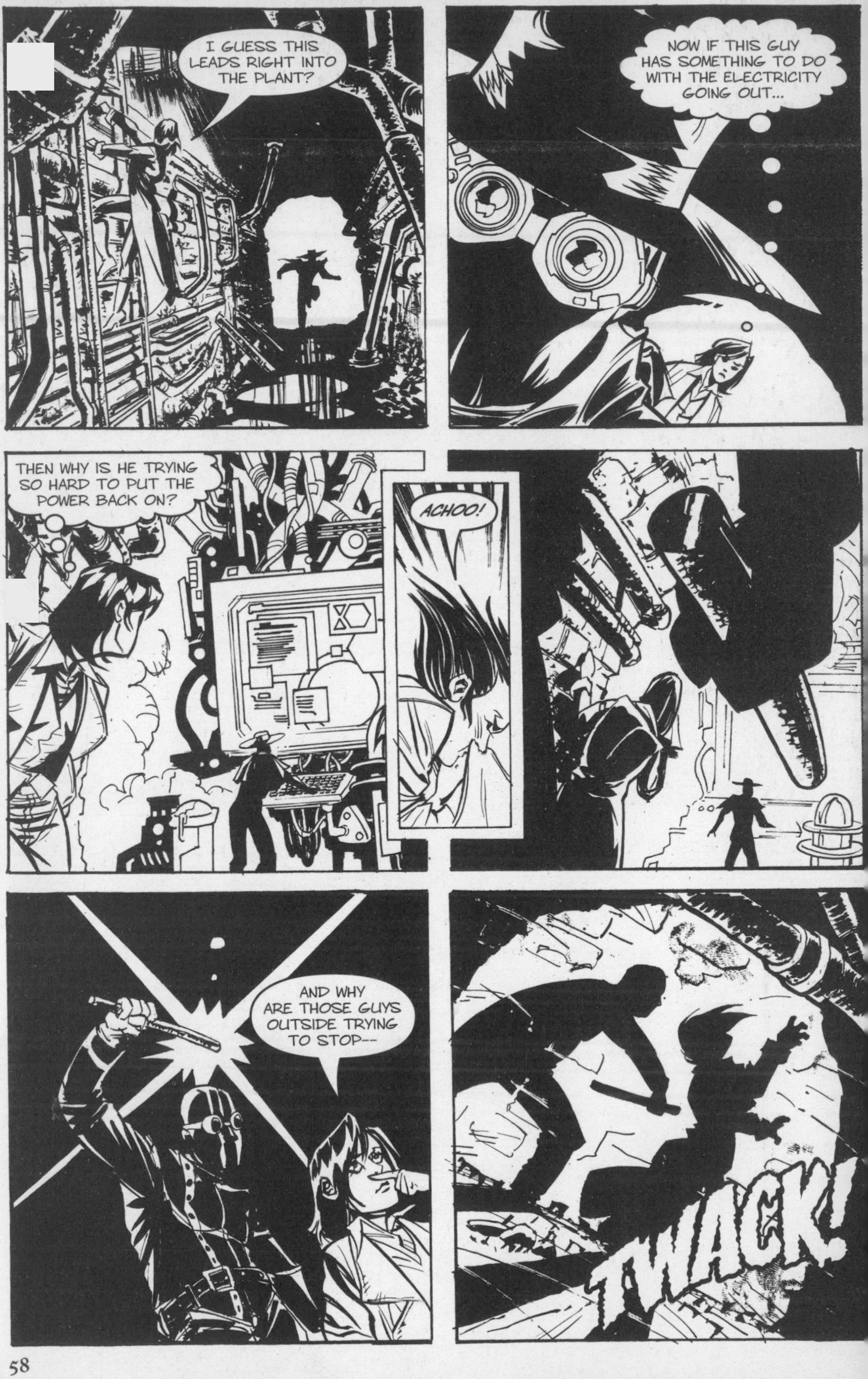
I GUESS THIS LEADS RIGHT INTO THE PLANT?
NOW IF THIS GUY HAS SOMETHING TO DO WITH THE ELECTRICITY GOING OUT...
THEN WHY IS HE TRYING SO HARD TO PUT THE POWER BACK ON?
ACHOO!
AND WHY ARE THOSE GUYS OUTSIDE TRYING TO STOP--
TWACK!

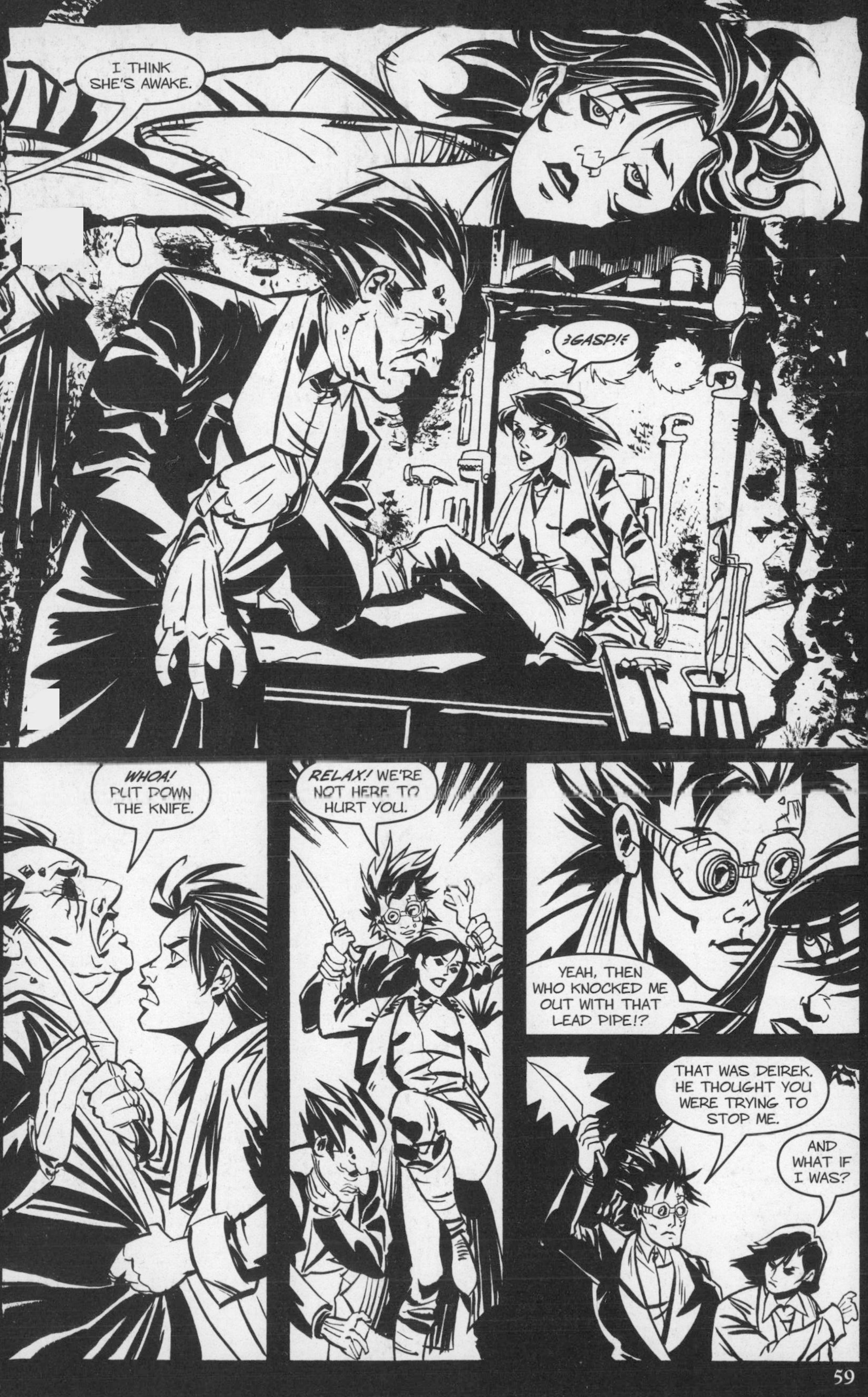
I THINK SHE'S AWAKE.
GASP!
WHOA! PUT DOWN THE KNIFE.
RELAX! WE'RE NOT HERE TO HURT YOU.
YEAH, THEN WHO KNOCKED ME OUT WITH THAT LEAD PIPE!?
THAT WAS DEIREK. HE THOUGHT YOU WERE TRYING TO STOP ME.
AND WHAT IF I WAS?

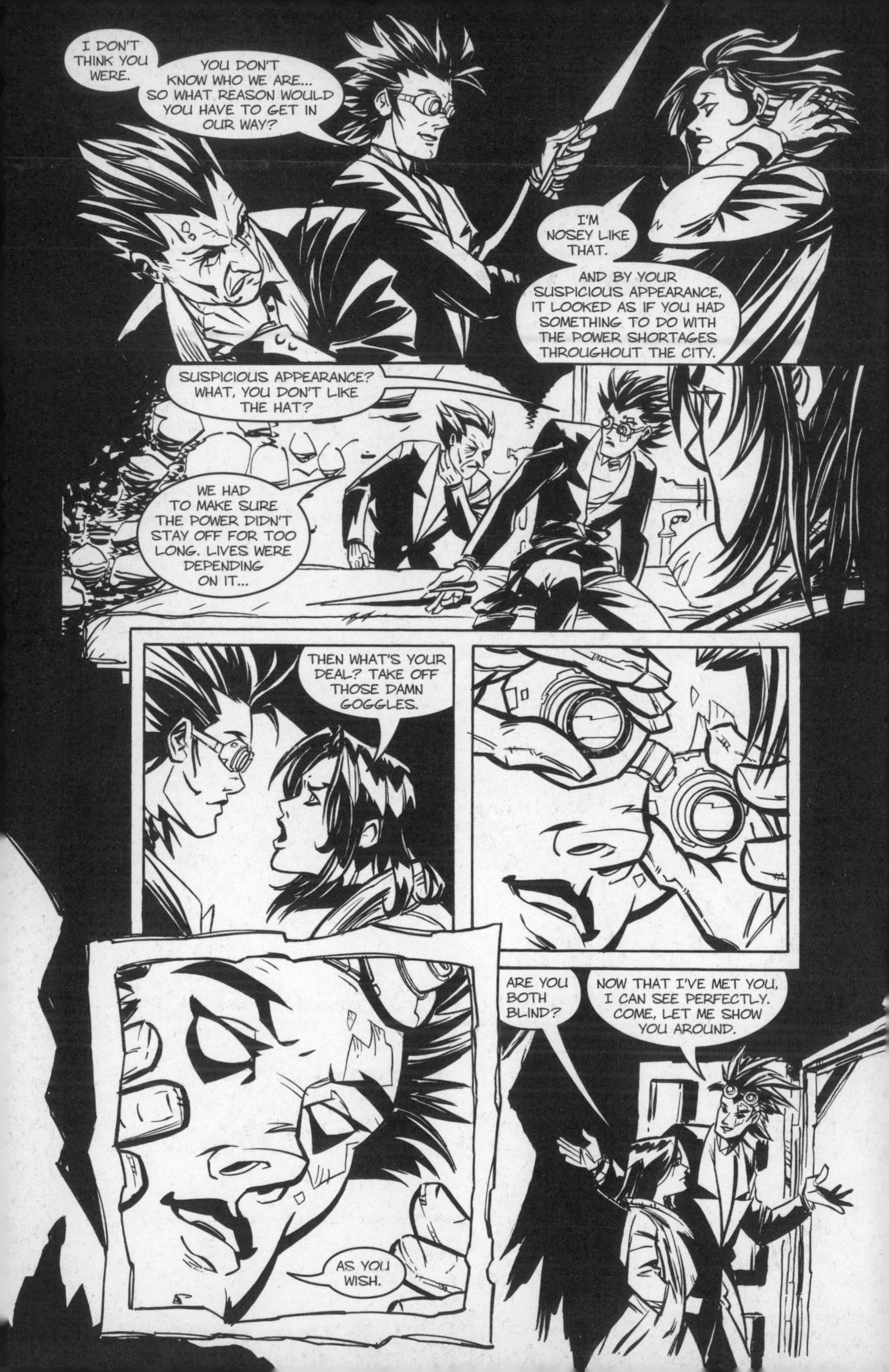
I DON'T THINK YOU WERE.
YOU DON'T KNOW WHO WE ARE... SO WHAT REASON WOULD YOU HAVE TO GET IN OUR WAY?
I'M NOSEY LIKE THAT.
AND BY YOUR SUSPICIOUS APPEARANCE, IT LOOKED AS IF YOU HAD SOMETHING TO DO WITH THE POWER SHORTAGES THROUGHOUT THE CITY.
SUSPICIOUS APPEARANCE? WHAT, YOU DON'T LIKE THE HAT?
WE HAD TO MAKE SURE THE POWER DIDN'T STAY OFF FOR TOO LONG. LIVES WERE DEPENDING ON IT...
THEN WHAT'S YOUR DEAL? TAKE OFF THOSE DAMN GOGGLES.
AS YOU WISH.
ARE YOU BOTH BLIND?
NOW THAT I'VE MET YOU, I CAN SEE PERFECTLY. COME, LET ME SHOW YOU AROUND.

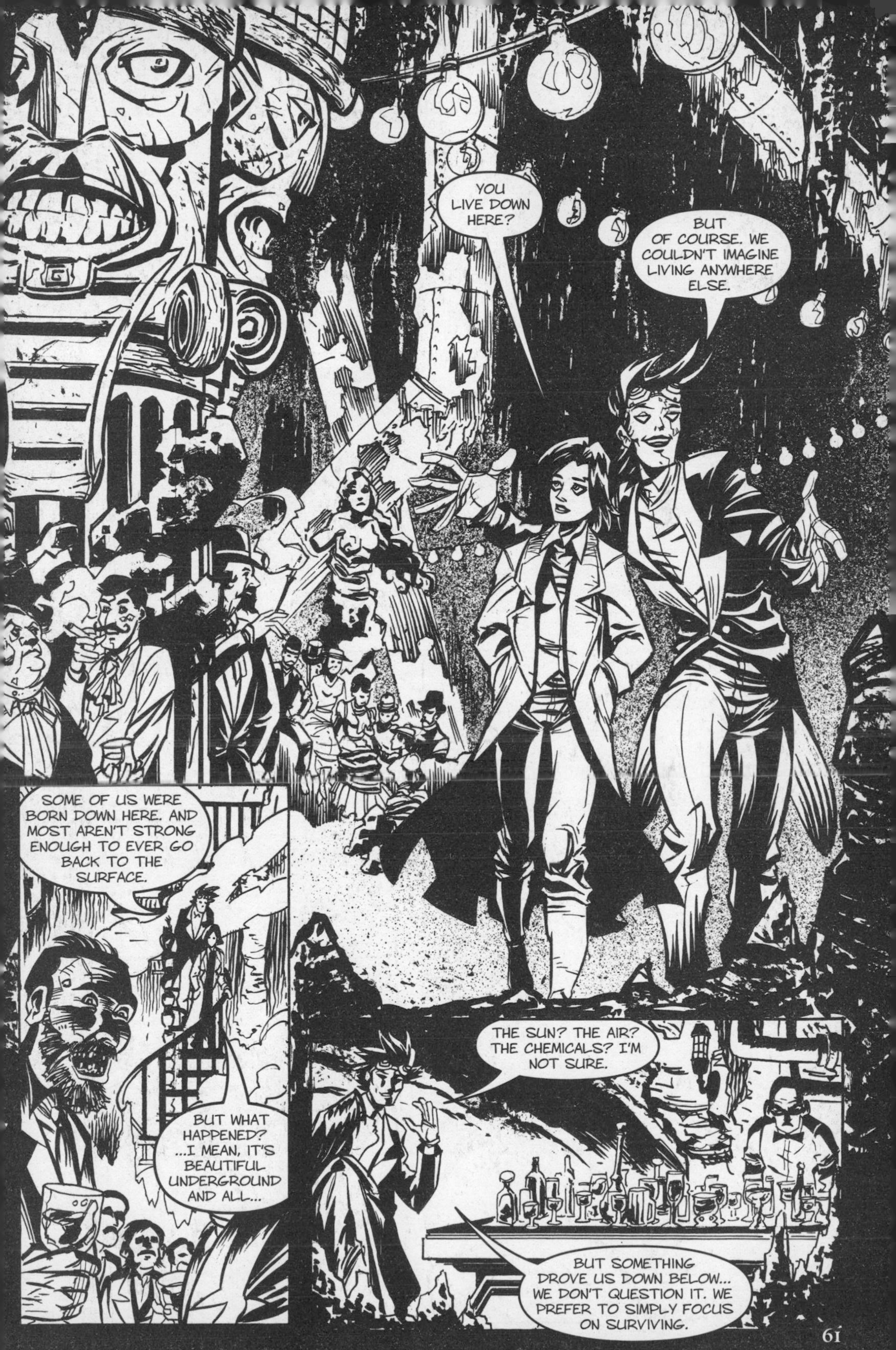
YOU LIVE DOWN HERE?
BUT OF COURSE. WE COULDN'T IMAGINE LIVING ANYWHERE ELSE.
SOME OF US WERE BORN DOWN HERE. AND MOST AREN'T STRONG ENOUGH TO EVER GO BACK TO THE SURFACE.
BUT WHAT HAPPENED? ...I MEAN, IT'S BEAUTIFUL UNDERGROUND AND ALL...
THE SUN? THE AIR? THE CHEMICALS? I'M NOT SURE.
BUT SOMETHING DROVE US DOWN BELOW... WE DON'T QUESTION IT. WE PREFER TO SIMPLY FOCUS ON SURVIVING.

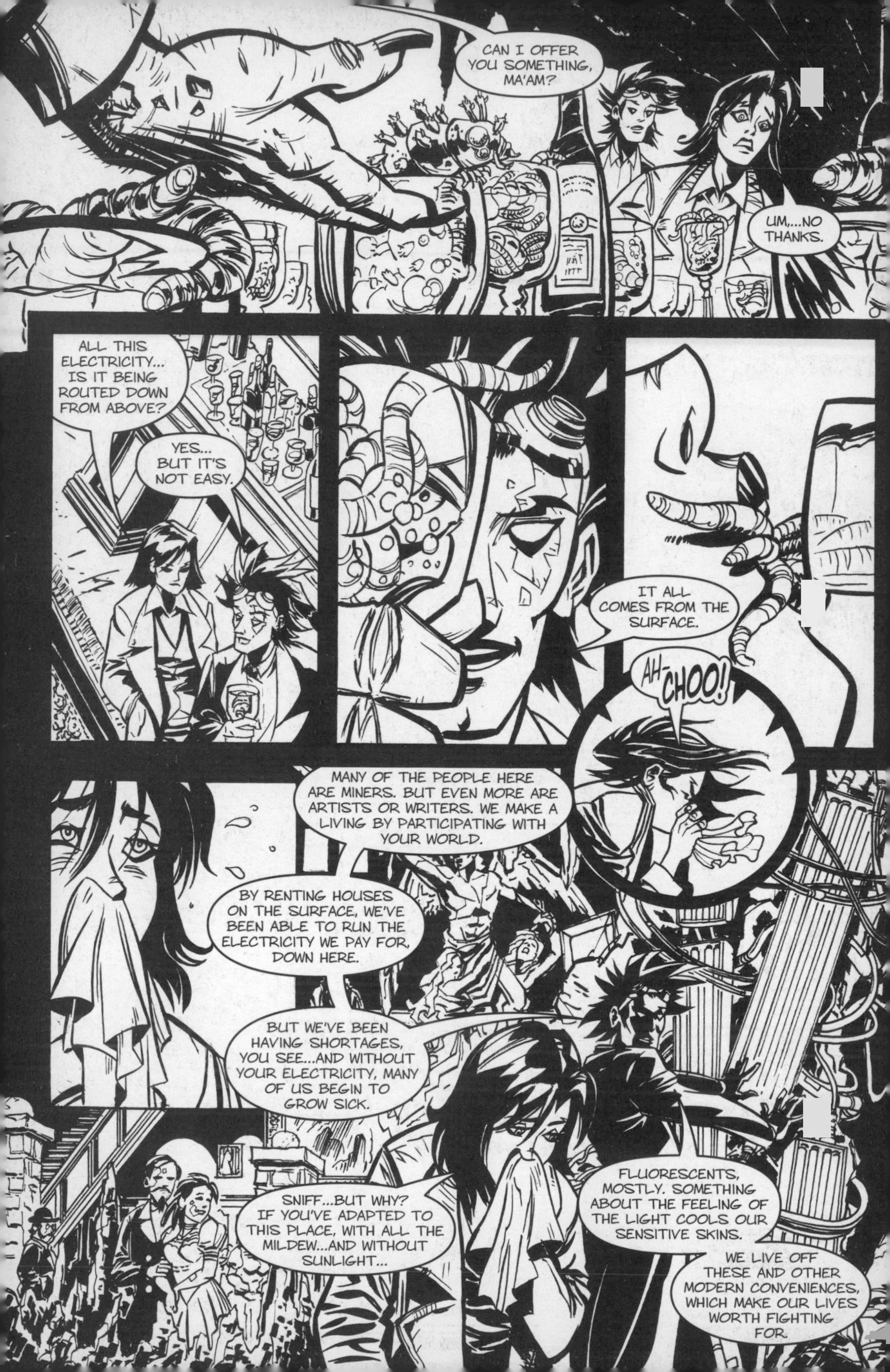
CAN I OFFER YOU SOMETHING, MA'AM?
UM,...NO THANKS.
ALL THIS ELECTRICITY... IS IT BEING ROUTED DOWN FROM ABOVE?
YES... BUT IT'S NOT EASY.
IT ALL COMES FROM THE SURFACE.
AH-CHOO!
MANY OF THE PEOPLE HERE ARE MINERS. BUT EVEN MORE ARE ARTISTS OR WRITERS. WE MAKE A LIVING BY PARTICIPATING WITH YOUR WORLD.
BY RENTING HOUSES ON THE SURFACE, WE'VE BEEN ABLE TO RUN THE ELECTRICITY WE PAY FOR, DOWN HERE.
BUT WE'VE BEEN HAVING SHORTAGES, YOU SEE...AND WITHOUT YOUR ELECTRICITY, MANY OF US BEGIN TO GROW SICK.
SNIFF...BUT WHY? IF YOU'VE ADAPTED TO THIS PLACE, WITH ALL THE MILDEW...AND WITHOUT SUNLIGHT...
FLUORESCENTS, MOSTLY. SOMETHING ABOUT THE FEELING OF THE LIGHT COOLS OUR SENSITIVE SKINS.
WE LIVE OFF THESE AND OTHER MODERN CONVENIENCES, WHICH MAKE OUR LIVES WORTH FIGHTING FOR.

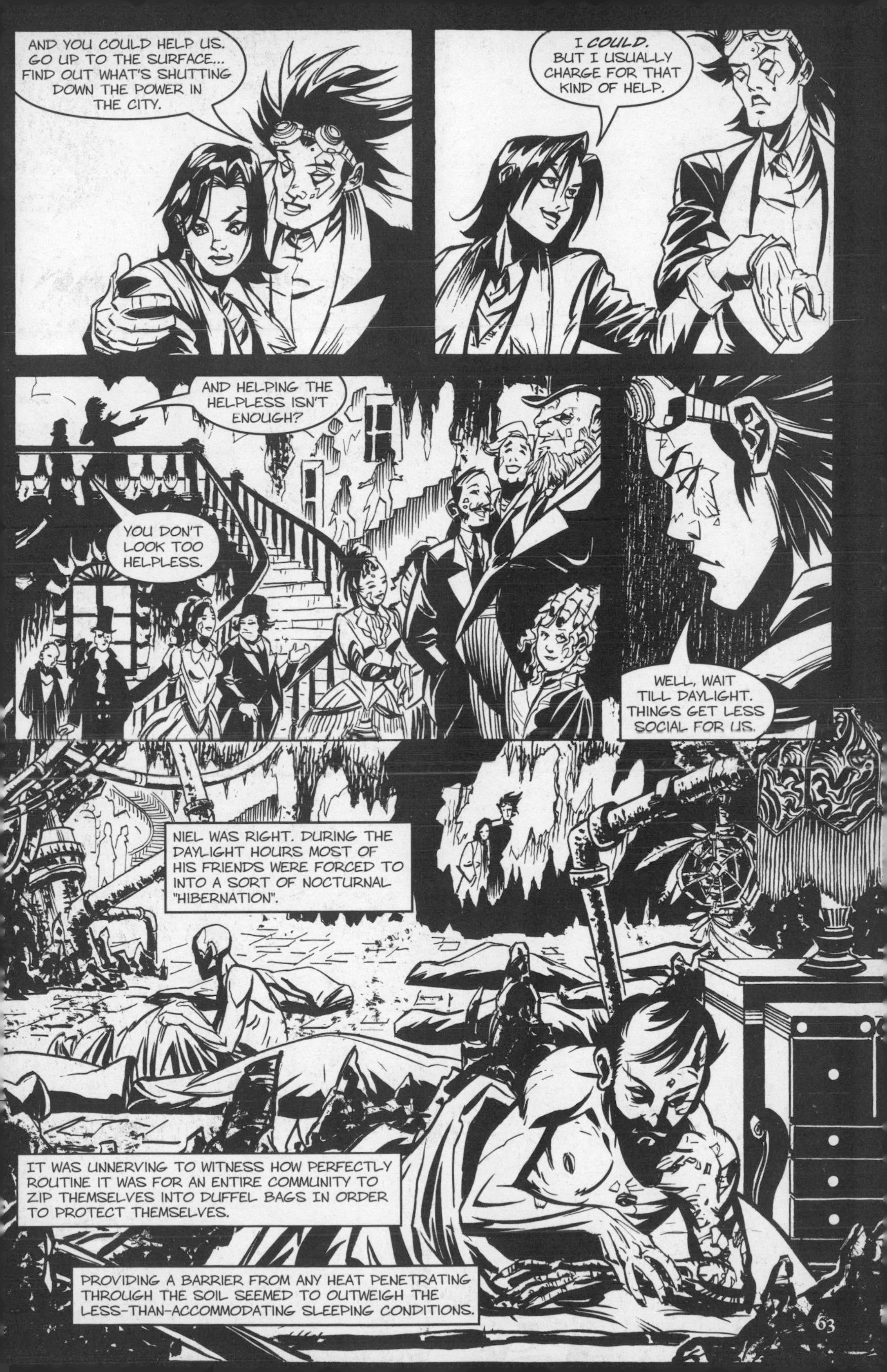
AND YOU COULD HELP US. GO UP TO THE SURFACE... FIND OUT WHAT'S SHUTTING DOWN THE POWER IN THE CITY.
I *COULD.* BUT I USUALLY CHARGE FOR THAT KIND OF HELP.
AND HELPING THE HELPLESS ISN'T ENOUGH?
YOU DON'T LOOK TOO HELPLESS.
WELL, WAIT TILL DAYLIGHT. THINGS GET LESS SOCIAL FOR US.
NIEL WAS RIGHT. DURING THE DAYLIGHT HOURS MOST OF HIS FRIENDS WERE FORCED TO INTO A SORT OF NOCTURNAL "HIBERNATION".
IT WAS UNNERVING TO WITNESS HOW PERFECTLY ROUTINE IT WAS FOR AN ENTIRE COMMUNITY TO ZIP THEMSELVES INTO DUFFEL BAGS IN ORDER TO PROTECT THEMSELVES.
PROVIDING A BARRIER FROM ANY HEAT PENETRATING THROUGH THE SOIL SEEMED TO OUTWEIGH THE LESS-THAN-ACCOMMODATING SLEEPING CONDITIONS.

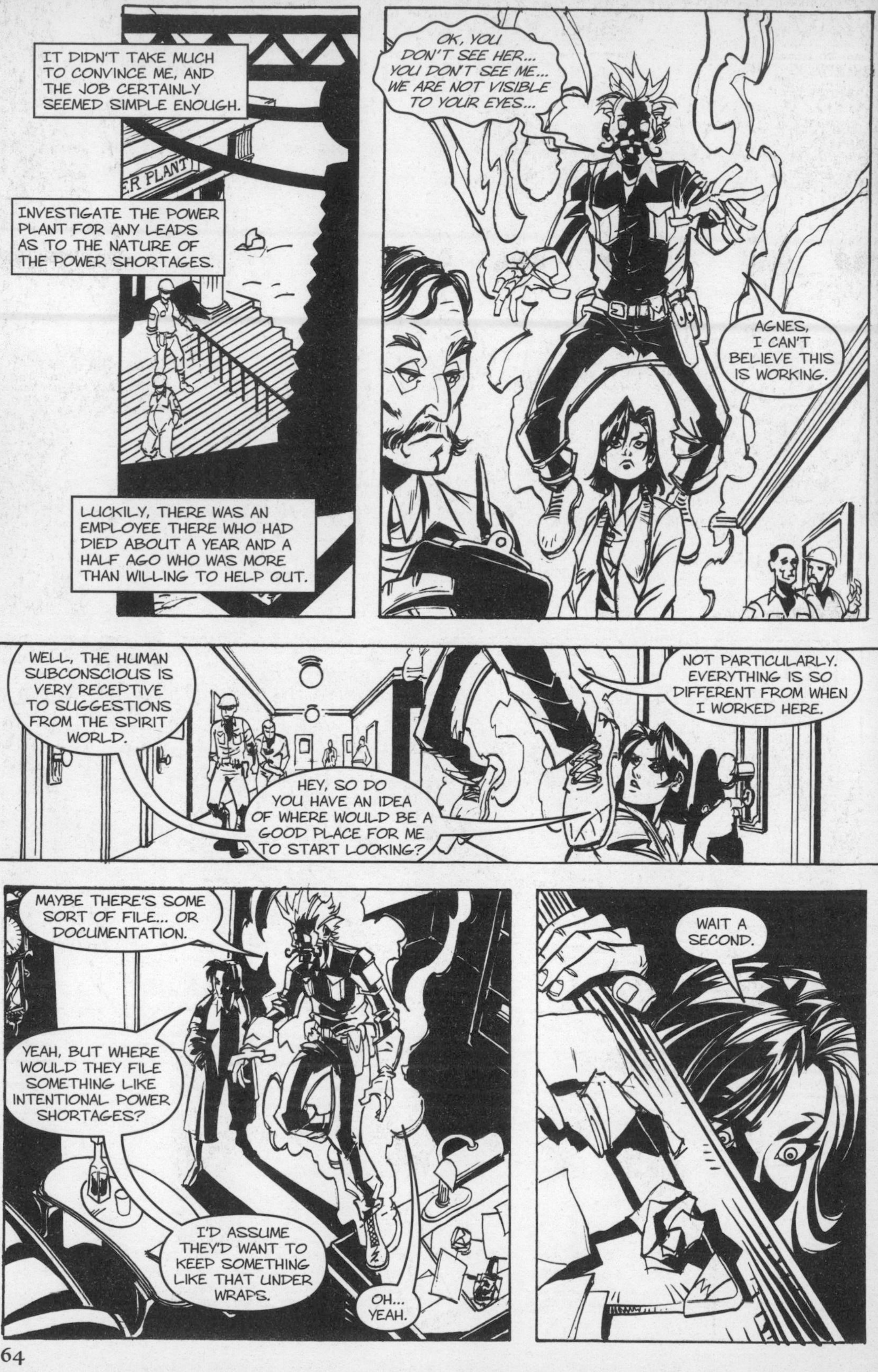
IT DIDN'T TAKE MUCH TO CONVINCE ME, AND THE JOB CERTAINLY SEEMED SIMPLE ENOUGH.
ER PLANT
INVESTIGATE THE POWER PLANT FOR ANY LEADS AS TO THE NATURE OF THE POWER SHORTAGES.
LUCKILY, THERE WAS AN EMPLOYEE THERE WHO HAD DIED ABOUT A YEAR AND A HALF AGO WHO WAS MORE THAN WILLING TO HELP OUT.
OK, YOU DON'T SEE HER... YOU DON'T SEE ME... WE ARE NOT VISIBLE TO YOUR EYES...
AGNES, I CAN'T BELIEVE THIS IS WORKING.
WELL, THE HUMAN SUBCONSCIOUS IS VERY RECEPTIVE TO SUGGESTIONS FROM THE SPIRIT WORLD.
HEY, SO DO YOU HAVE AN IDEA OF WHERE WOULD BE A GOOD PLACE FOR ME TO START LOOKING?
NOT PARTICULARLY. EVERYTHING IS SO DIFFERENT FROM WHEN I WORKED HERE.
MAYBE THERE'S SOME SORT OF FILE... OR DOCUMENTATION.
YEAH, BUT WHERE WOULD THEY FILE SOMETHING LIKE INTENTIONAL POWER SHORTAGES?
I'D ASSUME THEY'D WANT TO KEEP SOMETHING LIKE THAT UNDER WRAPS.
OH... YEAH.
WAIT A SECOND.

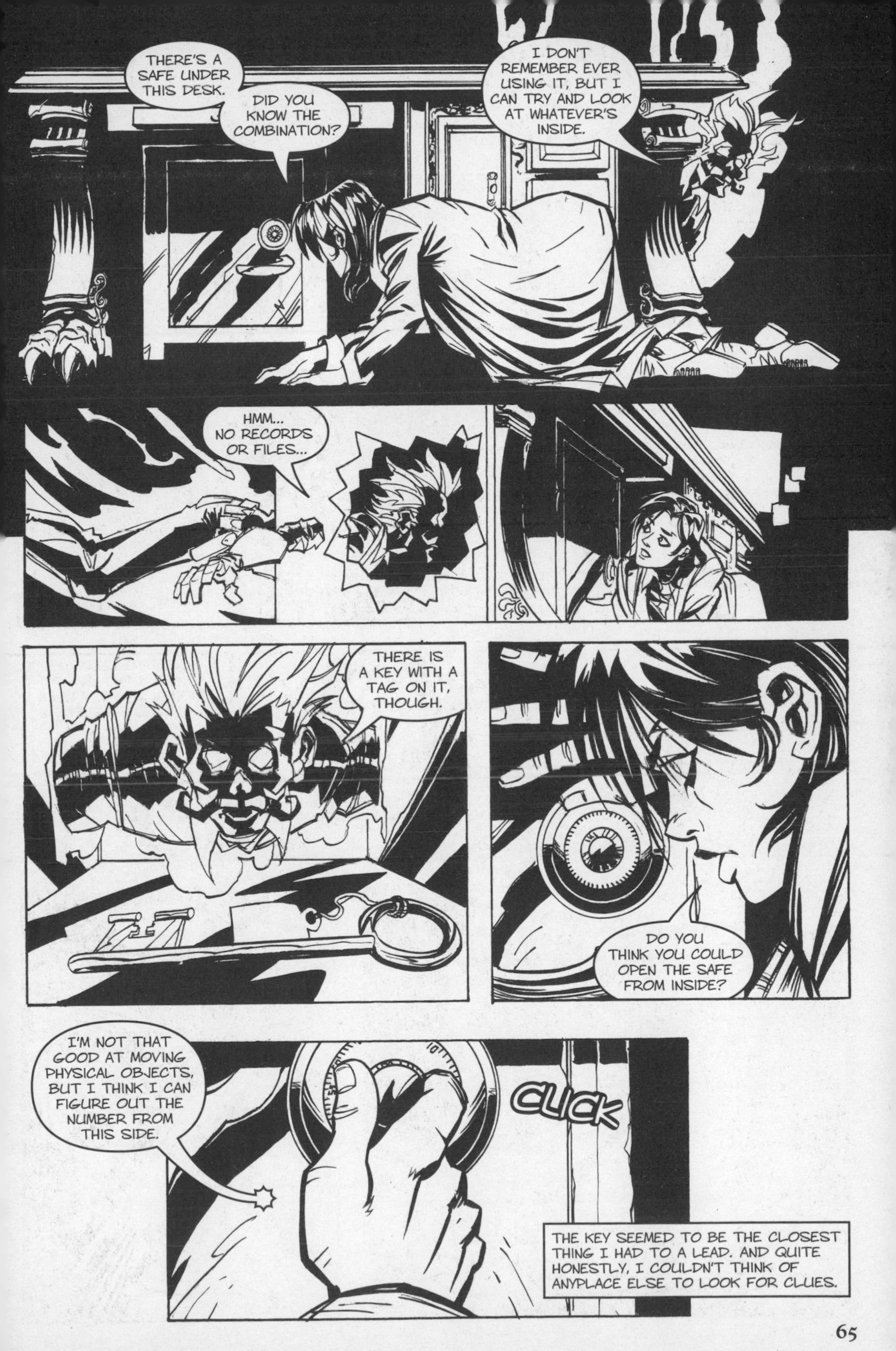
THERE'S A SAFE UNDER THIS DESK.
DID YOU KNOW THE COMBINATION?
I DON'T REMEMBER EVER USING IT, BUT I CAN TRY AND LOOK AT WHATEVER'S INSIDE.
HMM... NO RECORDS OR FILES...
THERE IS A KEY WITH A TAG ON IT, THOUGH.
DO YOU THINK YOU COULD OPEN THE SAFE FROM INSIDE?
I'M NOT THAT GOOD AT MOVING PHYSICAL OBJECTS, BUT I THINK I CAN FIGURE OUT THE NUMBER FROM THIS SIDE.
CLICK
THE KEY SEEMED TO BE THE CLOSEST THING I HAD TO A LEAD. AND QUITE HONESTLY, I COULDN'T THINK OF ANYPLACE ELSE TO LOOK FOR CLUES.

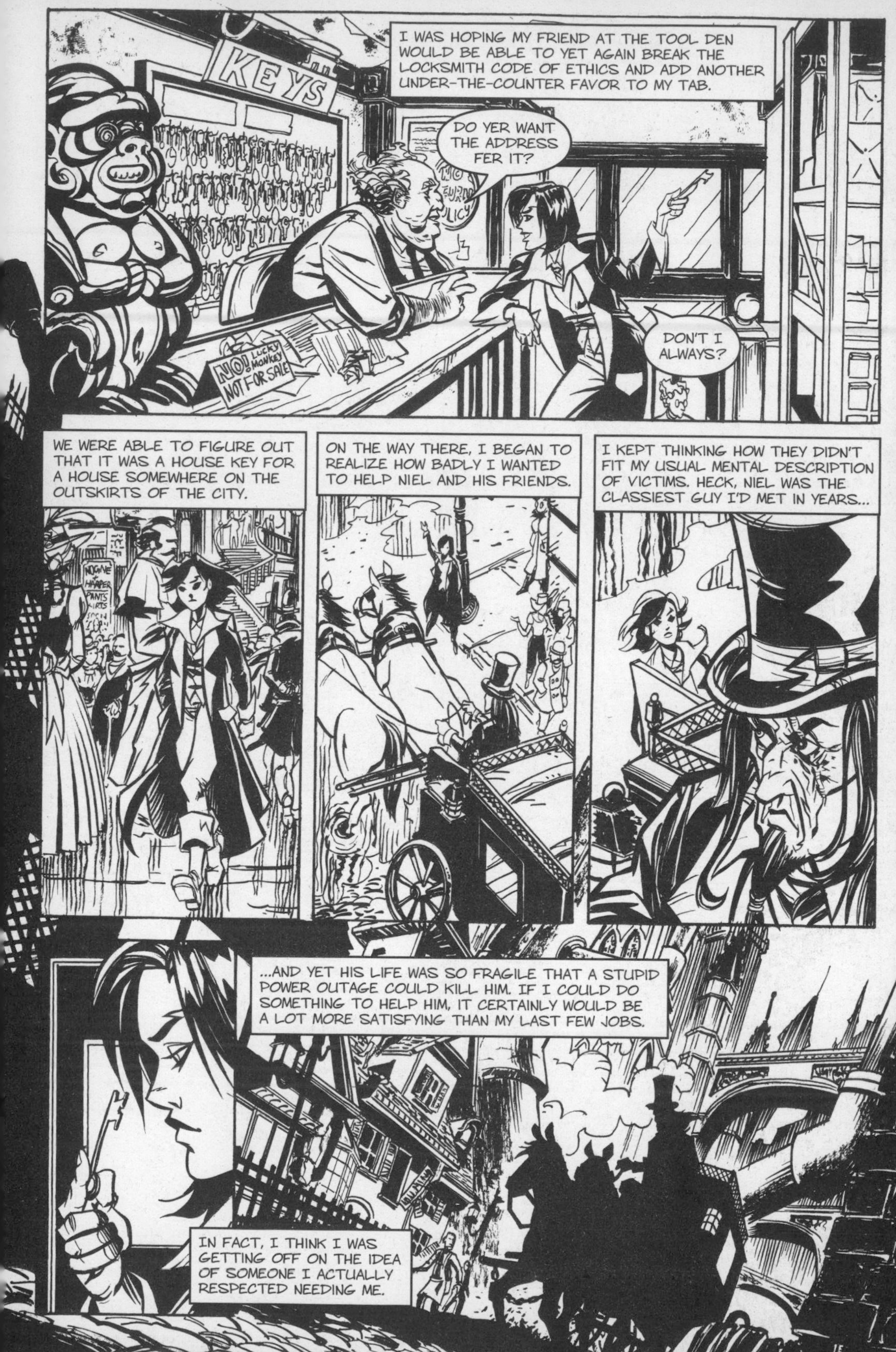

I WAS HOPING MY FRIEND AT THE TOOL DEN WOULD BE ABLE TO YET AGAIN BREAK THE LOCKSMITH CODE OF ETHICS AND ADD ANOTHER UNDER-THE-COUNTER FAVOR TO MY TAB.
KEYS
DO YER WANT THE ADDRESS FER IT?
NO! LUCKY MONKEY NOT FOR SALE
DON'T I ALWAYS?
WE WERE ABLE TO FIGURE OUT THAT IT WAS A HOUSE KEY FOR A HOUSE SOMEWHERE ON THE OUTSKIRTS OF THE CITY.
ON THE WAY THERE, I BEGAN TO REALIZE HOW BADLY I WANTED TO HELP NIEL AND HIS FRIENDS.
I KEPT THINKING HOW THEY DIDN'T FIT MY USUAL MENTAL DESCRIPTION OF VICTIMS. HECK, NIEL WAS THE CLASSIEST GUY I'D MET IN YEARS...
...AND YET HIS LIFE WAS SO FRAGILE THAT A STUPID POWER OUTAGE COULD KILL HIM. IF I COULD DO SOMETHING TO HELP HIM, IT CERTAINLY WOULD BE A LOT MORE SATISFYING THAN MY LAST FEW JOBS.
IN FACT, I THINK I WAS GETTING OFF ON THE IDEA OF SOMEONE I ACTUALLY RESPECTED NEEDING ME.

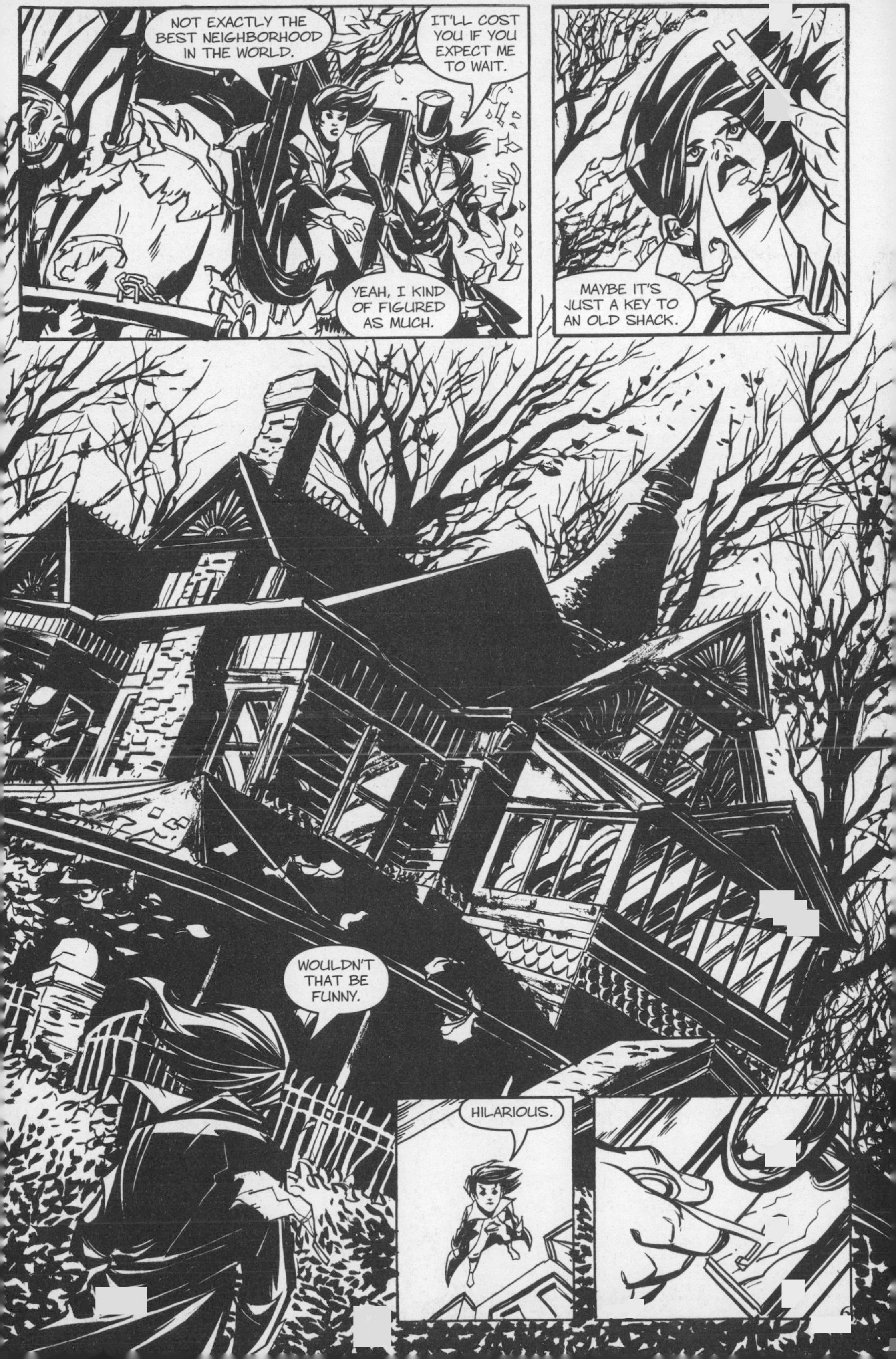
NOT EXACTLY THE BEST NEIGHBORHOOD IN THE WORLD.
IT'LL COST YOU IF YOU EXPECT ME TO WAIT.
YEAH, I KIND OF FIGURED AS MUCH.
MAYBE IT'S JUST A KEY TO AN OLD SHACK.
WOULDN'T THAT BE FUNNY.
HILARIOUS.

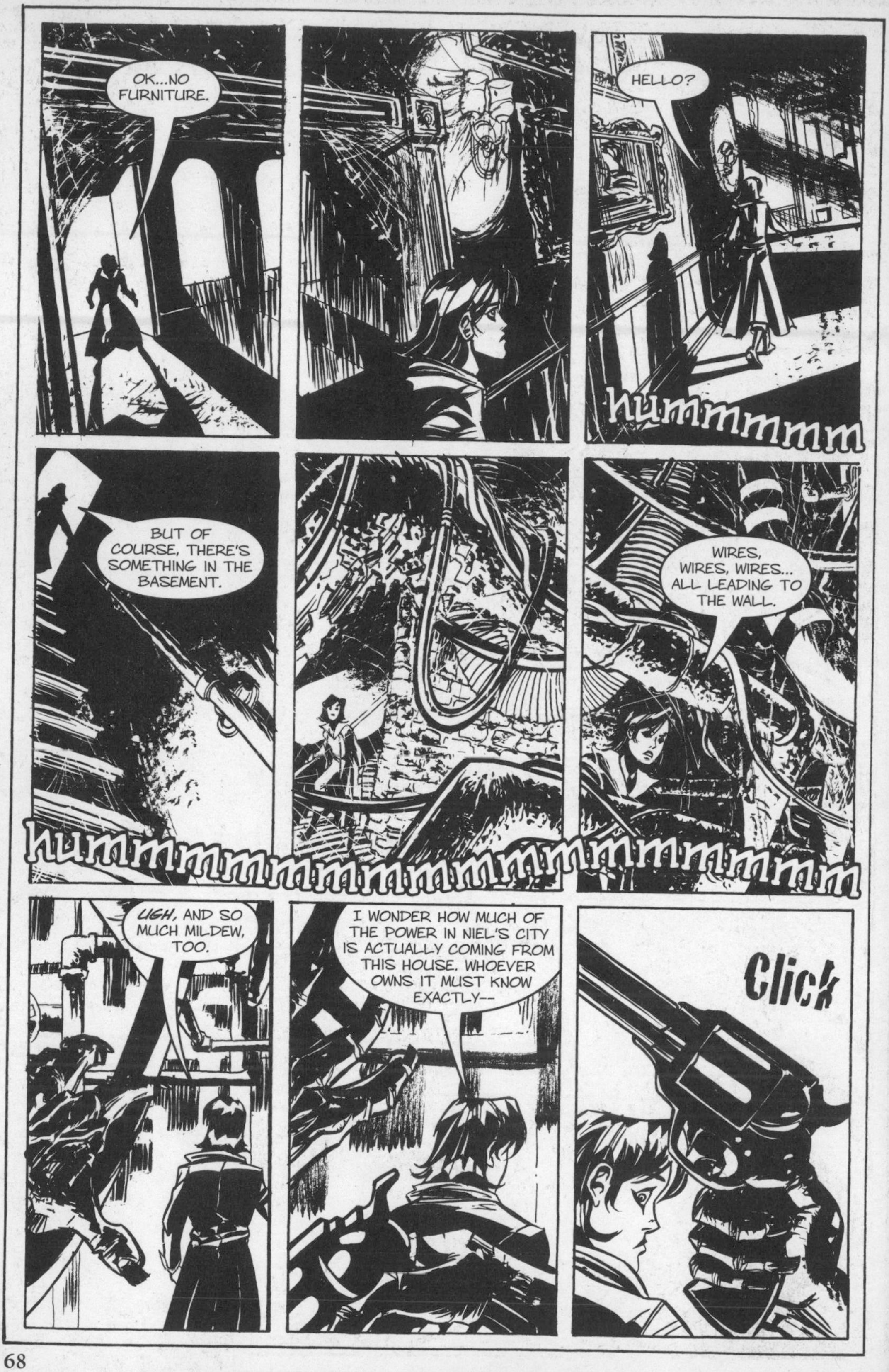
OK...NO FURNITURE.
HELLO?
hummmmmm
BUT OF COURSE, THERE'S SOMETHING IN THE BASEMENT.
WIRES, WIRES, WIRES... ALL LEADING TO THE WALL.
hummmmmmmmmmmmmmmmmmmmm
UGH, AND SO MUCH MILDEW, TOO.
I WONDER HOW MUCH OF THE POWER IN NIEL'S CITY IS ACTUALLY COMING FROM THIS HOUSE. WHOEVER OWNS IT MUST KNOW EXACTLY--
Click

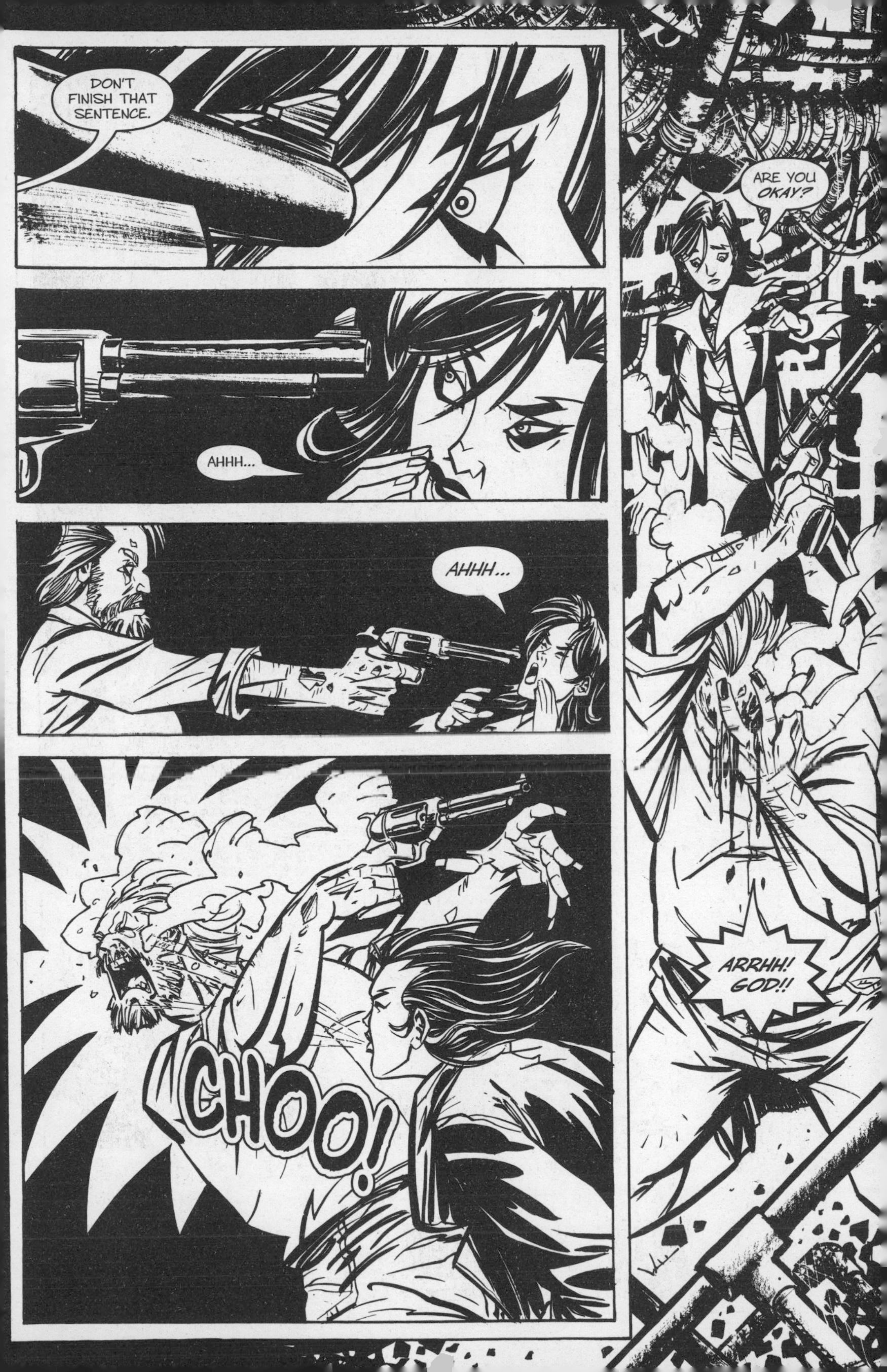
DON'T FINISH THAT SENTENCE.
AHHH...
AHHH...
CHOO!
ARE YOU OKAY?
ARRHH! GOD!!

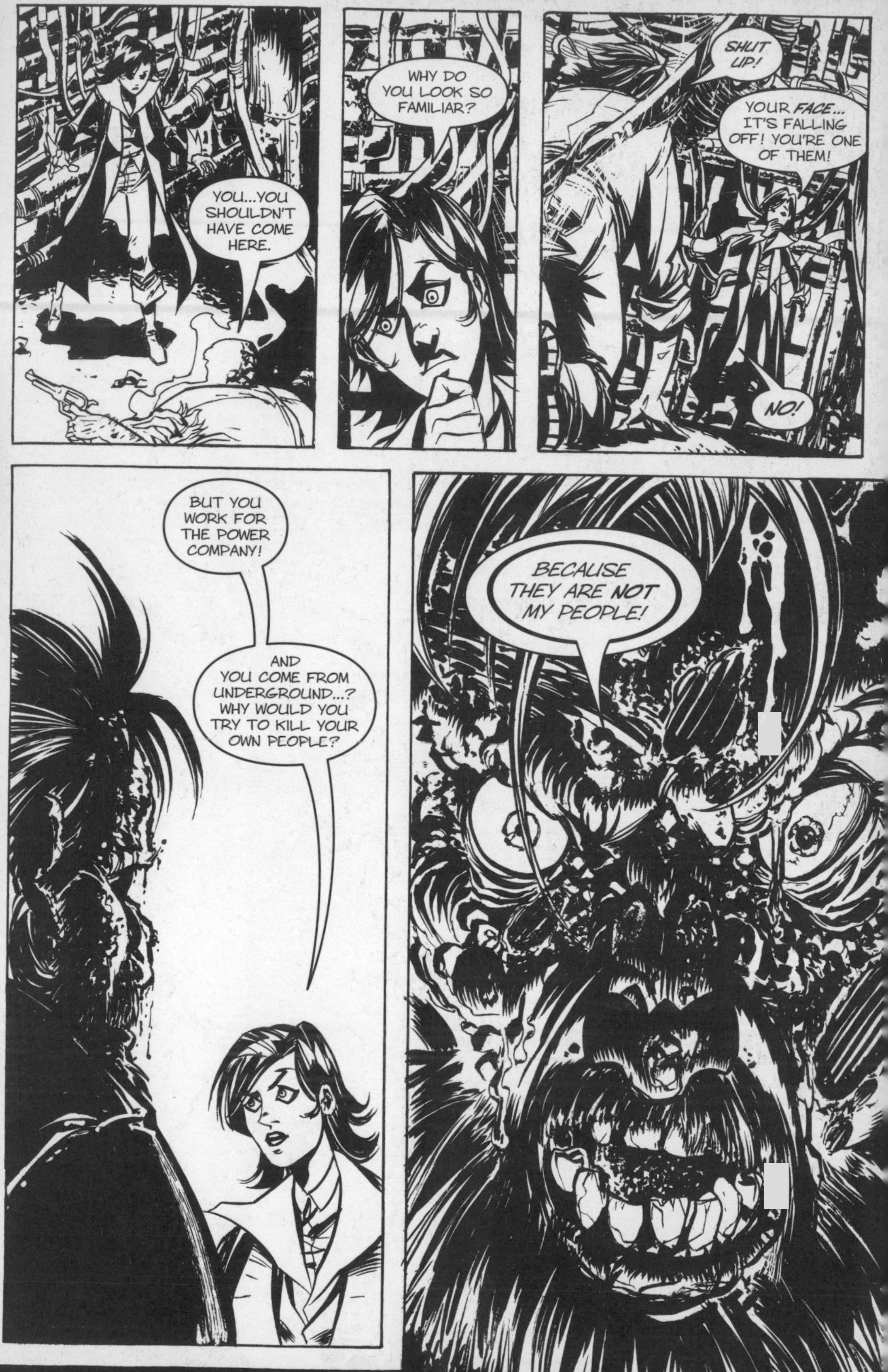
YOU...YOU SHOULDN'T HAVE COME HERE.
WHY DO YOU LOOK SO FAMILIAR?
SHUT UP!
YOUR FACE... IT'S FALLING OFF! YOU'RE ONE OF THEM!
NO!
BUT YOU WORK FOR THE POWER COMPANY!
AND YOU COME FROM UNDERGROUND...? WHY WOULD YOU TRY TO KILL YOUR OWN PEOPLE?
BECAUSE THEY ARE NOT MY PEOPLE!

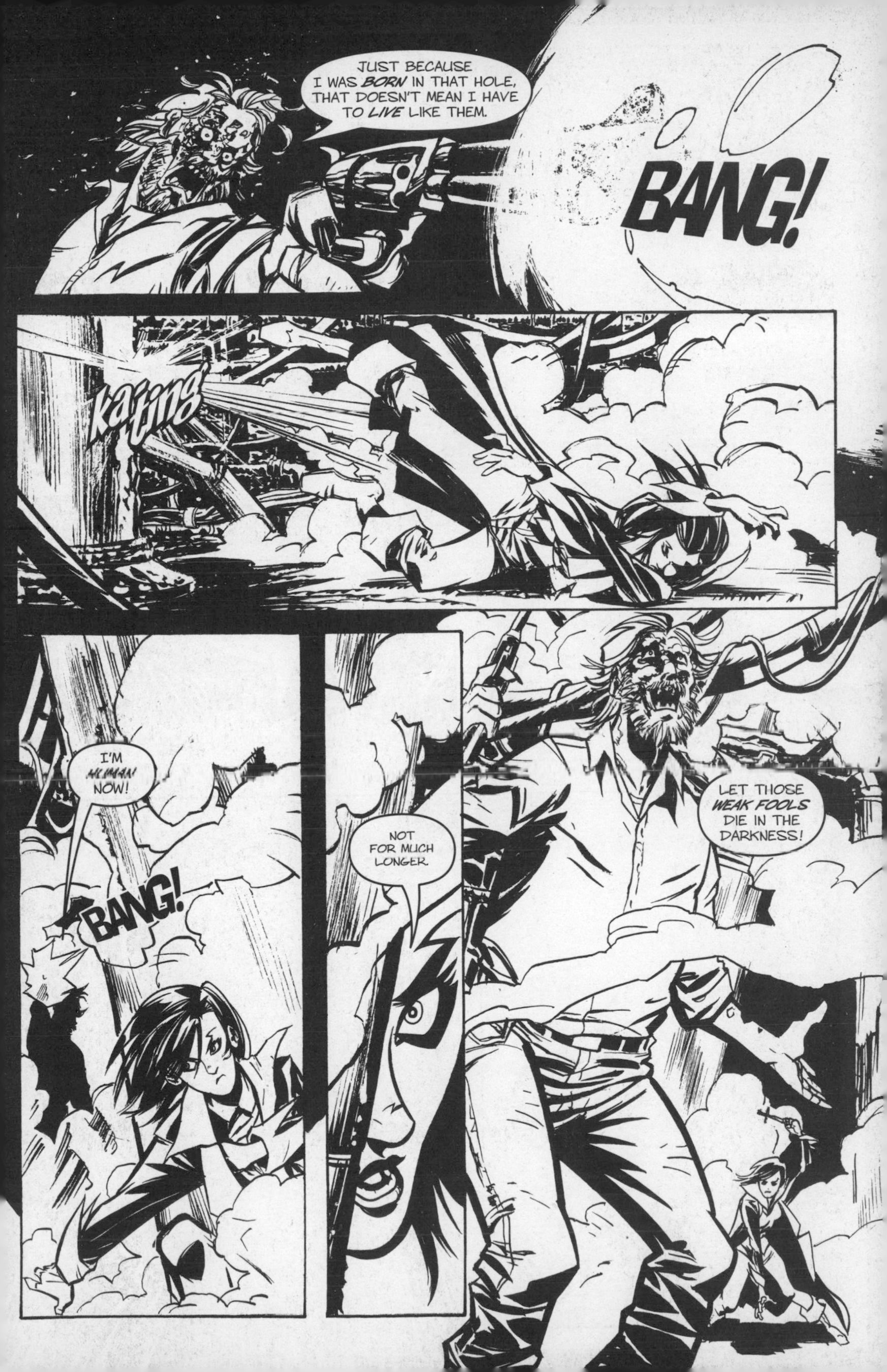
JUST BECAUSE I WAS BORN IN THAT HOLE, THAT DOESN'T MEAN I HAVE TO LIVE LIKE THEM.
BANG!
ka-ting
I'M HUMAN NOW!
BANG!
NOT FOR MUCH LONGER.
LET THOSE WEAK FOOLS DIE IN THE DARKNESS!

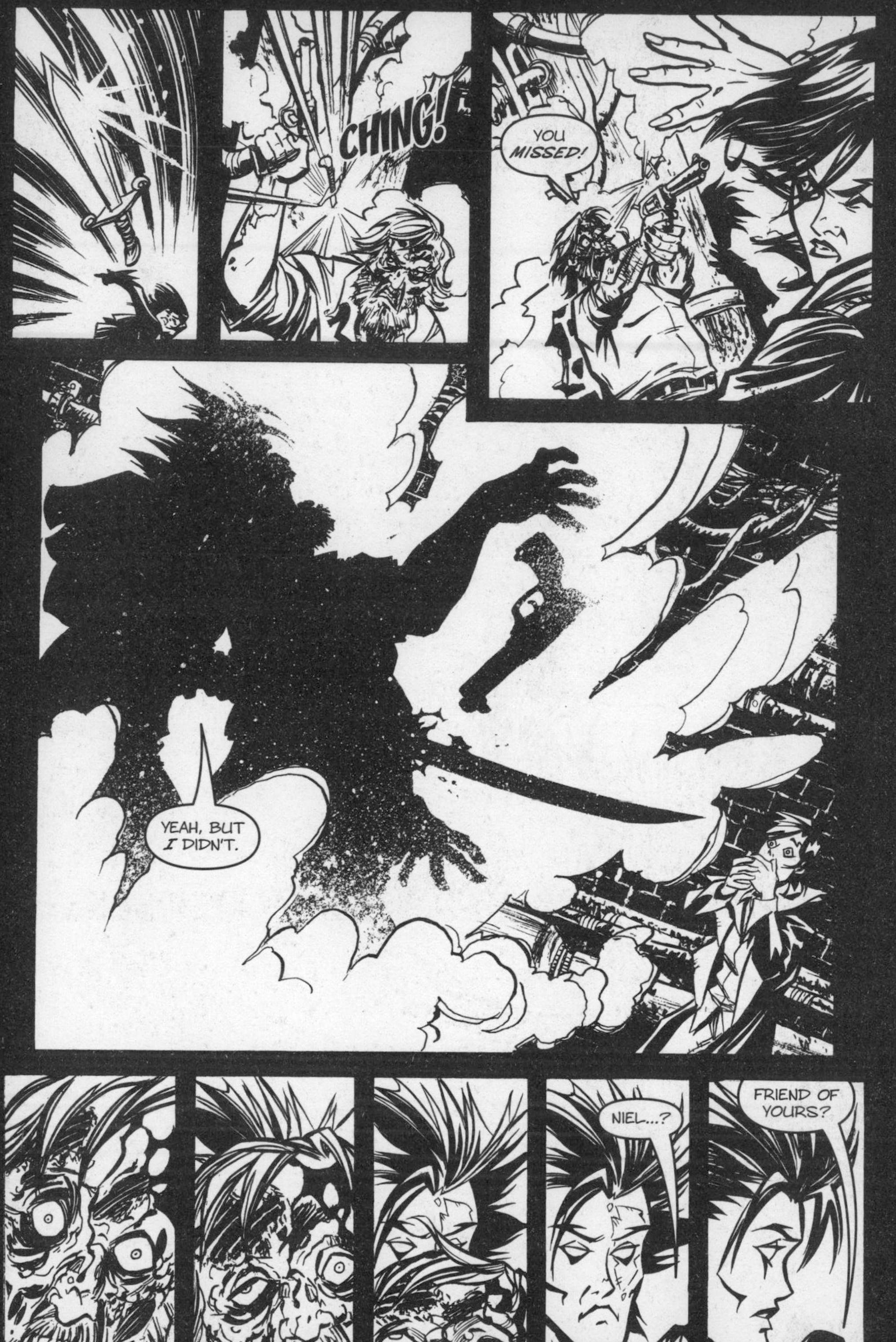

CHING!
YOU MISSED!
YEAH, BUT I DIDN'T.
COUGH COUGH
NIEL...?
FRIEND OF YOURS?

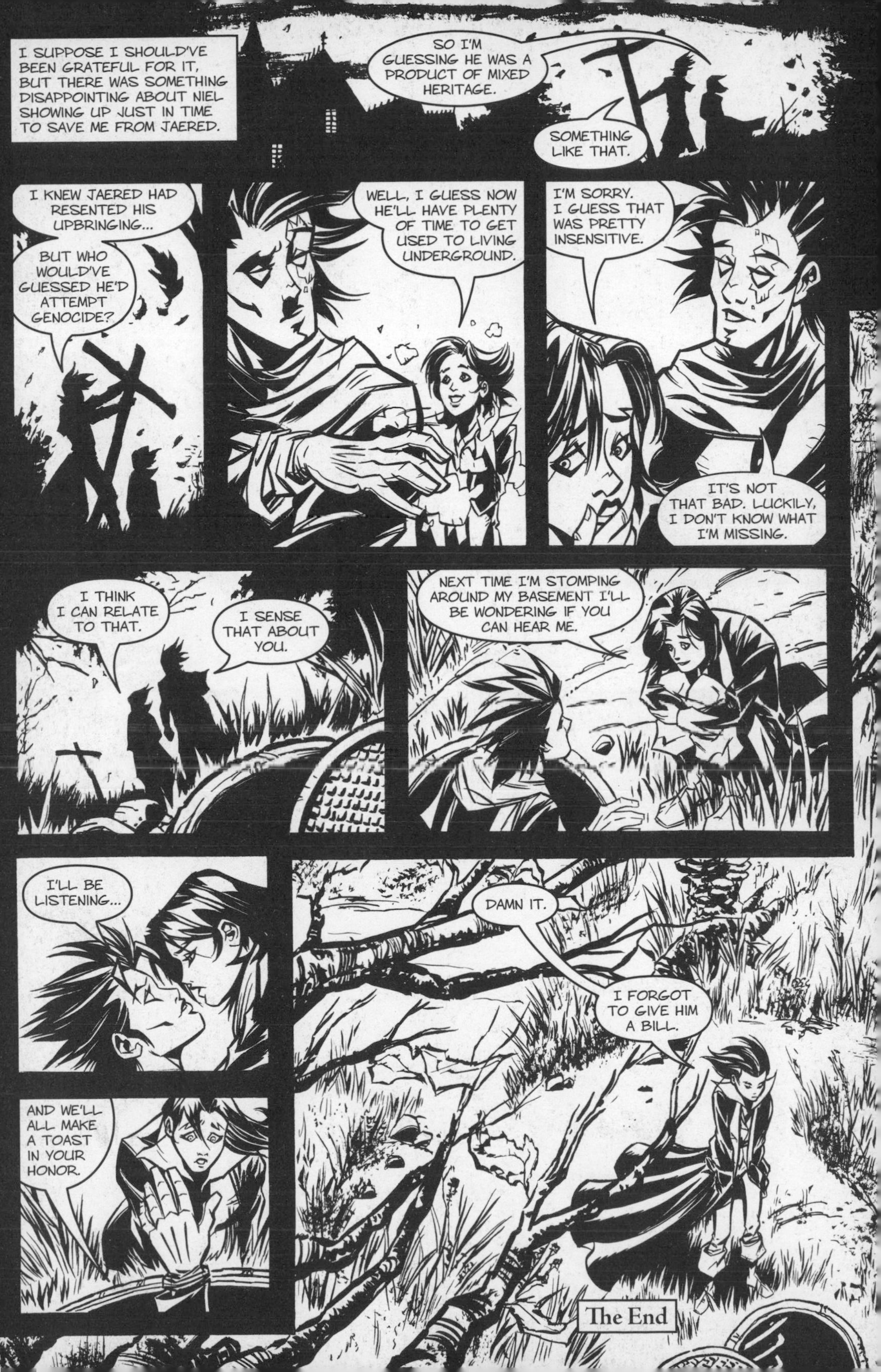
I SUPPOSE I SHOULD'VE BEEN GRATEFUL FOR IT, BUT THERE WAS SOMETHING DISAPPOINTING ABOUT NIEL SHOWING UP JUST IN TIME TO SAVE ME FROM JAERED.
SO I'M GUESSING HE WAS A PRODUCT OF MIXED HERITAGE.
SOMETHING LIKE THAT.
I KNEW JAERED HAD RESENTED HIS UPBRINGING...
BUT WHO WOULD'VE GUESSED HE'D ATTEMPT GENOCIDE?
WELL, I GUESS NOW HE'LL HAVE PLENTY OF TIME TO GET USED TO LIVING UNDERGROUND.
I'M SORRY. I GUESS THAT WAS PRETTY INSENSITIVE.
IT'S NOT THAT BAD. LUCKILY, I DON'T KNOW WHAT I'M MISSING.
I THINK I CAN RELATE TO THAT.
I SENSE THAT ABOUT YOU.
NEXT TIME I'M STOMPING AROUND MY BASEMENT I'LL BE WONDERING IF YOU CAN HEAR ME.
I'LL BE LISTENING...
AND WE'LL ALL MAKE A TOAST IN YOUR HONOR.
DAMN IT.
I FORGOT TO GIVE HIM A BILL.
The End

CHAPTER 4

"INVITE ONLY"

WRITTEN, ILLUSTRATED
and LETTERED
by **DAVE ROMAN**

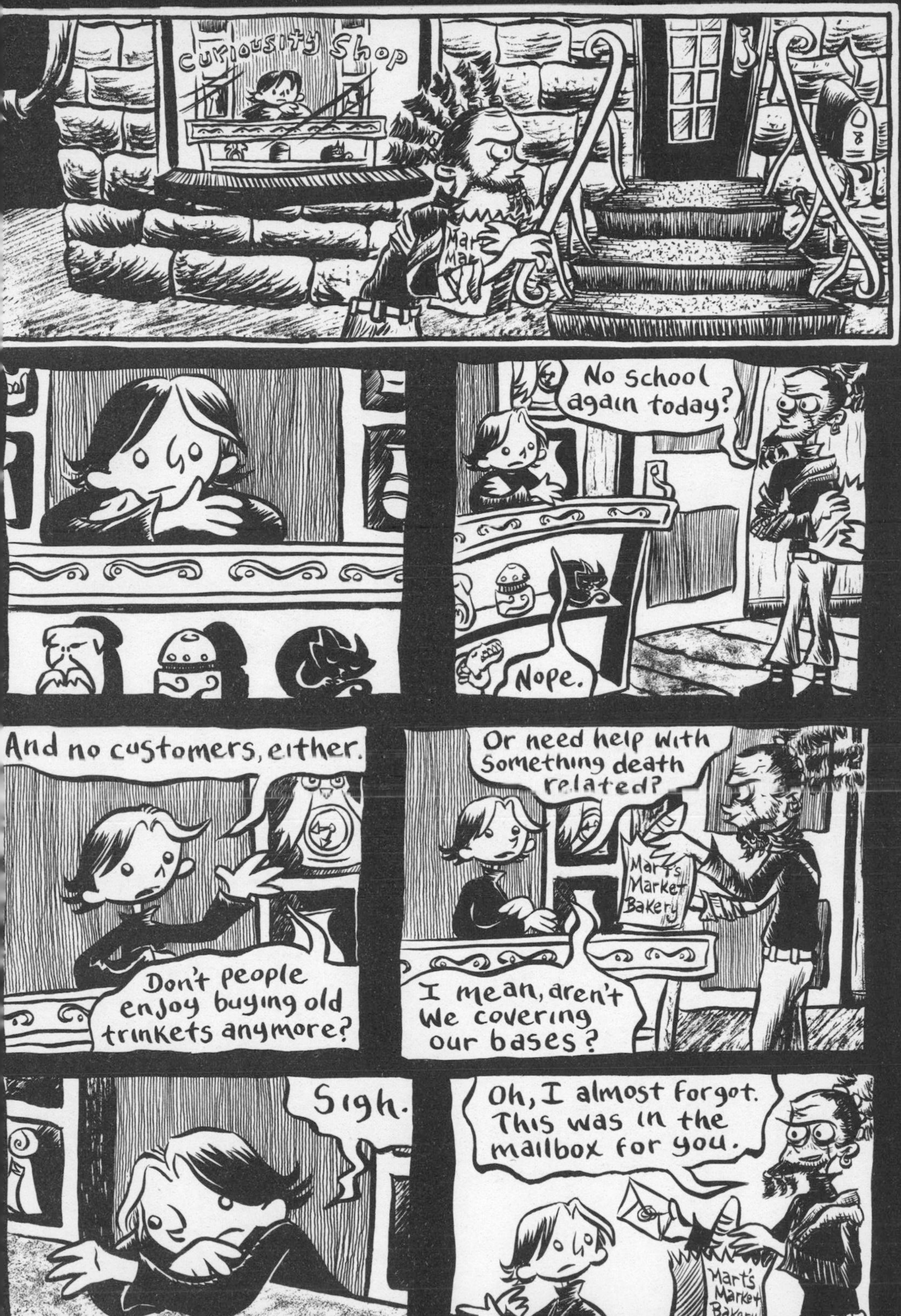
Curiousity Shop
Mart's Mar
No school again today?
Nope.
And no customers, either.
Don't people enjoy buying old trinkets anymore?
Or need help with something death related?
Mart's Market Bakery
I mean, aren't we covering our bases?
Sigh.
Oh, I almost forgot. This was in the mailbox for you.
Mart's Market Bakery

To: Miss Agnes Quill
c/o The New
Curiosity Shop

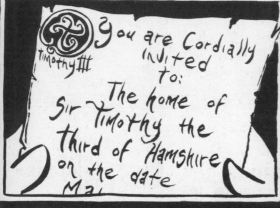

Timothy III

You are Cordially
Invited
to:
The home of
Sir Timothy the
third of Hamshire
on the date
Ma...

...a party?

Why would someone invite ME to a party?

I don't even have any friends.

None that are alive, anyway.

Except for Mr. Lorik. Could this just be a trick to get me out of the shop?

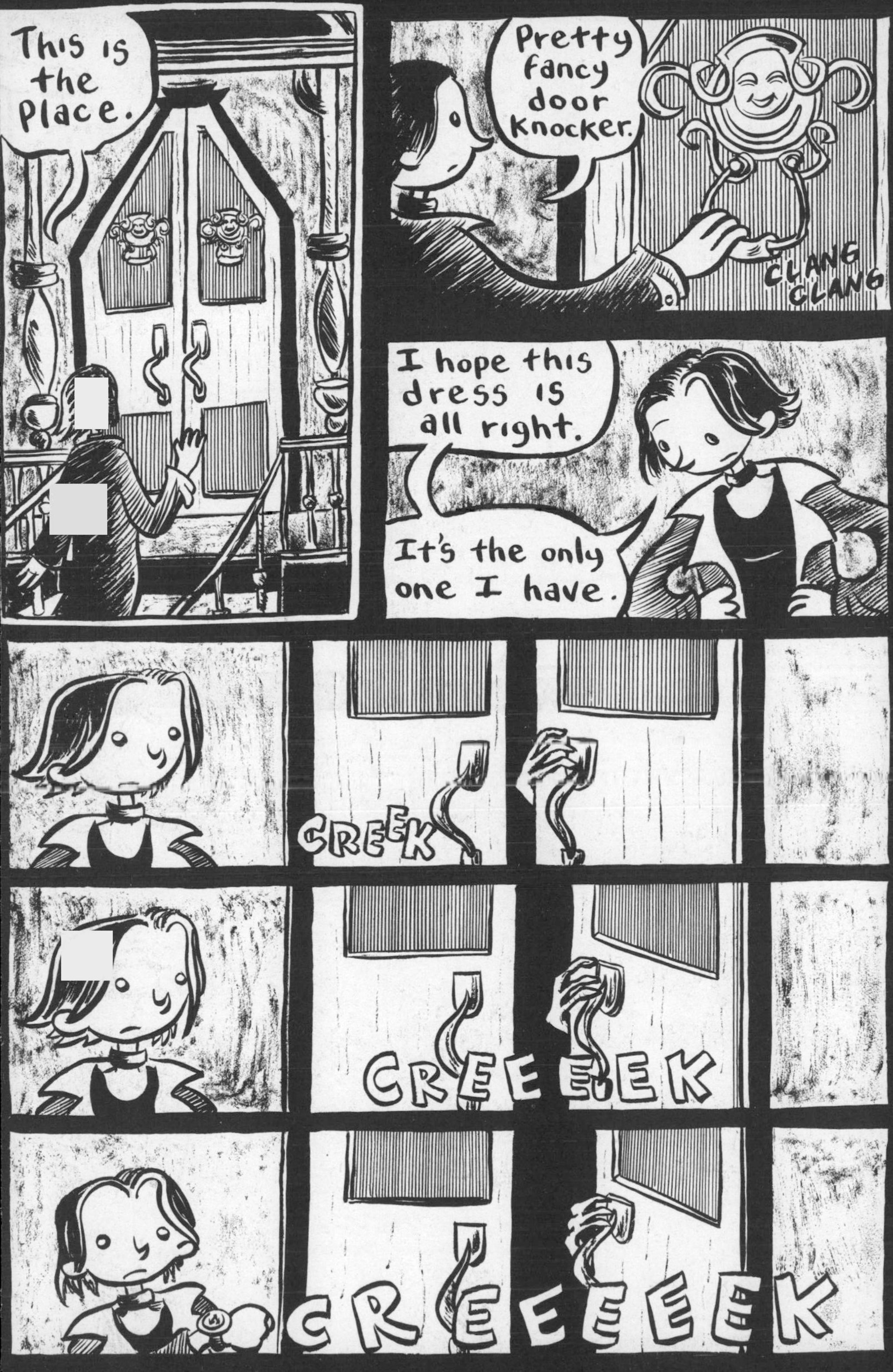
This is the Place.
Pretty fancy door knocker.
CLANG CLANG
I hope this dress is all right.
It's the only one I have.
CREEK
CREEEEK
CREEEEEK

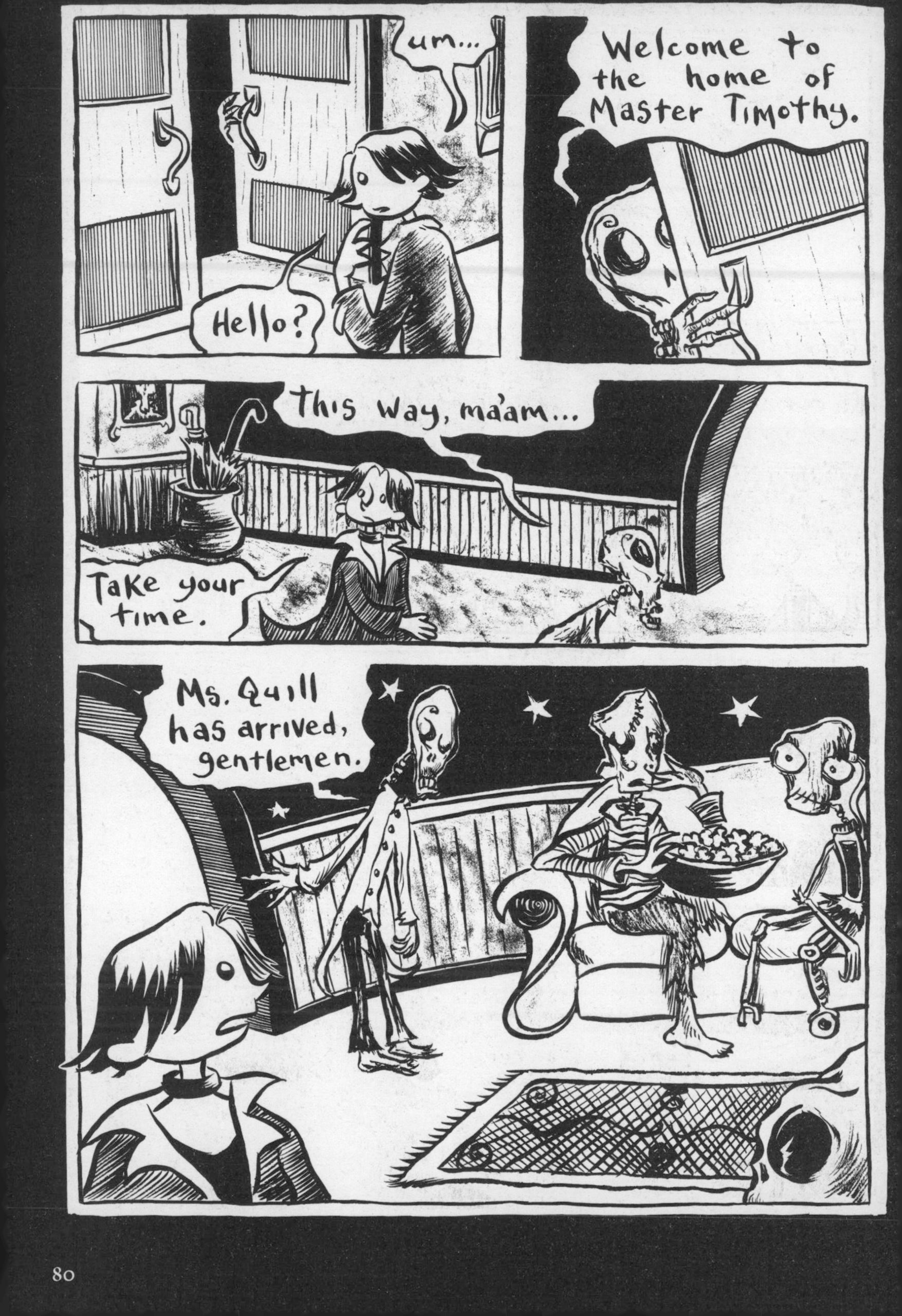

um...
Hello?
Welcome to the home of Master Timothy.
This way, ma'am...
Take your time.
Ms. Quill has arrived, gentlemen.

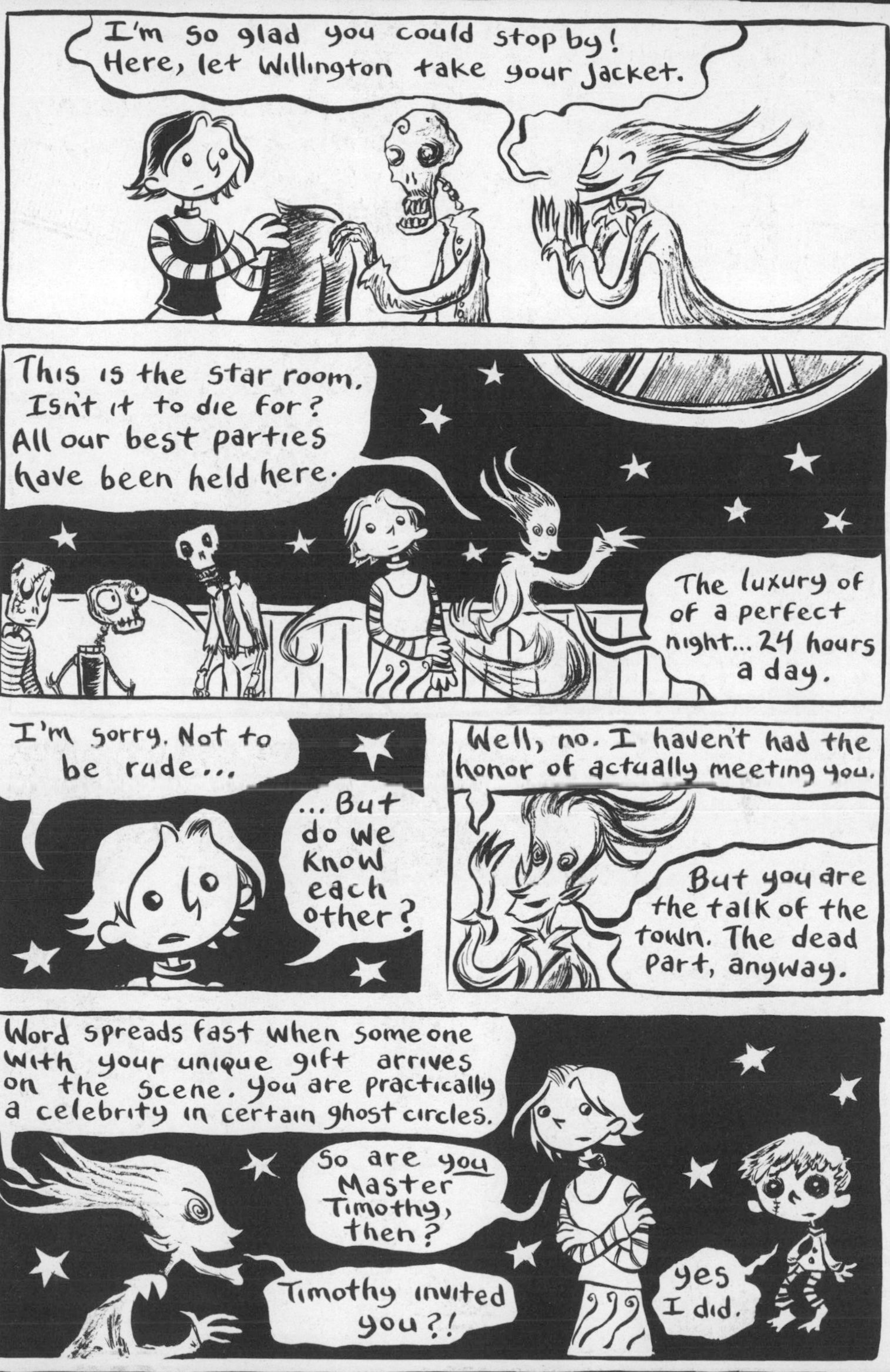

I'm so glad you could stop by! Here, let Willington take your Jacket.
This is the star room. Isn't it to die for? All our best parties have been held here.
The luxury of of a perfect night... 24 hours a day.
I'm sorry. Not to be rude...
... But do we know each other?
Well, no. I haven't had the honor of actually meeting you.
But you are the talk of the town. The dead part, anyway.
Word spreads fast when some one with your unique gift arrives on the scene. You are practically a celebrity in certain ghost circles.
So are you Master Timothy, then?
Timothy invited you?!
yes I did.

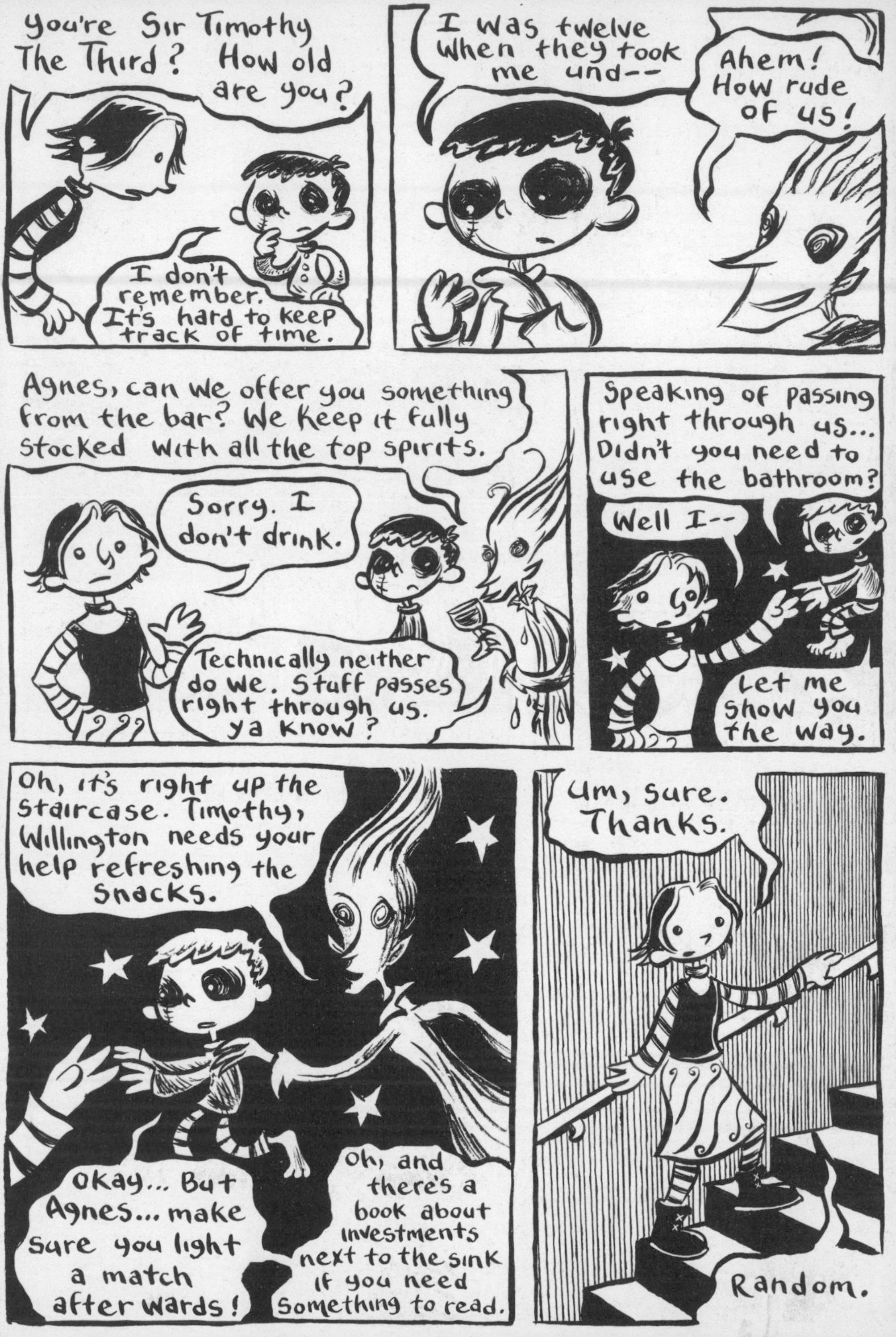

You're Sir Timothy The Third? How old are you?
I don't remember. It's hard to keep track of time.
I was twelve when they took me und--
Ahem! How rude of us!
Agnes, can we offer you something from the bar? We keep it fully stocked with all the top spirits.
Sorry. I don't drink.
Technically neither do we. Stuff passes right through us. ya know?
Speaking of passing right through us... Didn't you need to use the bathroom?
Well I--
Let me show you the way.
Oh, it's right up the staircase. Timothy, Willington needs your help refreshing the snacks.
Okay... But Agnes... make sure you light a match afterwards!
Oh, and there's a book about investments next to the sink if you need something to read.
Um, sure. Thanks.
Random.

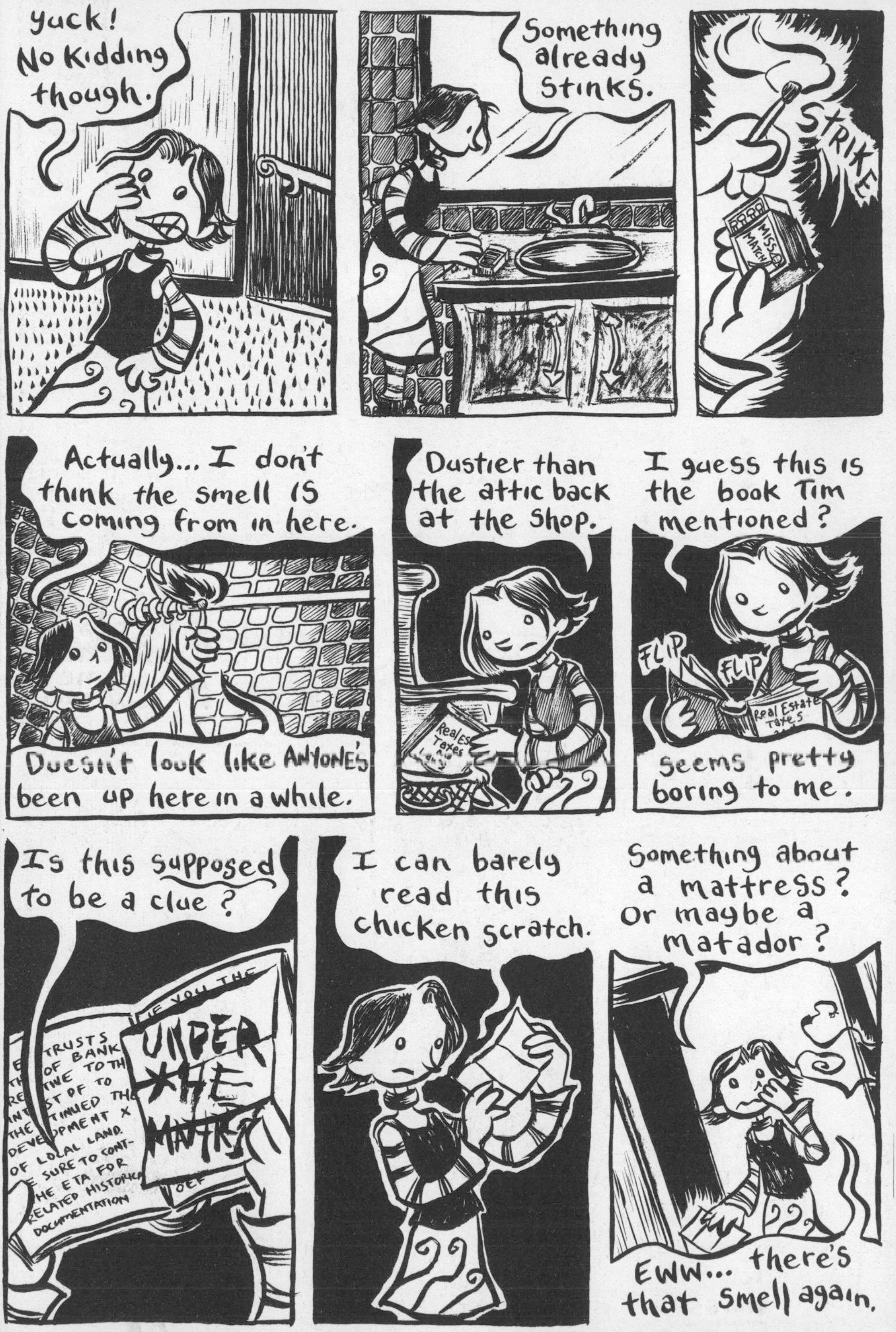

yuck! No Kidding though.
Something already Stinks.
STRIKE
Actually... I don't think the smell IS coming from in here.
Doesn't look like ANYONE's been up here in a while.
Dustier than the attic back at the Shop.
I guess this is the book Tim mentioned?
FLIP
FLIP
Real Estate Taxes
Seems pretty boring to me.
Is this supposed to be a clue?
I can barely read this chicken scratch.
Something about a mattress? Or maybe a matador?
Eww... there's that smell again.

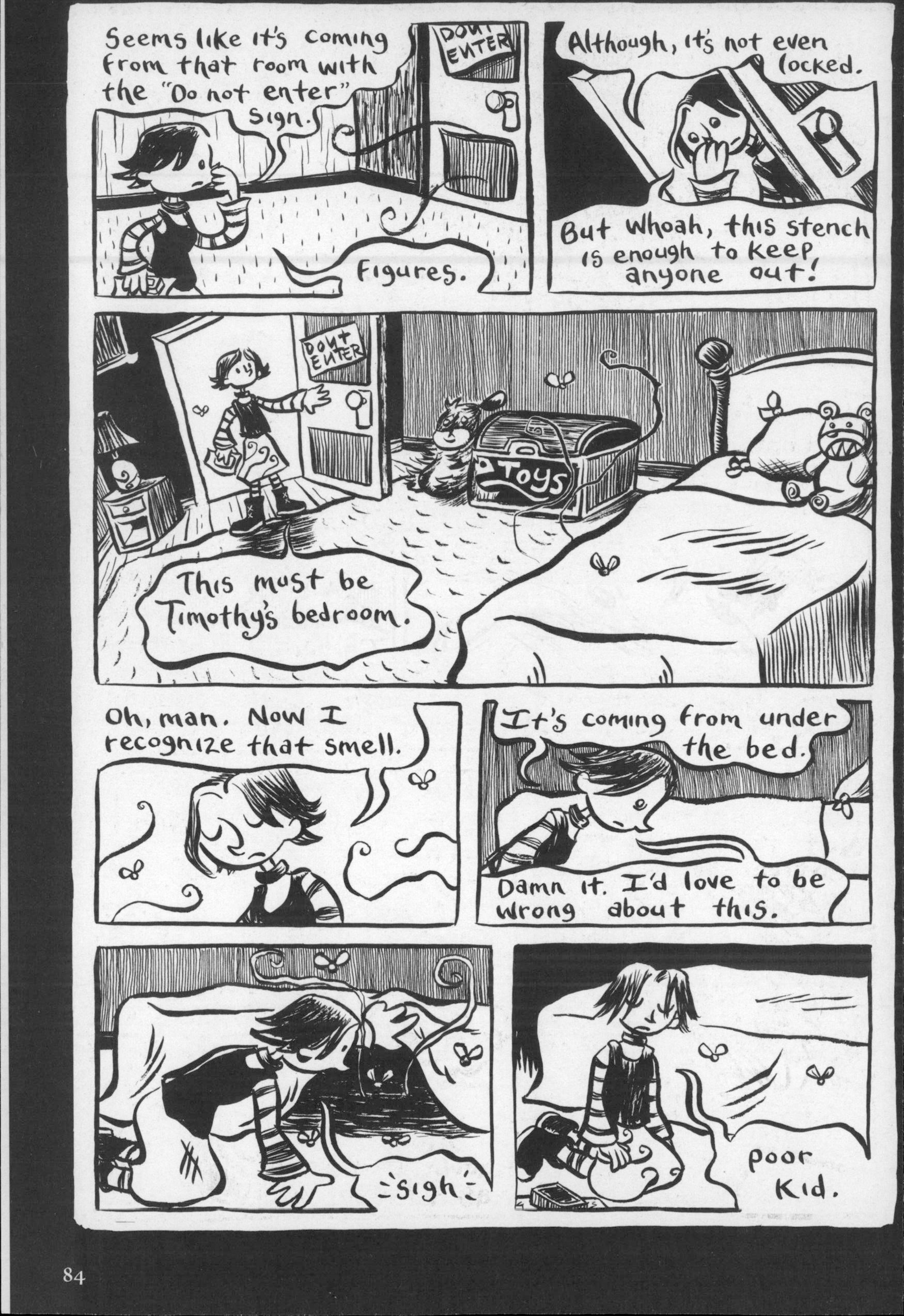
Seems like it's coming from that room with the "Do not enter" sign.
DON'T ENTER
Figures.
Although, it's not even locked.
But whoah, this stench is enough to keep anyone out!
DON'T ENTER
TOYS
This must be Timothy's bedroom.
Oh, man. Now I recognize that smell.
It's coming from under the bed.
Damn it. I'd love to be wrong about this.
sigh
poor Kid.

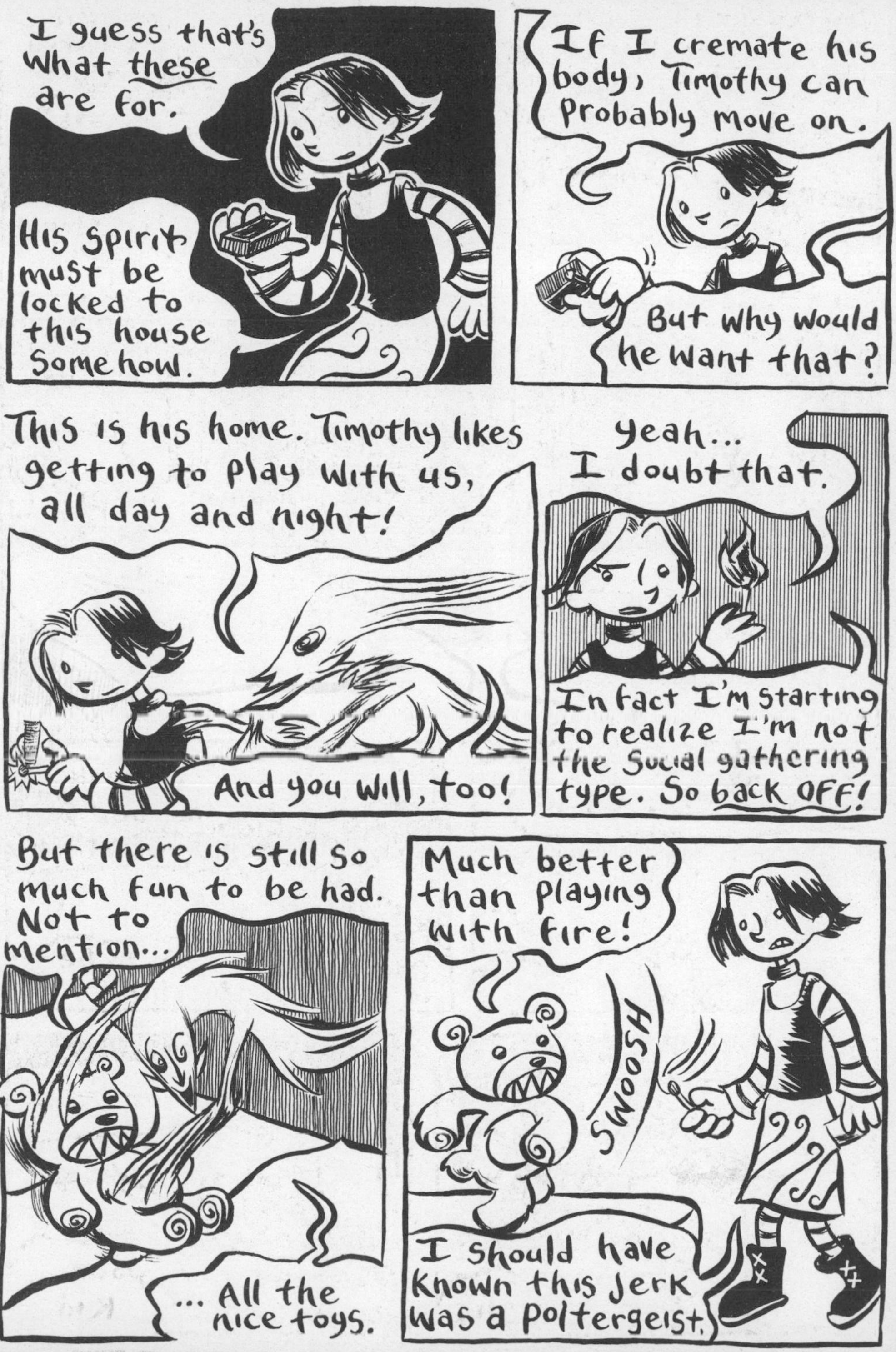

I guess that's what these are for.
His spirit must be locked to this house somehow.
If I cremate his body, Timothy can probably move on.
But why would he want that?
This is his home. Timothy likes getting to play with us, all day and night!
And you will, too!
yeah... I doubt that.
In fact I'm starting to realize I'm not the social gathering type. So back OFF!
But there is still so much fun to be had. Not to mention...
... All the nice toys.
Much better than playing with fire!
SWOOSH
I should have known this jerk was a poltergeist.

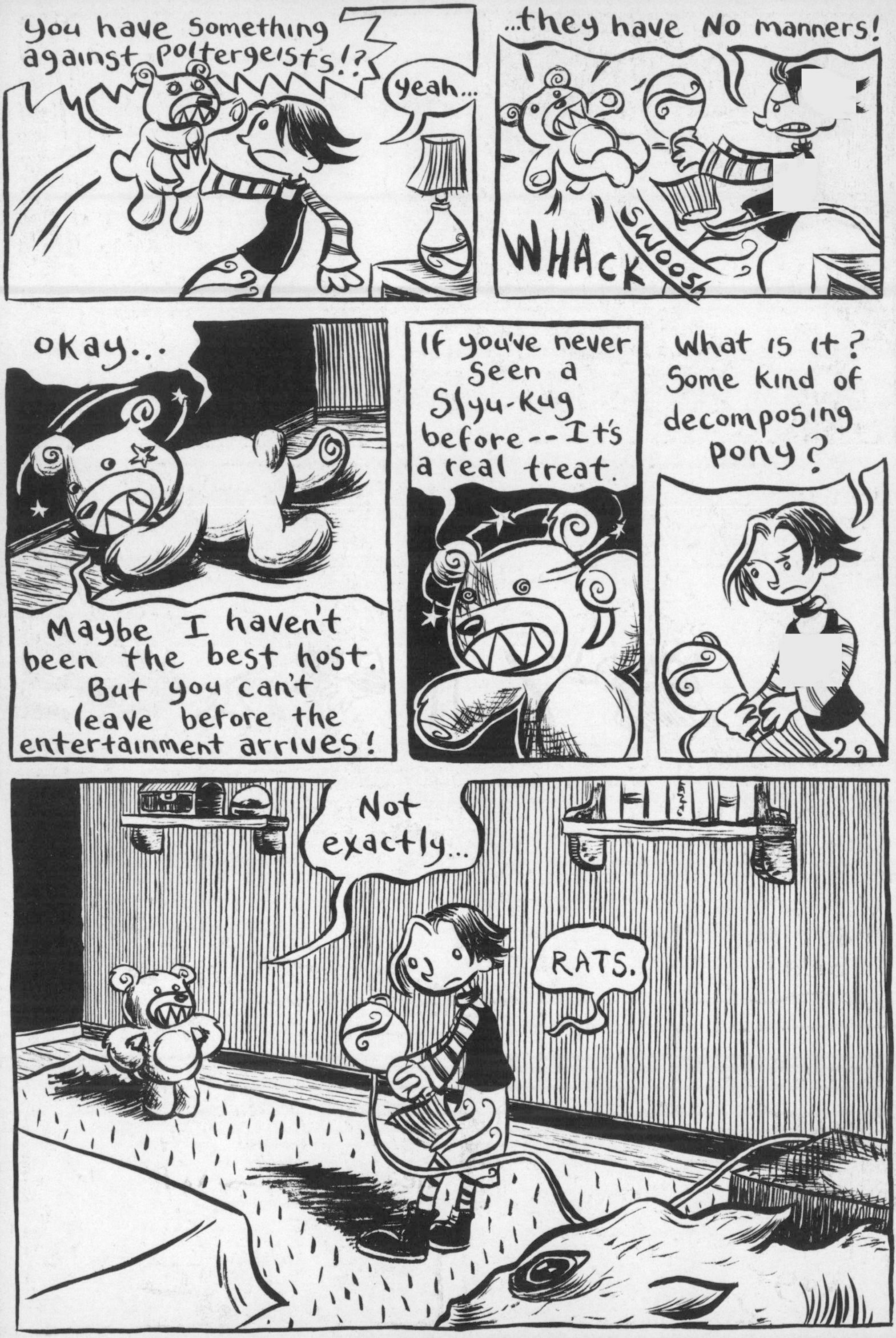
You have something against poltergeists!?
yeah...
...they have No manners!
WHACK
SWOOSH
okay...
Maybe I haven't been the best host. But you can't leave before the entertainment arrives!
If you've never seen a Slyu-Kug before--It's a real treat.
What is it? Some kind of decomposing pony?
Not exactly...
RATS.

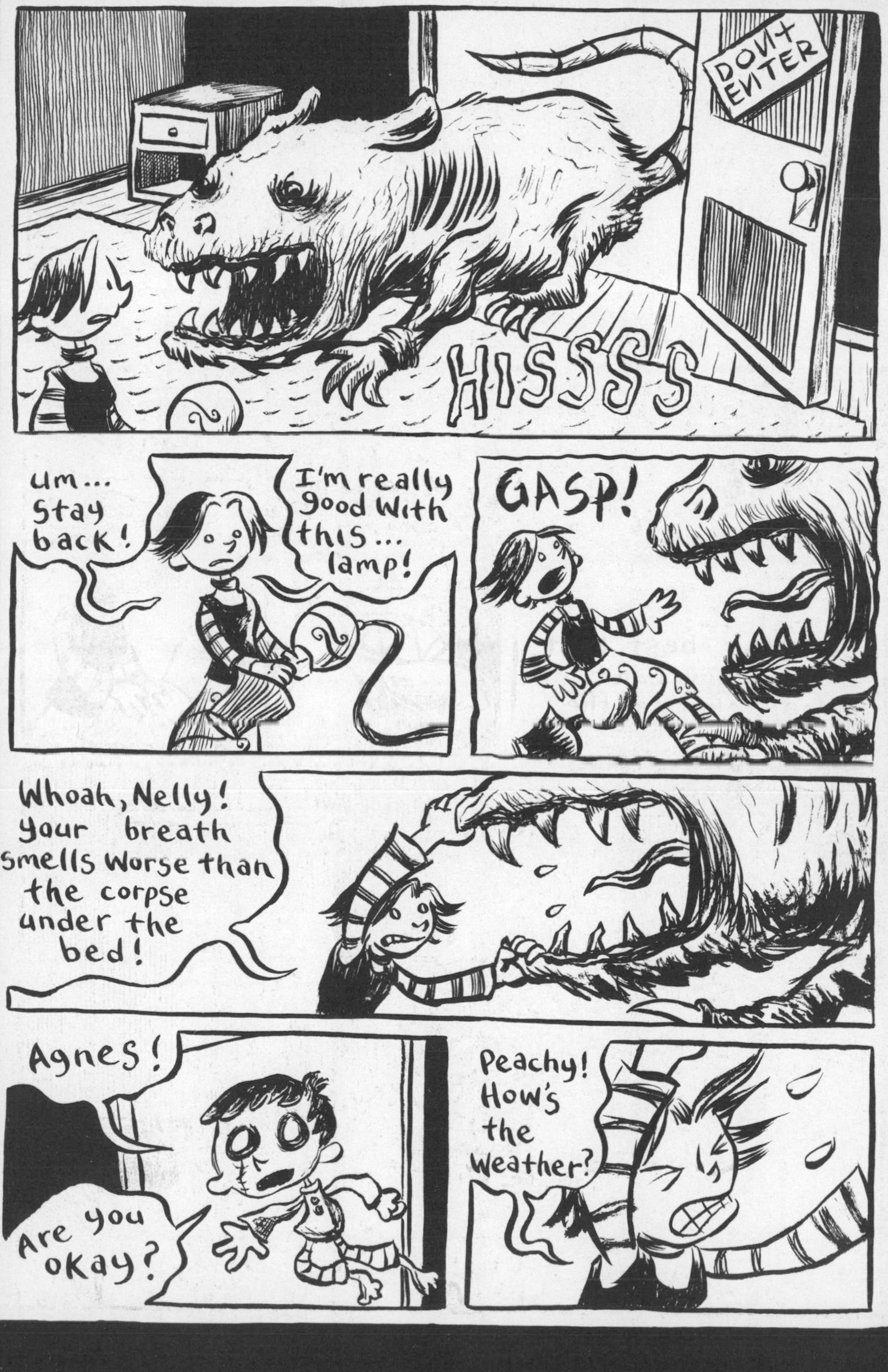
DON'T ENTER
HISSSS
um... Stay back!
I'm really good with this... lamp!
GASP!
Whoah, Nelly! your breath smells worse than the corpse under the bed!
Agnes!
Are you okay?
Peachy! How's the weather?

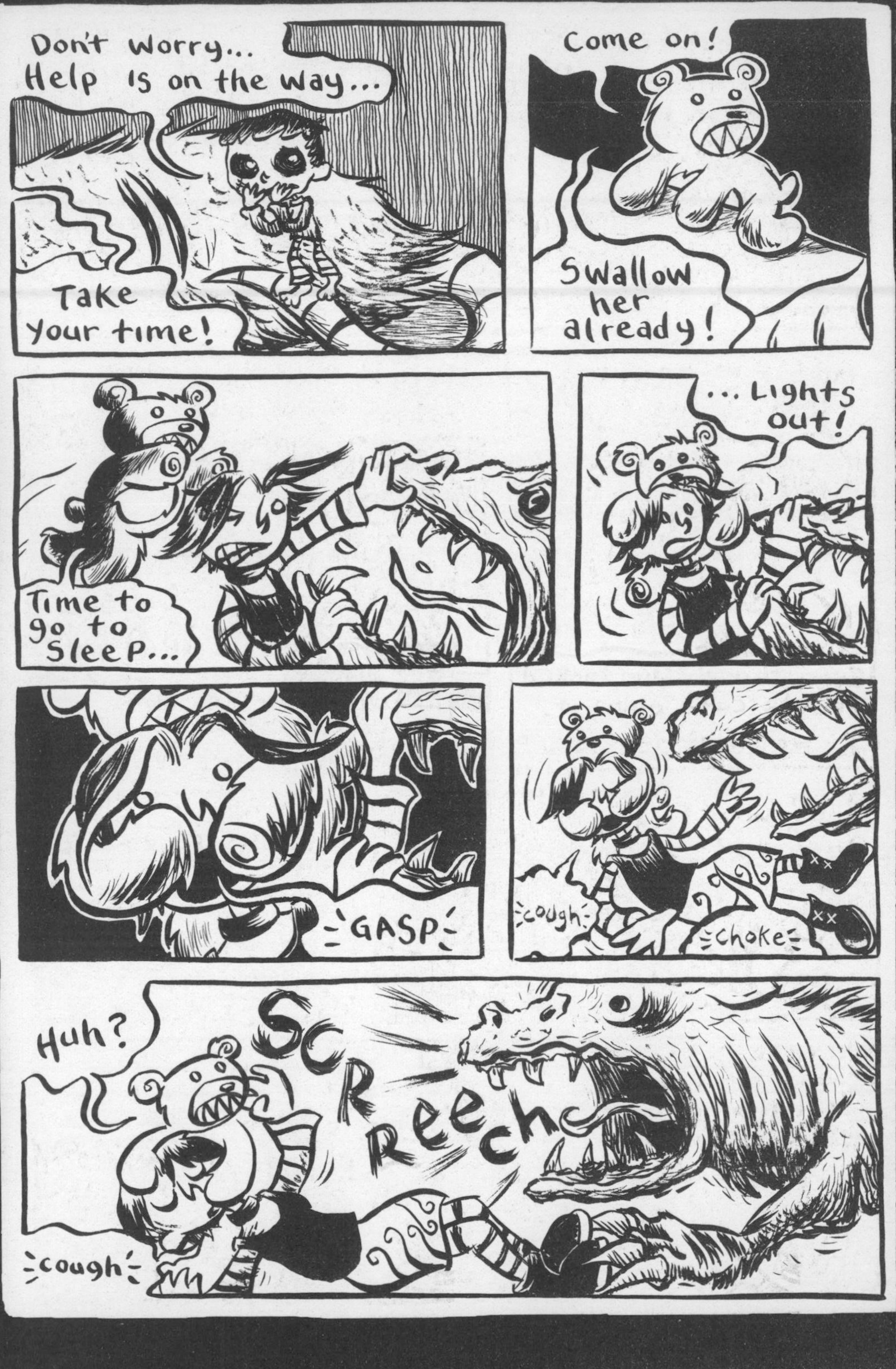
Don't worry...
Help is on the way...
Take your time!
Come on!
Swallow her already!
Time to go to sleep...
...Lights out!
GASP
cough
choke
Huh?
SCReech
cough

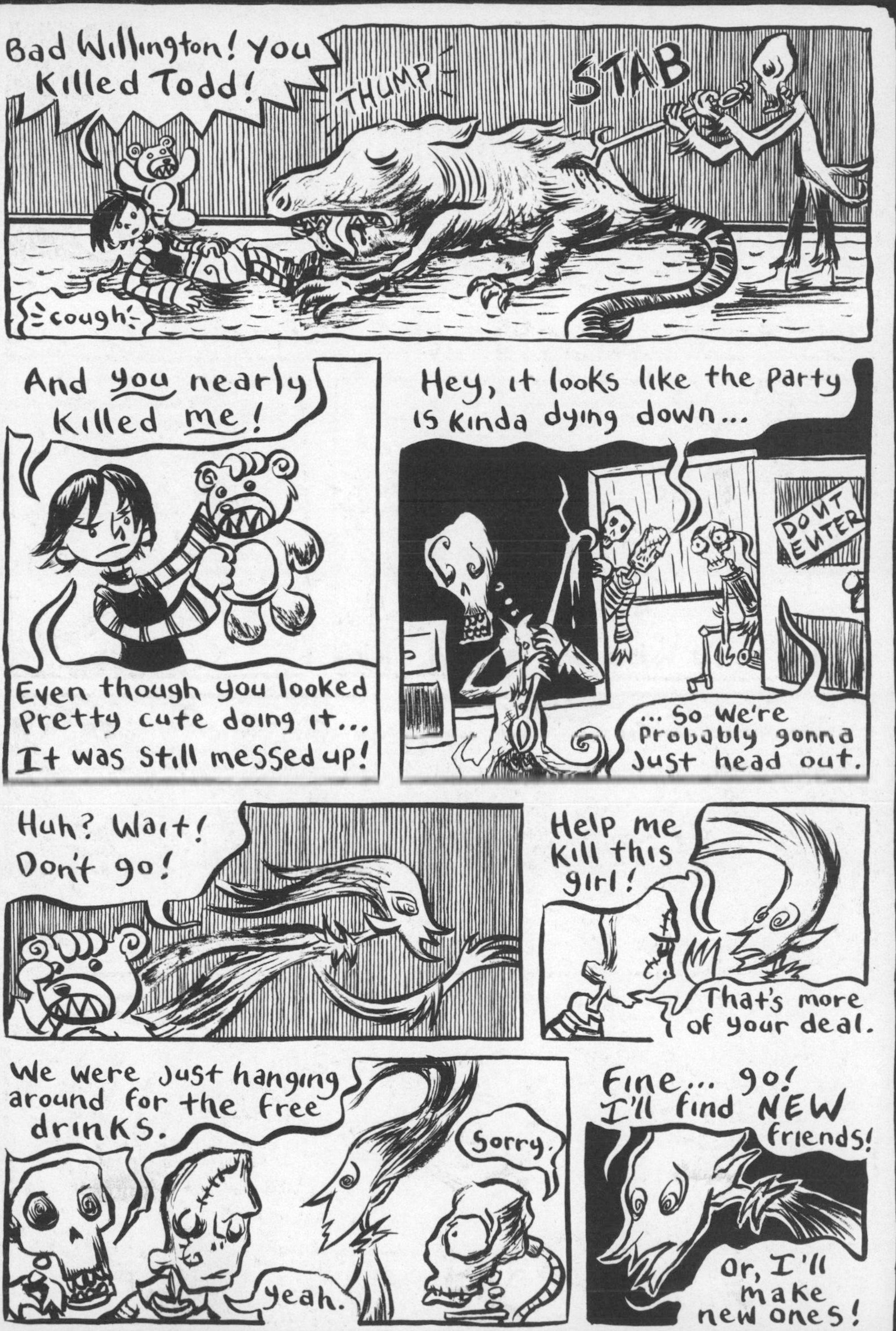
Bad Willington! You Killed Todd!
THUMP
STAB
cough
And you nearly Killed me!
Even though you looked Pretty cute doing it... It was still messed up!
Hey, it looks like the party is Kinda dying down...
DON'T ENTER
...So we're Probably gonna Just head out.
Huh? Wait! Don't go!
Help me Kill this girl!
That's more of your deal.
We were just hanging around for the free drinks.
Sorry.
Yeah.
Fine... go! I'll find NEW friends!
Or, I'll make new ones!

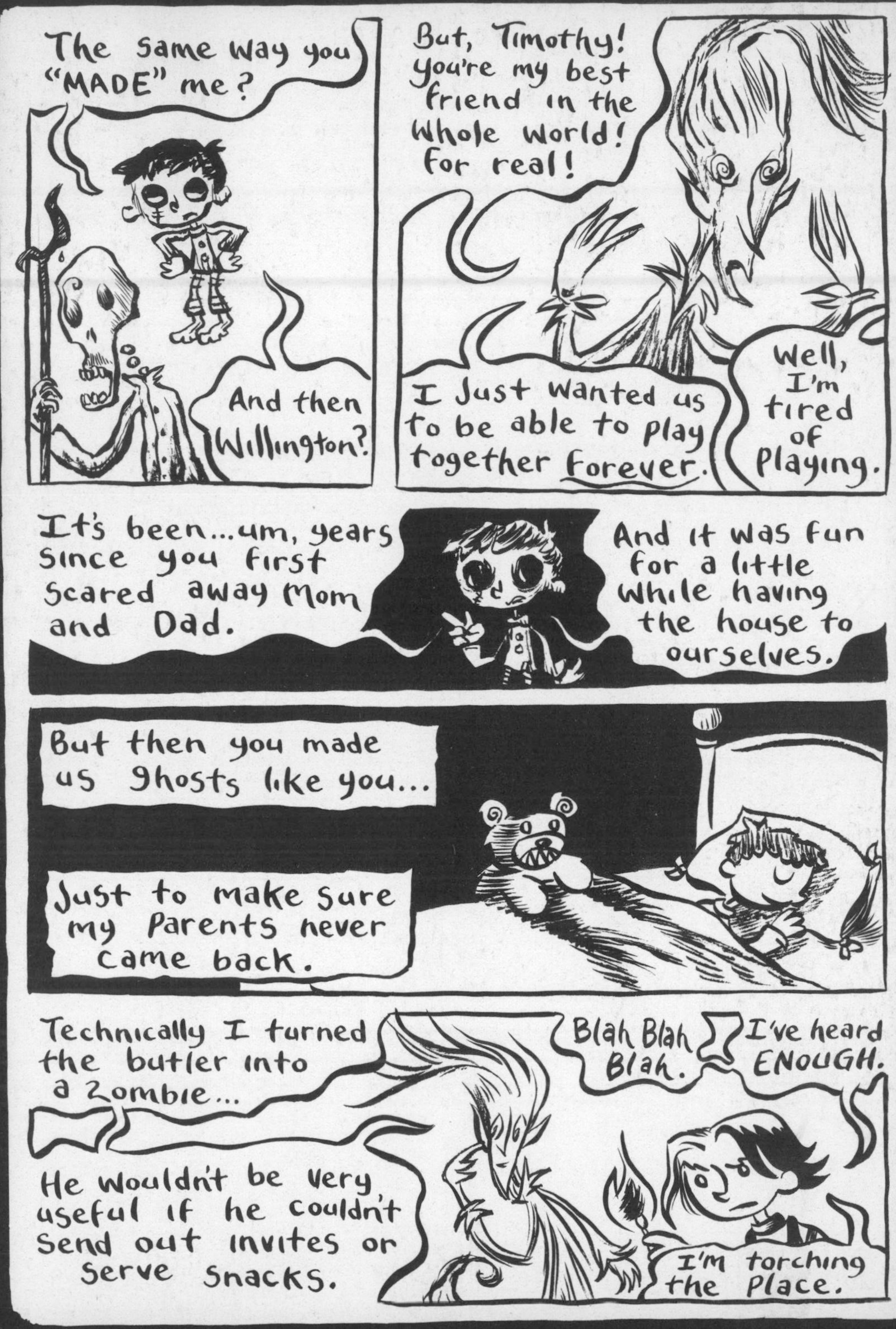

The same way you "MADE" me?
And then Willington?
But, Timothy! You're my best friend in the whole world! For real!
I just wanted us to be able to play together forever.
Well, I'm tired of playing.
It's been...um, years since you first scared away Mom and Dad.
And it was fun for a little while having the house to ourselves.
But then you made us ghosts like you...
Just to make sure my parents never came back.
Technically I turned the butler into a zombie...
He wouldn't be very useful if he couldn't send out invites or serve snacks.
Blah Blah Blah.
I've heard ENOUGH.
I'm torching the place.

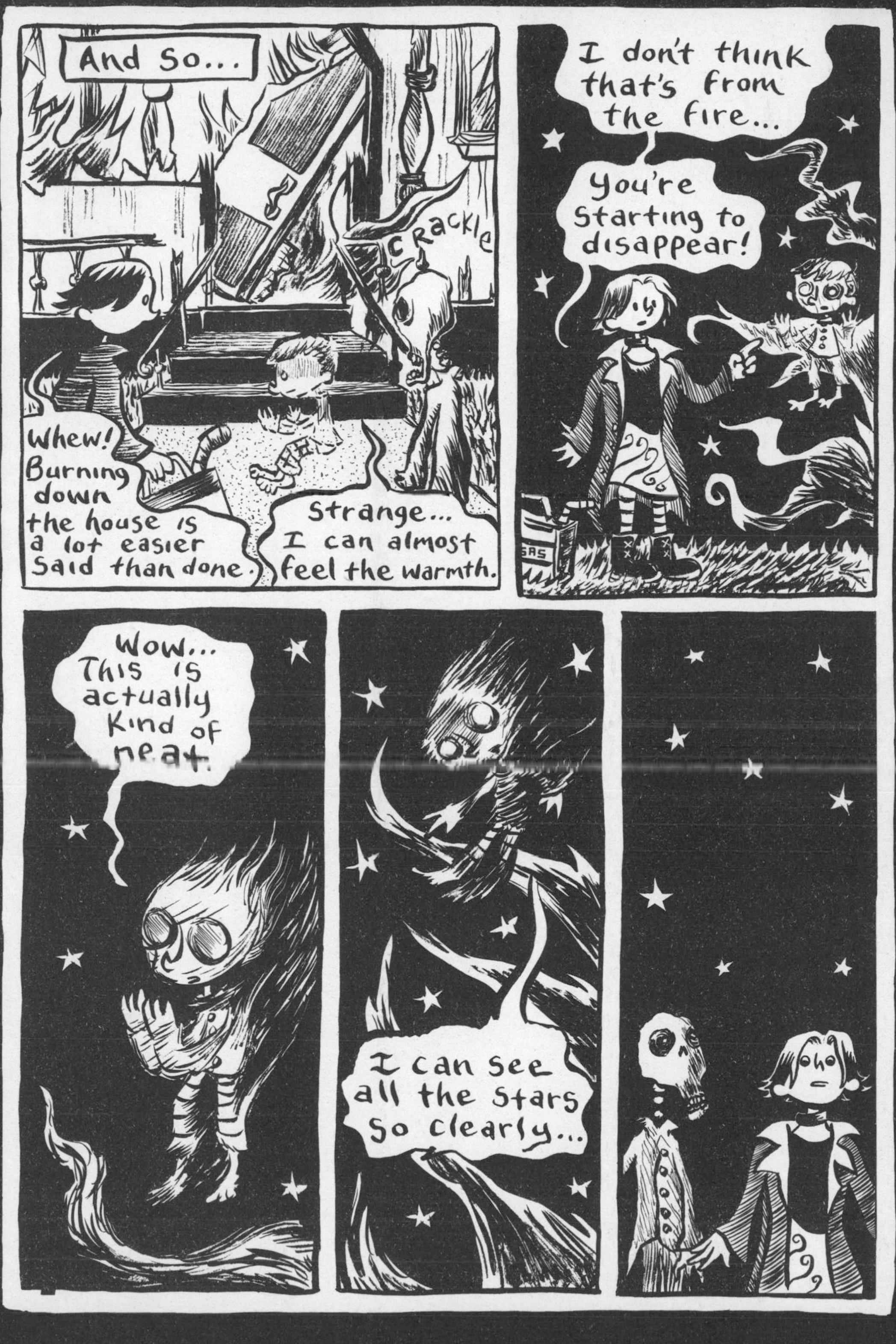

And so...
CRACKLE
Whew! Burning down the house is a lot easier said than done.
Strange... I can almost feel the warmth.
I don't think that's from the fire...
You're starting to disappear!
Wow... This is actually kind of neat.
I can see all the stars so clearly...

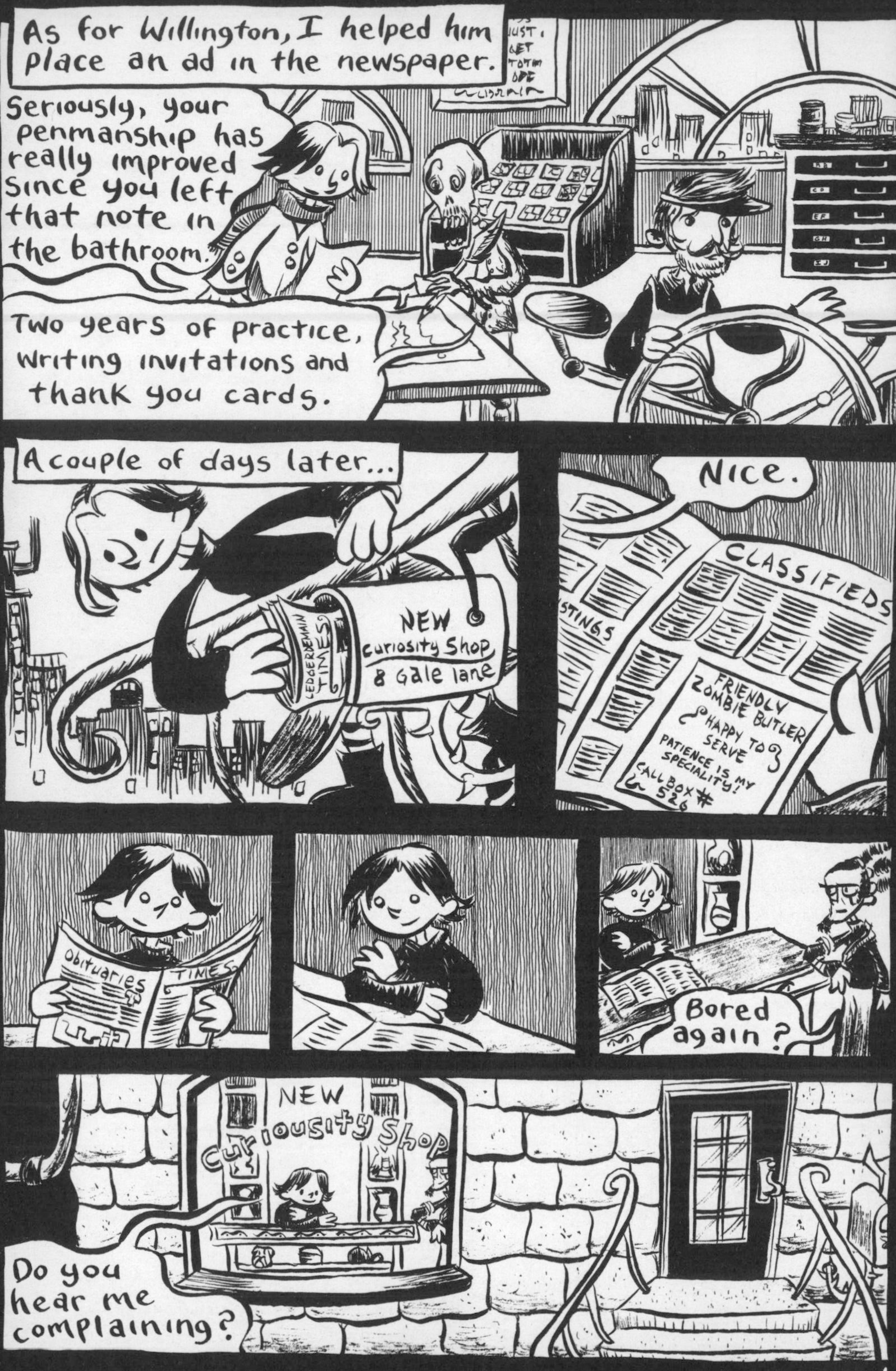
As for Willington, I helped him place an ad in the newspaper.
Seriously, your penmanship has really improved since you left that note in the bathroom.
Two years of practice, writing invitations and thank you cards.
A couple of days later...
LEDGERDEMAIN TIMES
NEW curiosity Shop 8 Gale lane
Nice.
CLASSIFIEDS
FRIENDLY ZOMBIE BUTLER
HAPPY TO SERVE
PATIENCE IS MY SPECIALITY!
CALL BOX # 526
Obituaries
TIMES
Bored again?
NEW Curiousity Shop
Do you hear me complaining?
end

the DATA ANALYSIS KEEP
FIELD GUIDE
to
AGNES QUILL

RESEARCH COMPILED
by **DAVE ROMAN**

ILLUSTRATED
by **JASON HO**
and **JEFF ZORNOW**

THE ORIGINS OF MS. QUILL'S TALENTS

Sixteen-year-old Agnes Quill has inherited an ancient family curse, brought about by the loss of her parents. Several of our key scholars have accounted for and confirmed that she has the ability to see and communicate with spirits trapped between worlds. In several confidential journal entries, Agnes describes the events of her parents' funeral, where the ghost of her Grandfather, Ages Quill, visited her. It was then that he explained the nature of specters and how he used his connections with them to great advantage throughout his career. He comforted Agnes by relaying that her parents died quietly, and had therefore moved on to a place where spirits can rest in peace. Agnes has come to realize that In contacting her, Ages Quill had not died in the same manner, for only specters that are still at great unrest can communicate with the living.

Avoiding life in a boarding home, Agnes ran away to Legerdemain to find the dilapidated castle her Grandfather had once called home. When she arrived, she discovered that at the base of the castle was is an old store called The New Curiosity Shop, which her Grandfather used to run his detective agency . It was there that she met Mr. Lorik, the caretaker, who confirmed that as the last living member of the Quill family, the castle and everything in it now belonged to her.

0.1. FINDINGS IN REGARDS TO
SPECIFIC ABILITIES

Agnes is fully cognizant and acquainted with the spirits that are trapped within our physical world. She can communicate with most of those who wander our streets and homes aimlessly, although occasionally there are spirits too far lost for her to reach. Agnes' own grandfather is, in fact, trapped between worlds, and has been known to help her out when she is in a desperate situation. Agnes wrote the following in one of journals:

> *The ghosts and spirits stuck in our world reflect all walks of life and even the souls of animals. Not all the ghosts are the haunting type; in fact, some are quite friendly and willing to cooperate with anyone who pays attention to them. This is especially helpful when I'm searching for clues or trying to get information from places most living people cannot access.*

0.2. IN REGARDS TO THE PERSONALITY OF MS. QUILL

A teenage detective following in her famous grandfather's footsteps, Agnes takes her work very seriously. She is extremely driven, throwing herself completely into her cases, almost out of necessity. Experiencing the sites and sounds of the spirit world on a regular basis can drive her crazy; only when she is engulfed by her work does she feel perfectly comfortable. Agnes gets excited easily, and often has a hard time staying still or keeping her mind on one subject. She is somewhat disorganized, which results in her becoming frantic when she cannot find what she is looking for.

Trying to connect to people in the living world is a constant challenge for Agnes. However, she has a natural gift for talking to spirits, which often gives her the upper hand while working on a hard-to-crack case. When she isn't caught up in a mystery, she is usually less confident, often distancing herself from the world around her.

Agnes attends school, but does not feel that she truly fits in. Although Agnes would like to make flesh-and-blood friends, she he is out of her element in social situations, unsure of what to do. Agnes worries about how the world perceives her and goes to great lengths to keep from attracting too much attention to herself.

Agnes is constantly learning to overcome her own self-doubt and make the best of the talents she has, while coming to grips with the responsibilities of growing up. Running her own business forces her to continuously reevaluate what she wants from life.

0.3. MS. QUILL'S REFLECTIONS ON THE CITY OF LEGERDEMAIN

Agnes often regards the city itself as a living being, with its own unique personality traits.

She wrote the following description in a letter to Ms. Dorothy Brosgol at the St.Vera orphanage:

fig. 0.1

> "…A chaotic melting pot of new and old, its buildings are stacked atop pre-existing structures and castles that have fallen to ruin. There is an eclectic mix of influences from different time periods, all built on top of a Victorian-era foundation. Cobblestone streets and immense steel pipes twist throughout the city, which is usually thick with dense fog. There are countless alleyways that seem to lead to nowhere, and plenty of shady creatures that lurk in them. In the center of the city there is a large cemetery, equivalent to the location and vastness of a valley. Central Park Graveyard takes up a good part of the city. Of course, it's haunted—there are endless accounts of people who walk in and never make it to the other side. Many historical archives claim that the City of Legerdemain started as a graveyard that everything else was gradually built around."

Agnes lives in a deserted castle in the middle of the city. The foundation level of the castle is small store called The New Curiosity Shop, run by a man named Mr. Lorik (an old friend of her grandfather's). The store sells items imported from other regions including sculpture, books, artwork and tools.

Agnes often speaks of protecting her home and her family heritage. She uses her unique talents not only to help the people and spirits who hire her, but also to preserve the things she holds dear. Before Agnes arrived in Legerdemain, The New Curiosity Shop was in danger of going out of business—Mr. Lorik, growing old and weak, found it hard to maintain on a daily basis, and even more difficult to resist the offers from outside developers who wished to buy the old building. By following in her Grandfather's footsteps and continuing to operate the business, Agnes has managed to keep the building in her family's name.

Agnes attends class at Marley's Schoolhouse, a small building with only a single room and teacher. Her classmates are of varying ages and grade levels, usually consisting of about 15 kids per year. Few people in Legerdemain can actually afford education (and the rich send their kids away for a better life outside Legerdemain). Agnes has a hard time connecting with most of the kids in her class, whom she fears won't accept her because of her unusual abilities and lifestyle. Regardless of Agnes' less than perfect attendance record she manages to do well on the tests she has taken.

fig. 0.2

1.1. THOSE DIRECTLY CONNECTED TO MS. QUILL

QUILL, Ages - Paternal grandfather (*fig. 1.1*)

File note: Since he is the subject of his own file and continuing investigation, we have included only information as it pertains to his granddaughter.

Mr. Ages Quill was a famous detective who helped many people during his lifetime. By all accounts and interviews, he was a good man that many people still feel they owe a great debt to. He has been the subject of extensive research by the Data Analysis Keep, but since he was not willing to cooperate directly with any of our scholars, our knowledge of his exploits are far from complete. Throughout his life many rumors circulated about his "talents," and it wasn't long into his career that he attracted the attention of our organization. Over the years many

1.1

fig. 1.2a

scholars have claimed to witness his use of phantoms and unclassified entities as allies in his work, but few have been able to obtain what would classify as documented proof.

According to his Last Will and Testament (which The Keep has taken the effort to copy for our own records), Ages Quill has left all his property and possessions to his granddaughter Agnes. It is not known why, but it seems Agnes' parents kept the fact of her inheritance a secret. Whether they were waiting for to her to come of age or were intending to hide the truth about her grandfather is not documented. Agnes did not learn about Ages Quill or his profession until his ghost came to visit, informing Agnes that there was a place that rightly belonged to her.

Ages Quill's death is still shrouded in mystery, and constantly seems to resurface in the work that Agnes has carried on. The one thing that is clear: Ages is still trapped between realms, and has yet to move on completely. Agnes is obsessed with uncovering the truth behind her grandfather's mysterious end, which seems connected to several powerful people who wish to remain in the shadows of the city.

fig. 1.2b

QUILL, Katrina and Oliver - Mother and father (figs. 1.2a, 1.2b)

Agnes' parents, Katrina and Oliver Quill, were killed when she was only seven. They were hard-working farmers who lived in the rural town of Calico Creek. Town records state that they passed away from a form of influenza that had spread through much of the area. According to Agnes' accounts, no ghosts or remnants of her parents have ever turned up in any of her adventures. It was upon her parents' death that Agnes first became aware of her unique abilities and her grandfather's legacy.

LORIK, "Mr." - First name unknown, aka The Lorik (*fig. 1.3*)

Mr. Lorik is the current caretaker of The New Curiosity Shop. Mr. Lorik appears as a dark skinned man in his mid-fifties, but is in fact a multi-dimensional being known as The Lorik. J. Epoch, an expert on inter-dimensional studies who has acted as a freelance agent for the Data Analysis Keep, wrote a brief description on her findings regarding this unique entity:

> "*The Lorik exists in several realms of existence simultaneously through separate bodies. I don't know how or why but I've seen enough of them to know it's true. I first met a man who called himself Thomas Lorik, and then watched him die in front of me. Not too long after, I discovered that he was very much alive. But he was not the same man . . . and he did not originate from the same place. When I confused him for my friend, he explained that he was 'connected,' but separate at the same time. He claimed to be conscious of many other pieces of himself spread out through different worlds. It creeped me out so I stopped asking him questions.*"

The Mr. Lorik that resides with Agnes at The New Curiosity Shop acts as Agnes' guardian and living connection to the history of her grandfather. He is always there to offer advice, although usually in a cryptic manner that leaves Agnes asking even more questions. Mr. Lorik always maintains a calm and reserved appearance, especially when Agnes is at her most frantic. Those who have spent time with them can attest that Agnes is extremely protective of Mr. Lorik and the Curiosity Shop they both call home. Many locals have speculated Mr. Lorik's attachment to the store runs deeper than loyalty.

> "That old man has been working in that store forever. No one even remembers when the place was built. And no one can remember a time that he wasn't employed there. When the store fell on hard times, the old man got sick. When the shop was prospering, so too the man. He is made from the walls of its foundation. If you burn the store down only then will the man die."
> -**Traver Marts**, *owner of the Marts family-owned bakery*

fig. 1.3

Regarding Mr. Lorik's Skills and Abilities: Mr. Lorik is fairly experienced in several forms of magic and voodoo—often useful for Agnes, who is still learning to handle the supernatural. It is not documented where Mr. Lorik acquired his knowledge of the mystic arts, but he seems to have various connections to local shaman as well as tribesmen clerics, who pass through Ledgerdemain.

Additional note: There is no birth record on file for Mr. Lorik in any of the Legerdemain Municipal buildings, and there seems to be no documentation of a first name ever used.

HECKS, Harland (*fig. 1.4*)

Harland Hecks is currently a ghost who haunts the back corner of Marley's schoolhouse. Harland died over fifty years ago when he was sent to the back of the class for misbehaving, and was accidentally left there over winter break (during one of the worst winters in recorded history). Although dead, Harland hardly ever seems to acknowledge it, as he is usually more concerned with keeping up his role as the class clown year after year.

fig. 1.4

STROSSGHAN, Niel (*fig. 1.5*)

A native of the underground city known as the Buried Homes and Gardens (see excerpt below), Niel is openly infatuated with Agnes, constantly trying to win her affection. Agnes is admittedly attracted to his good looks and elegant style, but is equally put off by Niel's arrogance and forward nature, which often gets him on her bad side. However, Agnes pities his people's inability to live above the ground, and continues to help Niel on a regular basis.

fig. 1.5

EXCERPTS
from the
JOURNALS
of
AGNES QUILL

TRANSCRIBED *by* **DAVE ROMAN**

ILLUSTRATED *by* **JASON HO,
JEFF ZORNOW,**
and **JEN WANG**

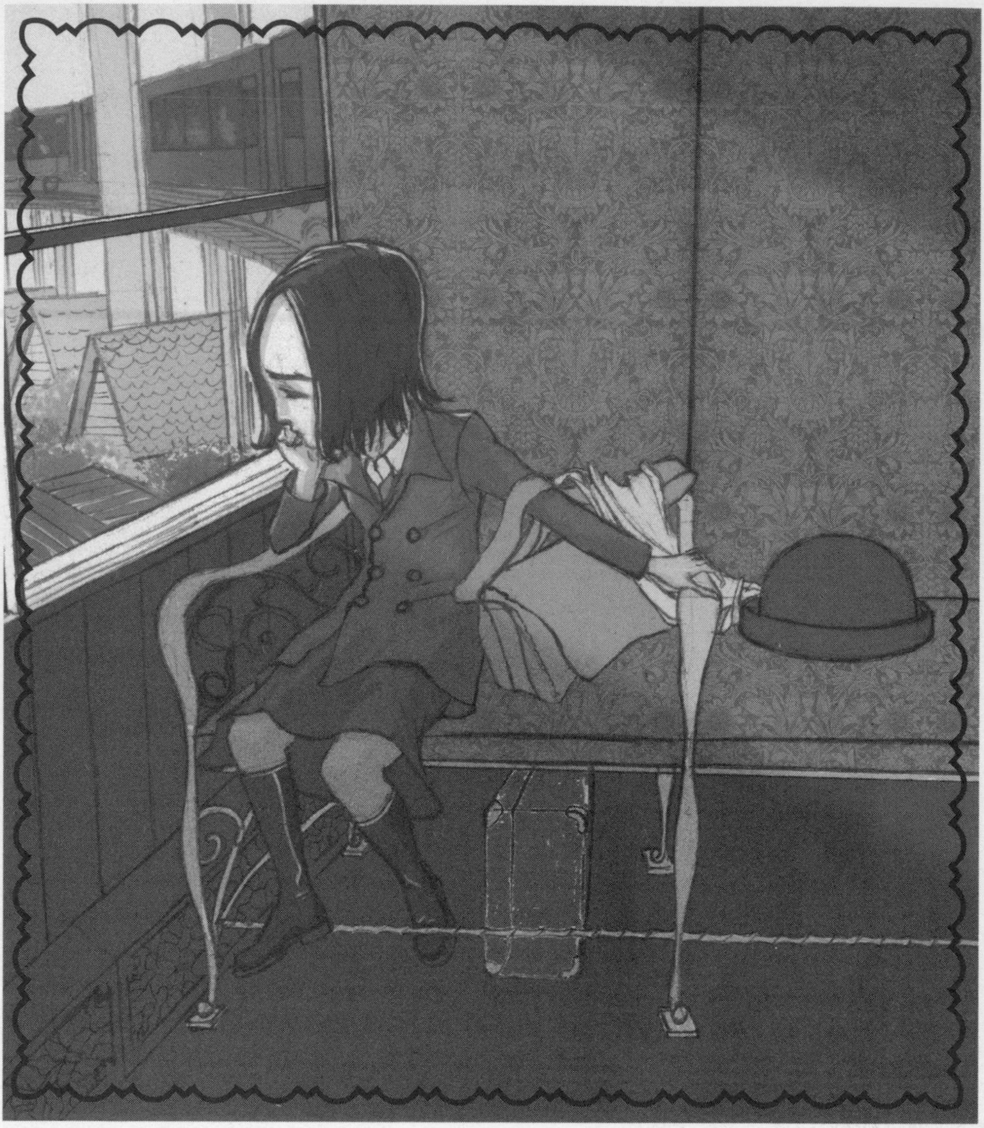

ENTRY #1

I finally have a chance to start a new journal...though I don't know how much I should write about. There has been so much happening so quickly. And a lot has been SCARY. Yet I'm trying my best not to act afraid. That's what Grandfather asked of me. He warned about those that can feed on people's fear—which makes me panic more instead of calming me down. So I'll try and just focus on the trip here.

Riding a train for the first time was both exciting and strange—as was arriving at the station and everything that's happened since. I knew it wouldn't be anything like home here, and in some ways I'm okay with that. Anything is better than growing up in an orphanage. But this city is so loud and overwrought with smoke, I can barely tell if my senses are responding correctly. If I stick my tongue out in the fog, there is a taste to it that reminds me of burning fuel or working machinery. I've already had three nosebleeds today and my hair feels like it hasn't been washed in forever (it's only been 2 days.) I didn't talk to anyone on the train ride, but I could hear voices traveling through the aisles in a way that felt as if a draft were passing over my body. It was creepy, so I tried to focus on the changing scenery out the window and imagine what Grandfather's castle would look like.

Now that I am here, I can say it's less like the ones I remember from fairytale books and more like something that survived a war. I always assumed castles to be big, with endless rooms of wonder and grandeur—I never realized they can also be small and damp. Not that I don't love it, because it is wonderful in so many ways! I can't wait to explore through all its junk and clutter. And just knowing that this is where my grandfather used to live makes the whole place seem familiar.

I'm very grateful to Mr. Lorik. He doesn't say much, but just knowing he's downstairs in the store is comforting. His is the good kind of quiet.

ENTRY #4

I took a walk though the city today. Mostly just staring at the crowds trying to get a sense of the character of people who live here. I kept getting distracted by the OTHER THINGS though. Mostly ghosts.

There's way more here in Legerdemain compared to back home. Lots of the scary types, with mean faces and horrible sounds. Like the ones at the orphanage that kept begging me to follow them in circles. But here in the city there are different kinds, too. Some just appear lost, while others seem more adjusted to being dead. When I got back to the Curiosity Shop, I tried talking with Mr. Lorik, but he just kind of ignored me. But as I was heading back up to my room he called me over to the kitchen to eat some soup he made. It was the best thing I've had to eat since Mom died.

ENTRY #5

It's been a few weeks and I wonder if I'm finally getting used to city life. I know I really don't have any choice, so I'm trying my best to get over all the overwhelming feelings. It's like being dropped in the middle of the ocean and learning to swim on the spot. In the city, there's always someone there, just out of sight. And everywhere there are voices. Sometimes screams and screeches. It is easy to forget I was ever at peace.

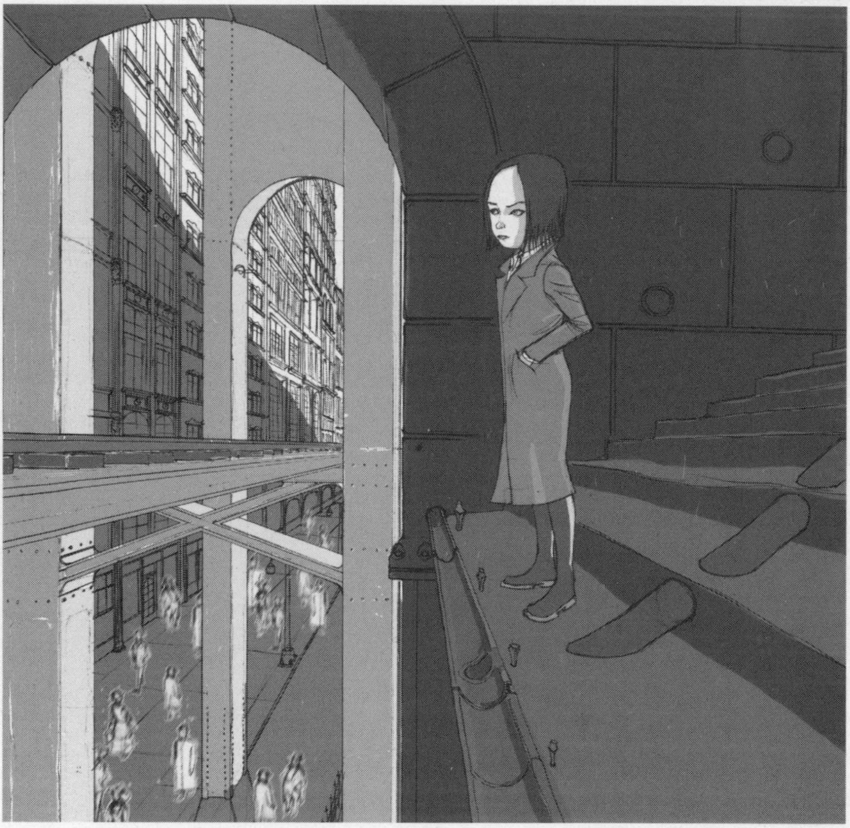

ENTRY #10

I need to find a way to make some money. I actually saw Mr. Lorik looking nervous this morning, which is so out of character for him that it seemed supernatural. I think he's worried about the Curiosity Shop. There seem to be a lot of people coming by during the day, talking with him in a weird business speak. I know that technically the castle belongs to me now...but I don't know what that really means or how mortgages work. And since I haven't seen my grandfather since that day at the funeral, I feel like there isn't anyone who can tell me what I should do.

Did grandfather feel these spirits as strongly as I do now? I never considered how spirits have a physical presence, but I guess they really do. Walking down the streets of Legerdemain I can feel them against me, even when I can't see anything there. It's as if there are layers or levels to the afterlife somehow. I often imagine I can sense the walls between our worlds opening and closing with the shifting of the earth. I don't really know if that makes any sense or not. I just get these strange feelings. So many things moving in different ways. I wish there were a better way to distinguish what is real and what isn't.

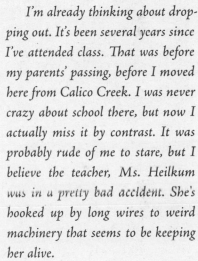

I started school today.

I'm already thinking about dropping out. It's been several years since I've attended class. That was before my parents' passing, before I moved here from Calico Creek. I was never crazy about school there, but now I actually miss it by contrast. It was probably rude of me to stare, but I believe the teacher, Ms. Heilkum was in a pretty bad accident. She's hooked up by long wires to weird machinery that seems to be keeping her alive.

But it's the students that really creep me out. They just seem so different than the kids I knew back home. Seems like they don't care about anything or ANYONE. And of course the classroom is haunted. Some trickster spirit, who seems to revel in playing pranks on the student body. Since it was my first day and I had to introduce myself in front of the class, the ghost took extra satisfaction in embarrassing me by trying to pull my skirt down, using my hair to perform a puppet show, and pouring ink in my mouth while I was talking. I would have to imagine that the other students are completely used to this by now, and yet they acted like it was the funniest thing they've ever seen. The smiles on their faces as I was coughing black ink still burns me up. I've been living that moment over and over all day. And each time I seem to resent the students even more than I do that stupid ghost.

ENTRY #15

I stayed home today. No reason to go out really. Except school. But I feel like I can get a better education here. There are so many books in the Curiosity Shop that are probably better reading than anything in that schoolhouse. Maybe I'll go back tomorrow. But only if Mr. Lorik makes me.

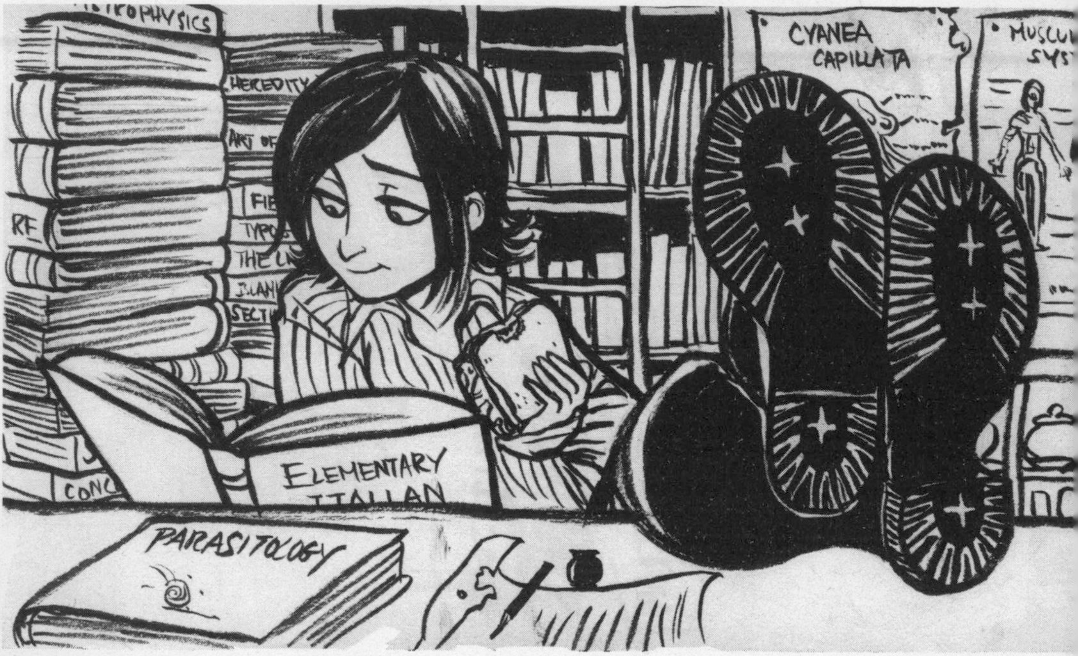
HEREDITY
CYANEA
CAPILLATA
ELEMENTARY
PARASITOLOGY

ENTRY #16

It's rather unfair that the few ghosts whose company I might actually enjoy are the ones who rarely haunt my surroundings. Obviously, my grandfather being the best example of a specter I'd like to see more often. Meanwhile, certain deceased personalities like Sir Ridley the Fifth (of what?) seem to make it their hobby of late to pay me a daily visit. All spirits love to hear themselves speak, and Sir Ridley speaks in volumes. He goes on and on about being a renowned gentleman in his day, but now he is nothing short of repulsive. Even if he still had his missing left arm and leg, his sense of humor would be enough to warrant avoiding him whenever possible. But since I'm the only person who can even pay attention to him after his execution, he loves nothing more than to pop up and yell "Surprise!" at the most inappropriate of times.

ENTRY #17

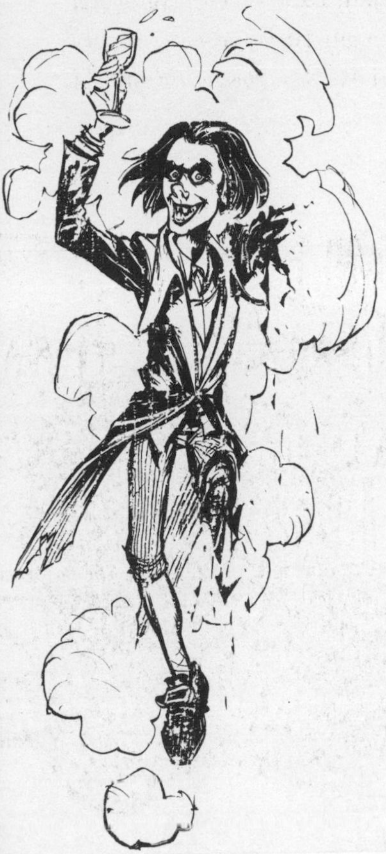

I really need to stop procrastinating and start cleaning up all the unorganized stuff in the attic. There are so many boxes and artifacts. Who knows what things up there might be useful or valuable. Originally I was avoiding it because it's haunted, which is funny coming from me since everything in my life is haunted. But I just get the sense that there's something stranger than just ghosts up there. I get a sudden piercing sensation even walking underneath the drop ladder. I keep meaning to mention it to Grandfather, but of course every time he materializes, it's so unexpected that I never think it is important enough to bring up.

ENTRY #18

I was thinking again about my first trip to Legerdemain. Back then, I knew nothing of this city or the thousands of ghosts that inhabit it. I was so unaware of all the things I can't avoid now, no matter how hard I try. The train that brought me from Calico was filled to the brim with roaming spirits that I convinced myself were just city folk. I remember thinking something was "off" about many of the passengers, but at the time I didn't really know how to process it. Even though it wasn't too long ago, it feels like I was so much younger.

I wonder why so many ghosts travel from the country to Legerdemain? It's as if they're drawn here, the same way I was after my parents passed away. Was there anyone else on that train that was still alive besides me?

Does it really matter whether I'm talking to myself out loud or to some stupid ghost? I'm tired of people staring at me (whether it's in class or on the streets) as if I'm some rickety fool. If I could stop every phantom from interrupting me in the middle of going to the toilet, I surely would. But it seems that as soon as you pass away, you lose all sense of respect for the living. Personal space has no definition when you float in and out of wherever you please.

So yes, I went back to class today and can't say it was really much better than my first day two weeks ago. Nobody even asked me why I didn't show up for all those days. Not that I really care what they were doing in school while I was home.

I got a lot of sleep today. Too bad it was during class. I dreamt about leaving Calico Creek and the few days I spent in the orphanage. It looked a lot nicer than I actually remember it. I wonder what would have happened to me if I had stayed there. Could I have ended up in a home with new parents of some kind? It didn't seem too likely. That place had enough kids—most younger than me—who deserved something better. I'm so grateful to Ms. Dorothy for sneaking me out of there, taking me all the way to the station at the edge of town. I can still remember the hopeful look in her face as she waved goodbye as the train was leaving. I hope she didn't get in any trouble trying to help me. Before I woke up, I remember wondering if Ms. Dorothy ever knew how scary it is to live alone. The only real difference between the city and the orphanage is that the city is a LOT bigger.

So I learned the name of our school specter today. He told me his name is Harland. And compared to my classmates, he's actually starting to seem not so bad. He feels this intrinsic need to be obnoxious and rowdy that is starting to seem downright rational. But I get the sense that there's more to him than he's really letting on—a sad side, that seems to humanize him. I can certainly relate to his loneliness even though I hate to admit it. I'd rather keep myself busy than think about things like not having friends or feeling alone in the world.

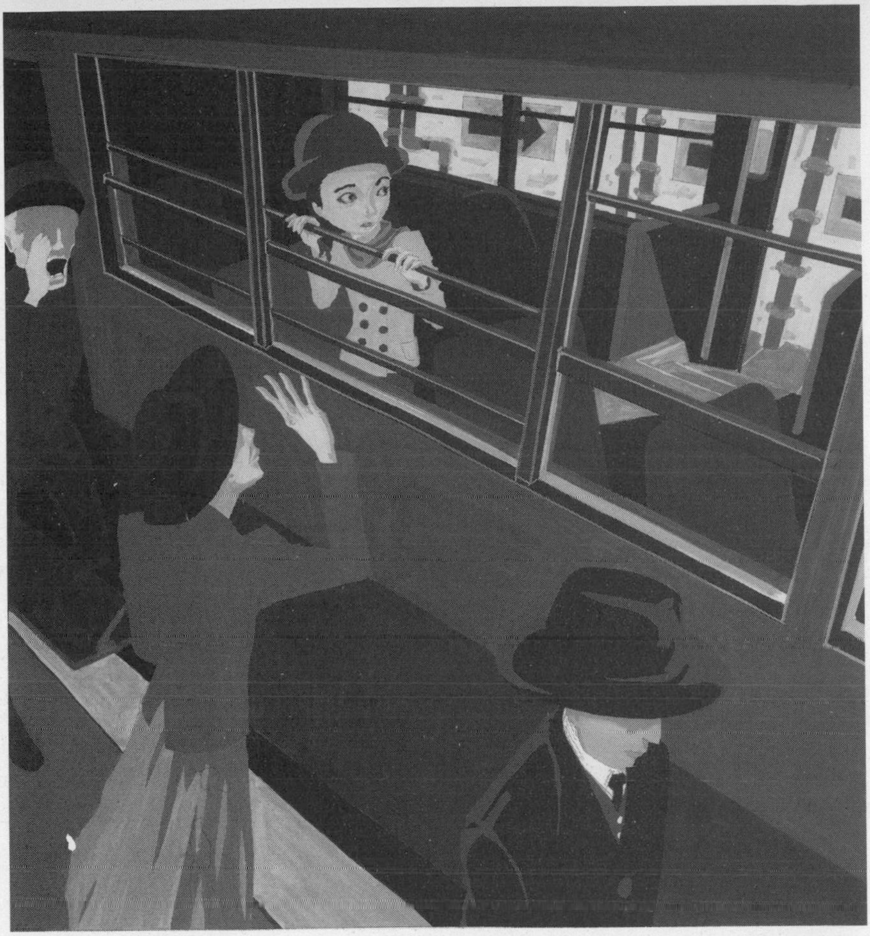

ENTRY #25

So I just did something crazy. I'm out of breath just thinking about it. I helped this guy. His name was Adam Farain. He wasn't alive...but I helped him. And he gave me money! Or at least he led me to a safe deposit box that was filled with money that used to belong to him. He said it didn't matter to him anymore, which I guess makes sense since I don't think ghosts can use money. But what DID matter were these people that he hated. When I first noticed him, he was moaning and wailing like someone had stolen his child or something. But I guess I was the first person to actually hear his voice since he died, because he started following me and begging me to listen. I really didn't want to, but he kept showing up wherever I went. So just to shut him up I agreed to take pity on him. He showed me where these people lived and told me more about how they were driving him crazy. I'll admit they did come across as rather snobbish, but certainly not worth killing oneself over. But it really seemed like life or death for him...which is hard to argue with a ghost about. He insisted that "order must be restored"—his words, not mine.

So I broke into their house, which was more like a museum. These people had a lot of money and a lot of junk. Tacky stuff, mostly—even more tacky than anything in the Curiosity Shop. But Adam only cared about one thing, which was a painting. According to him it was his final masterpiece—painted just before he died. This old couple had won it in an auction, or maybe their kids did. Anyway, they had it stuffed in a damp closet in their basement. And that's what Adam said was tearing him up inside, making him so enraged. I never imagined an artist would be so picky about who bought their work or where it ended up. But I guess for Adam, it was something that weighed deeply on his soul, even after passing away. I went out of my way to be sneaky as we headed out the back window with the painting. My heart was beating like crazy and I kept thinking we'd get arrested. It would be interesting to see them try to keep a ghost in jail.

Anyway, we left the painting on the front stoop of some swanky gallery on Gashon Blvd. I'm curious to check back and see if it ends up on their walls or in their trash.

ENTRY #26

The more I think about it, the more convinced I am that there must be other ghosts out there like Adam. I just need to figure out how to go about finding them. There are so many ghosts out there, how do I know which ones can use my help? And what if they ask me to do something I can't? Am I inviting trouble by encouraging ghosts to haunt me forever? I really wish Grandfather would show up so I could talk to him about it. He must have gone through all this kind of stuff when he first started his detective agency.

ENTRY #29

I've been going through Grandfather's filing cabinets and reading all his old case files. Either he didn't keep the best records, or a lot of information seems to be missing. There's much to absorb, and hopefully some of it will prove useful now that I've seriously considered re-opening the family business.

ENTRY #31

I spent most of the day in class doodling ideas for possible company names. "Agnes Quill: Dead Detective" sounded cool before I realized it sounded like I was the deceased, rather than the potential clients.

ENTRY #32

Mr. Lorik said it's okay if I use the old Curiosity Shop as a lobby for my clients, just the way he and Grandfather did in the old days. I think Mr. Lorik misses my grandfather as much as I do, even though he still won't say more than a sentence or two about him. The more I learn about him, the more unanswered questions I have. There's got to be someone living or dead who can help me understand why my grandfather's spirit still visits our world. I hate to think of him being tormented like the other trapped spirits in this city.

ENTRY #49

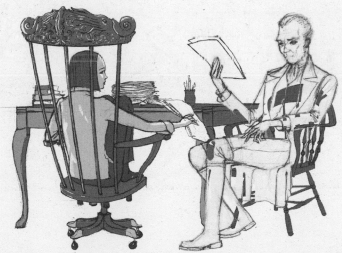

It seems like I've been working every night on some case or other.

I can no longer sleep, even during the day. At this point I would give anything just to be unconscious...not because I'm terribly tired (which I honestly should be after all the research I've been doing), but just to escape from the voices that keep penetrating my head. It's so hard to even separate them anymore. They all seem to bleed into each other. I hear them so much more lately. Even inconsequential

JW/05

conversations seem to travel from the spirit realm into my ears. Too many voices! Some are just stuck mumbling the same few lines over and over, with maddening repetition. I can barely take two steps without feeling them shifting around me. Like walking through a sea of quilts that are pulling in every direction. They wander so aimlessly through this city, I wonder how anyone could possibly help them all.

ENTRY #63

It feels so good to be back at the Curiosity Shop. I've spent the past two days trapped in the basement of Sechrist Manor. Luckily they had more food in storage than Lorik and I have eaten over the past year.

The old man who hired me should have known that he wouldn't be safe in that house, no matter how many ghosts I convinced to haunt it. I still don't even know why those masked men wanted to break in so badly—they moved so fast... I was knocked out and thrown down the staircase before I had a chance to strike up a conversation. The old man died the minute he reached the basement floor, and left without even a peep of thanks for my trouble. Of all the people not to turn into a ghost! If he had, I could have used his help to break free. Instead, I ended up blasting my way out with some gunpowder stored in wooden crates. Might have also blasted my eyebrows.

As soon as I got home, I took a shower and collapsed into bed...but of course I still had trouble sleeping. So here I am writing away. I can't really complain, because like I said, I am grateful to be back above ground.

ENTRY #65

It's difficult to write because my arm is still in a lot of pain. Why? Because some damn monster tried to bite it off, that's why. Something called a Slyu-kug with drool so thick that it completely soaked through the sleeves of my only dress. And I guess I never stopped to think about it before, but sometimes monsters have names like Todd.

ENTRY #67

Today I stopped by the mansion where Willington was just hired. It seems like he's settling in and getting used to having a new home to serve after all these years. The family seems pretty okay with whole zombie thing, but I think their cat is a little wound up by him. I told Willington I'd check up on him every now and then, just in case. Maybe I'll invite him over to the shop on his next day off.

ENTRY #68

It's amazing how being pushed out of the window of a three-story building can get rid of a headache. But it's totally true. I don't feel like going into all the details of my latest job, but let's just say it didn't end so well.

ENTRY #70

I'm still working hard on the Talasca case. It's taken me a few weeks, but I think I'm finally close to tracking down where the amulet is hidden. I just need to get there quickly because I know I'm not the only one looking for it. There are at least two other people who have been inquiring about the penthouse apartment that used to belong to the gypsy thief. If I can sneak in tonight before anyone signs a lease I may have a chance of beating them to it.

ENTRY #71

I've been thinking that the Curiosity Shop could really use a dog. I guess that would just be one more mouth to feed, though, and we still aren't exactly turning profit. Not enough of the cases I've taken on have really paid me for helping them. And it's hard to follow up with them after they've left this dimension. It wouldn't bother me if we didn't keep getting so many threatening notices about unpaid bills. Maybe I should look into a real part time job. Something a bit more reliable than detective work, that doesn't involve dumpster diving or exploring sewers.

ENTRY #75

Beatrice Osteri came by the shop again today. She thinks I'm gonna help set her up with one of those ghosts that haunt the shipping yards. Even with all her jewels and wealth she couldn't pay me enough to play matchmaker to spirits. It's too creepy to even humor the idea.

ENTRY #76

The power went out again. Luckily this time it was only for an hour or so. But still long enough to make me nervous. I'm positive we paid that last bill, but not sure how we'll cover the next one...

ENTRY #77

I turned down another job today. This really sleazy guy who may be the worst person I've ever met. He fully admitted how he cheated on his wife with all these other women. And I wish I threw him out of the shop as soon as he told me that, because it got a lot worse. He told me how he killed these women afterwards. Paid to cover it all up because he works for this big company that has the money to do stuff like that. Well, I guess his wife finally wised up because not only did she kick him to the curb, but left him with a curse to boot. The idiot didn't even realize his wife was studying black magic while he was out slumming. Serves him right, I say. I also called the cops.

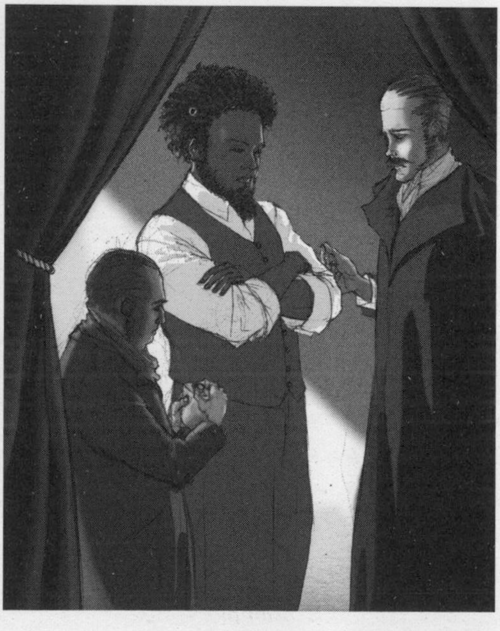

ENTRY #78

J.H., the mass murderer I mentioned, came back to the store today. He only stopped in for a few minutes and was more paranoid than anyone I'd ever seen. Scared out of his wits; he said he'd been running around the city all night. He offered me an insane amount of money to help him. I don't know what he expects me to do! I told him to keep running.

I only feel bad because it really was a lot of money... and Mr. Lorik still hasn't found a way to pay off those men that keep threatening to close us down.

ENTRY #79

At some point I'll write a detailed description of my trip to the Buried Homes and Gardens. Right now I just need some sleep.

ENTRY #80

So much for getting any sleep. I've been tossing and turning all night. For the brief moments that I am able to doze off I keep having disturbing dreams. Mostly about having to drink down glasses full of maggots and worms...and even worse, being zipped up in burlap bags and buried alive. Obviously it's me just reflecting on all the horrible things I've witnessed over the past few days. Sometimes it's impossible to shake these things off.

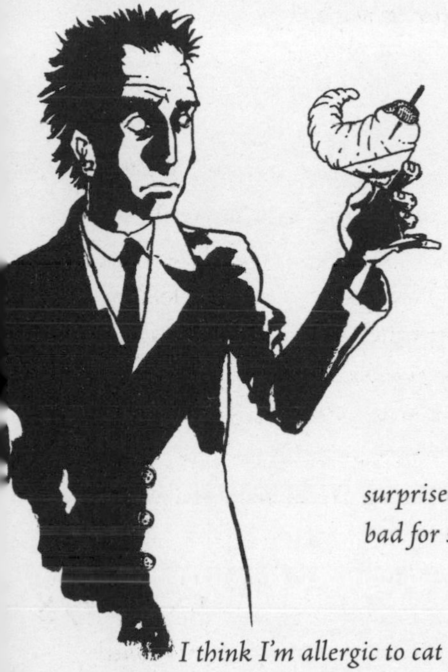

ENTRY #86

I spent most of the past week helping Niel rebuild a passageway that collapsed during the recent earthquakes. It was a lot of work, but I think they should have everything back in working order soon. Niel can actually be pleasant company when he's too busy to open his mouth.

ENTRY #90

I actually had a pretty uneventful day! I'm as surprised as anyone else. Even school didn't feel THAT bad for some reason. I must be getting old and boring.

ENTRY #94

I think I'm allergic to cat hair. Or at least girls who can transform into cats.

ENTRY #95

Is it possible to survive on a non-bread diet? I don't think I can stomach the stuff after all this business with spirit-body transfers. As if I wasn't paranoid enough! To think that even food could be haunted!

ENTRY #100

Somehow I got invited to another ghost social event. You'd think I would have learned my lesson years ago, but I felt obliged to go to this one, on account of it being a surprise for Reverend Hansard, the roguish spirit who helped me out of at least three recent scrapes. The party was mostly people long dead and out of touch with the living. (In fact, one lady claimed to be a thousand years dead.) But the most interesting part of the evening was meeting a cross-dimensional warlock who showed me how to cast a Manifest Spell. It was sort of like pulling a rabbit

out of your hat. Only in my case, I created a griffin, and I didn't need a hat; just some special talc powder and a melody. It was tricky to hum the song without some practice, but after a few tries I felt a strange vibration in my wrists, channeling some far off current. When I clapped my hands just right, the lights in the room flickered and the griffin spiraled out of them like smoke, before fading away. The warlock explained that the Manifest Spell is mostly a parlor trick, but I can see how it could prove useful in the right context. I wonder if Mr. Lorik would teach me any enchantments? Or at least let me go through his private book collection...

ENTRY #100

Today I was visited by some interesting people who were alive (rare enough), not interested in closing down the shop (whew!), or killing me (always nice). They said they worked for a group of teachers or something called the Data Analysis Keep, which claims to have been around for a long, long while. At any rate, one of them told me he knew a ghost that recommended we meet. I'm not sure why exactly, but they seem really interested in learning everything about me. It was like I was some mystery that they wanted to solve (kind of ironic). I'm not sure if client confidentiality applies to ghosts, but I ended up telling a few stories, like how Beatrice and I first met, and how she helped against the sentient legs that tried to kill me. They wanted to know more, but I thought it best to not give them too much information right away. Before

they left, they mentioned something about artists illustrating some of my accounts. But by that point it was already pretty late and I didn't know how to respond. I just told them I'd think about it. If they really have as many resources as they say they do, I'm wondering if they can help me find out who killed my grandfather. Certainly something to think about.

But I really SHOULD be trying to get some sleep...

ART GALLERY
(further renderings of the subject)

JESS FINK

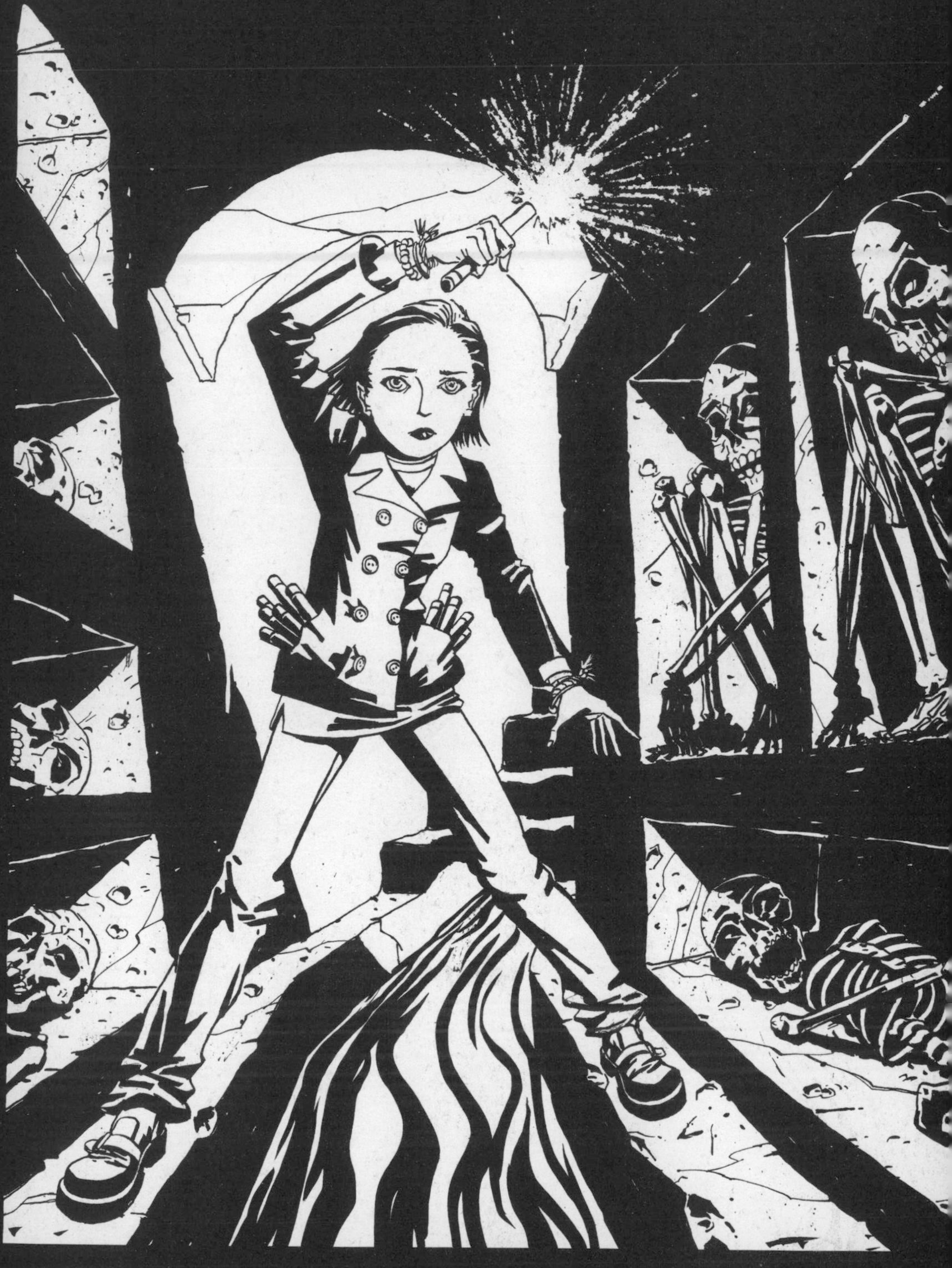

JASON HO

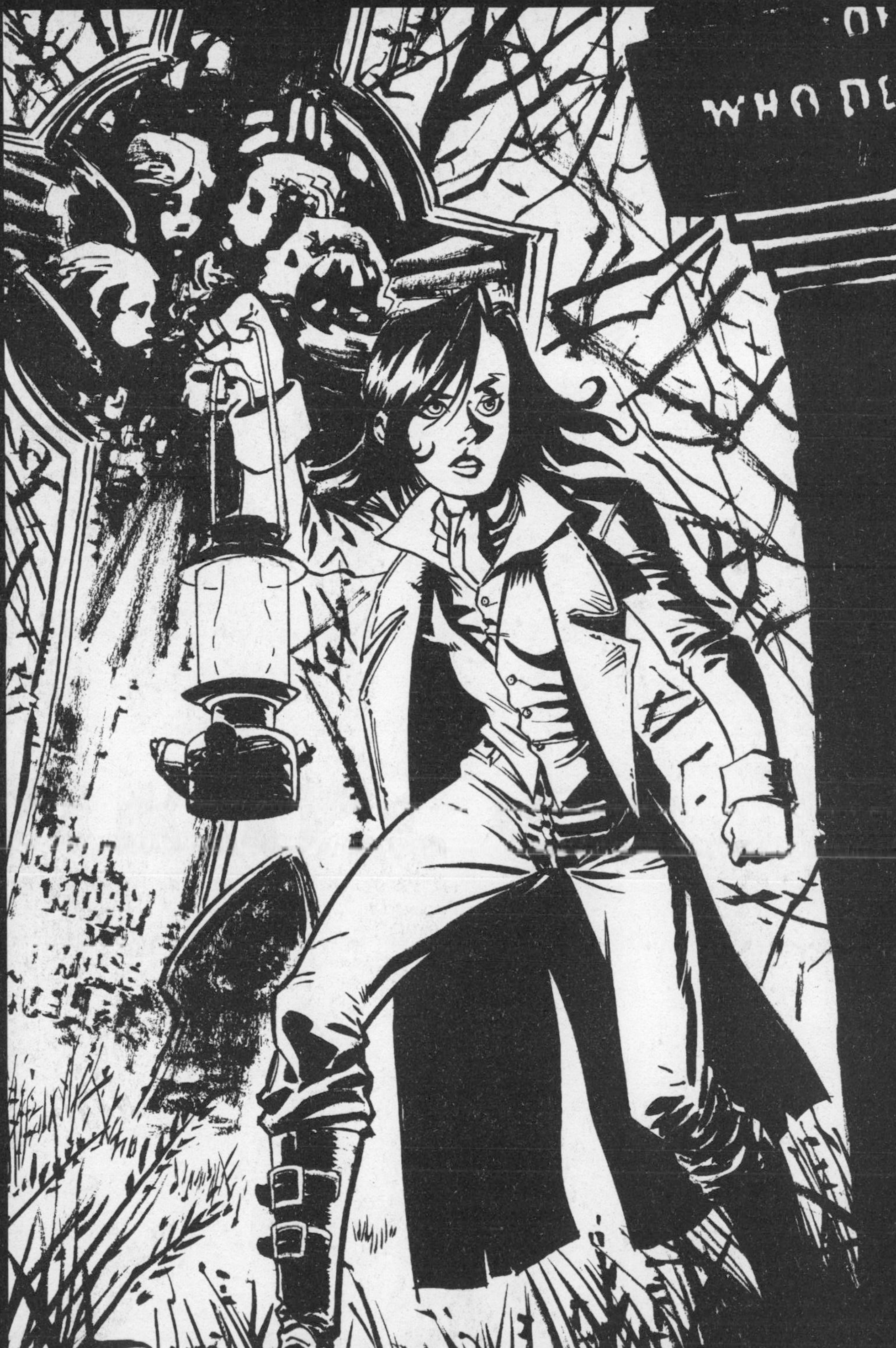

JEFF ZORNOW

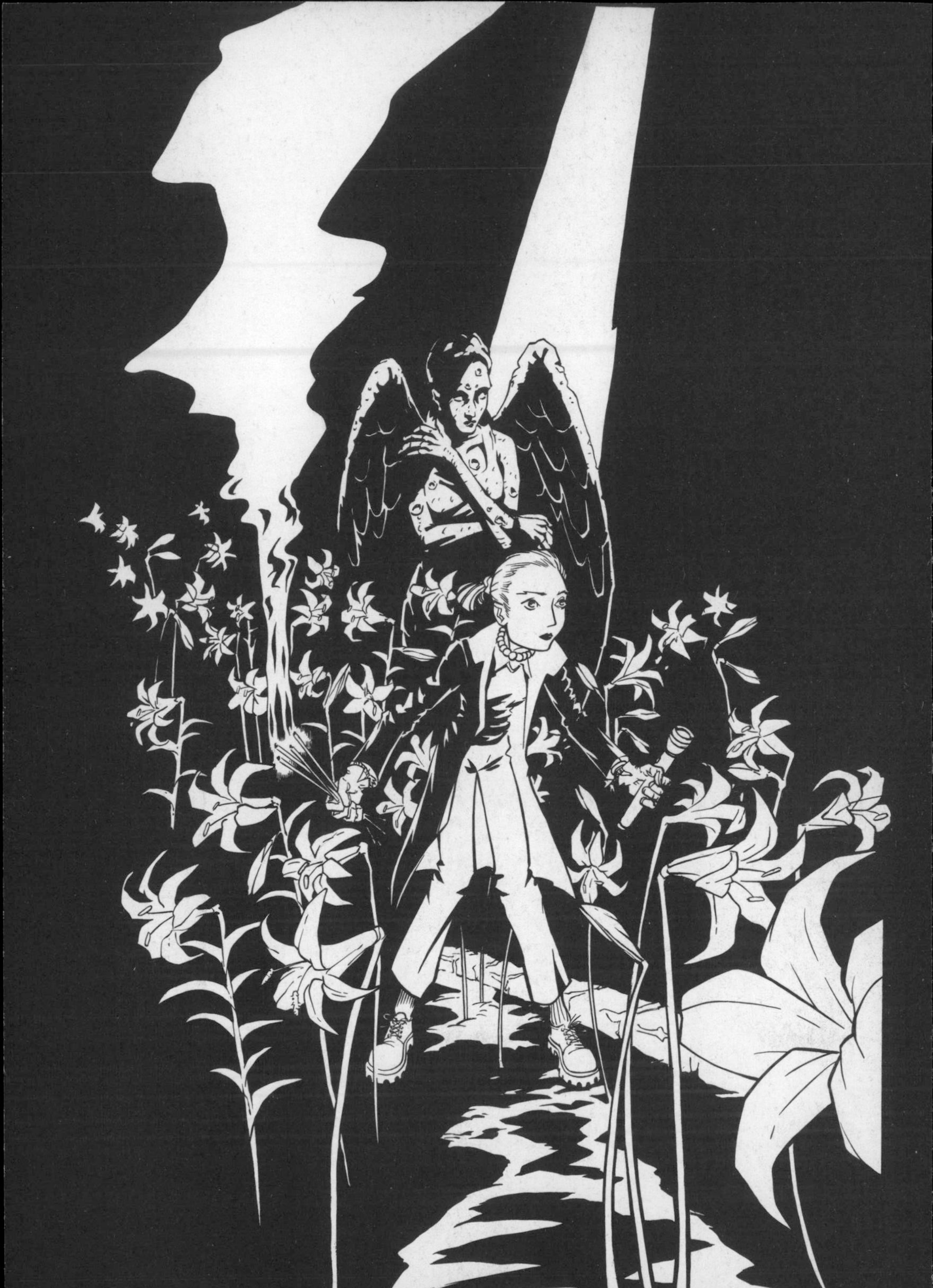

JASON HO *and* ADAM DEKRAKER

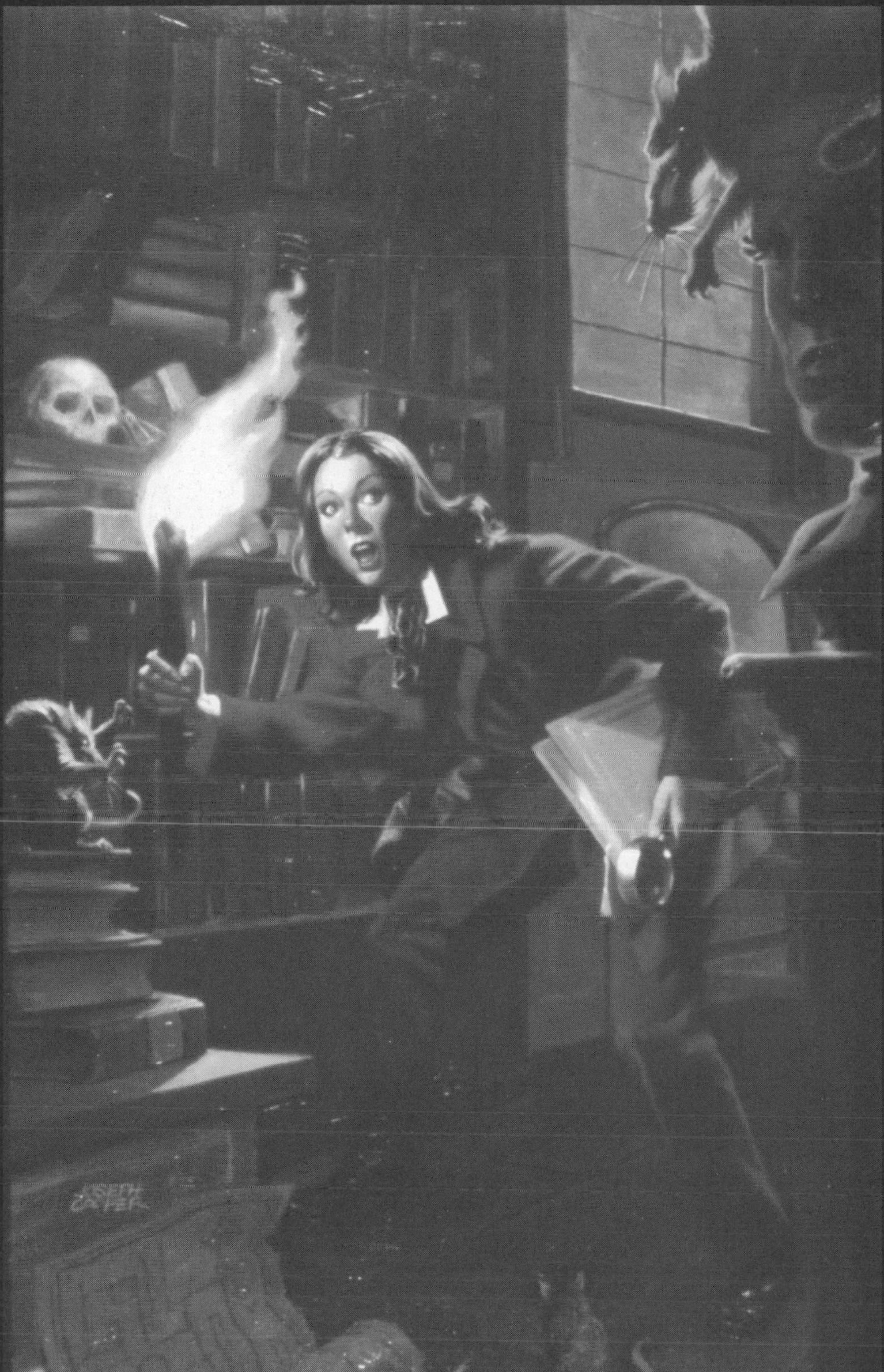

JOSEPH COOPER

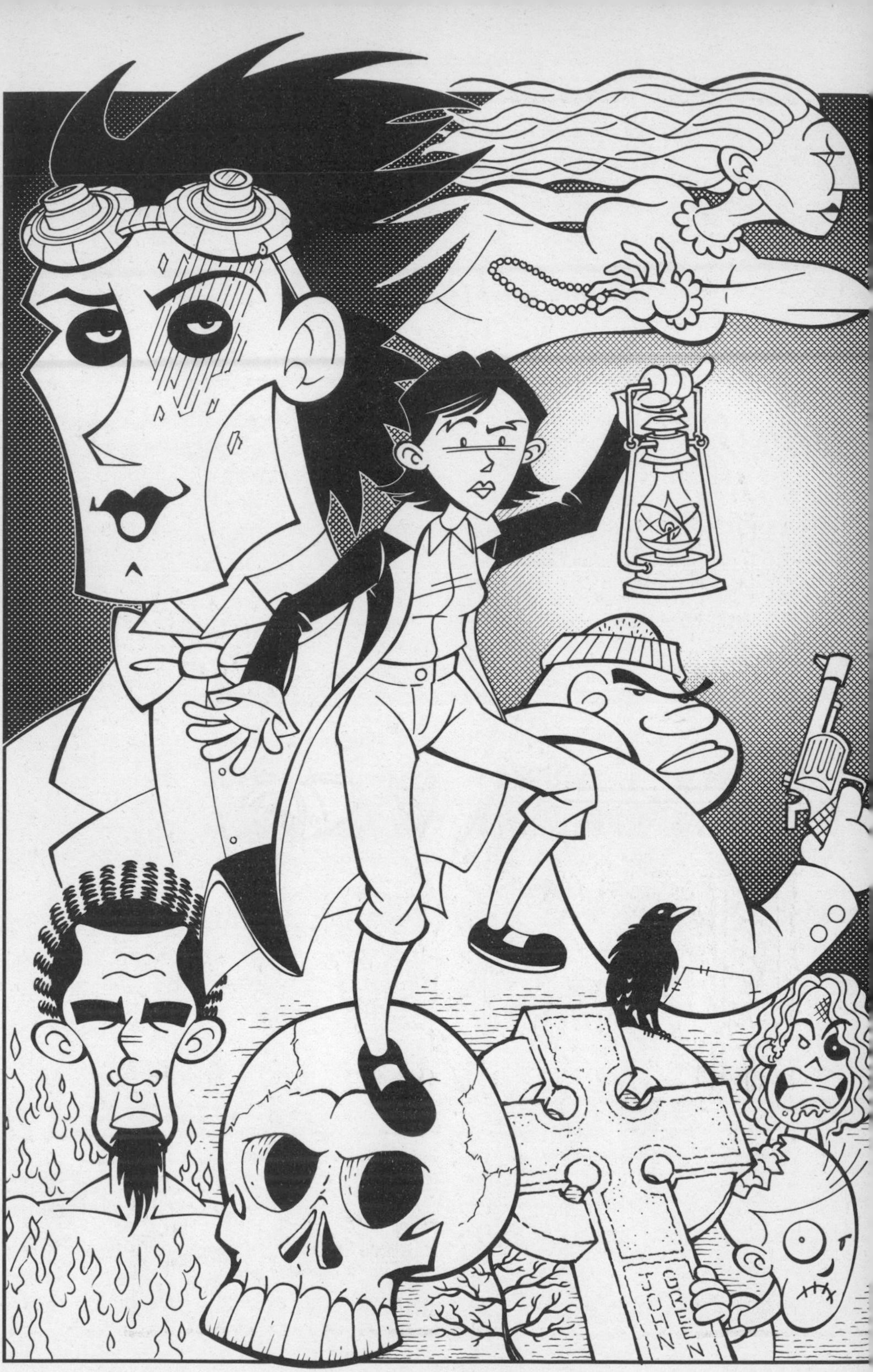
JOHN GREEN

JOHN GREEN

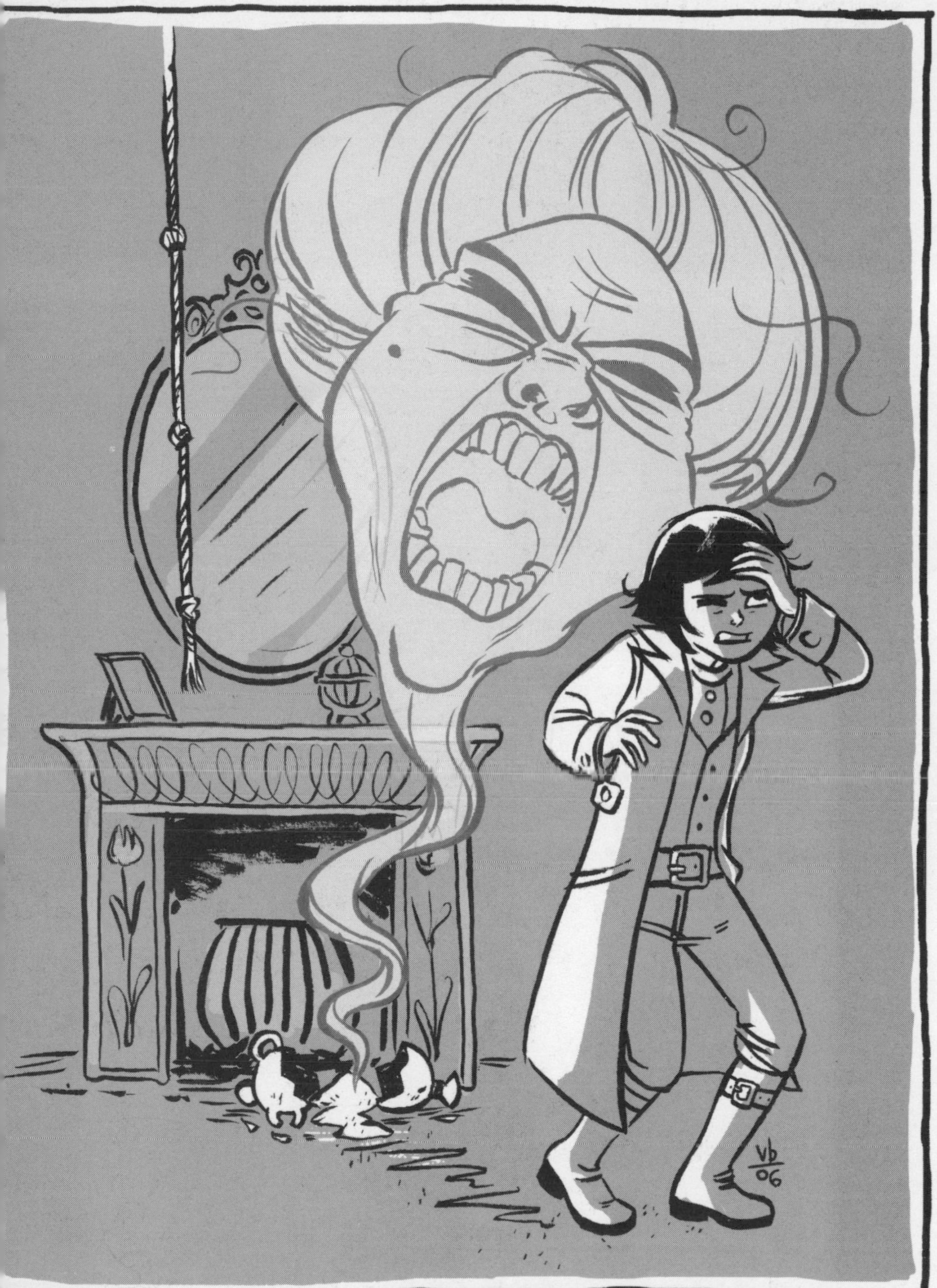

VERA BROSGOL

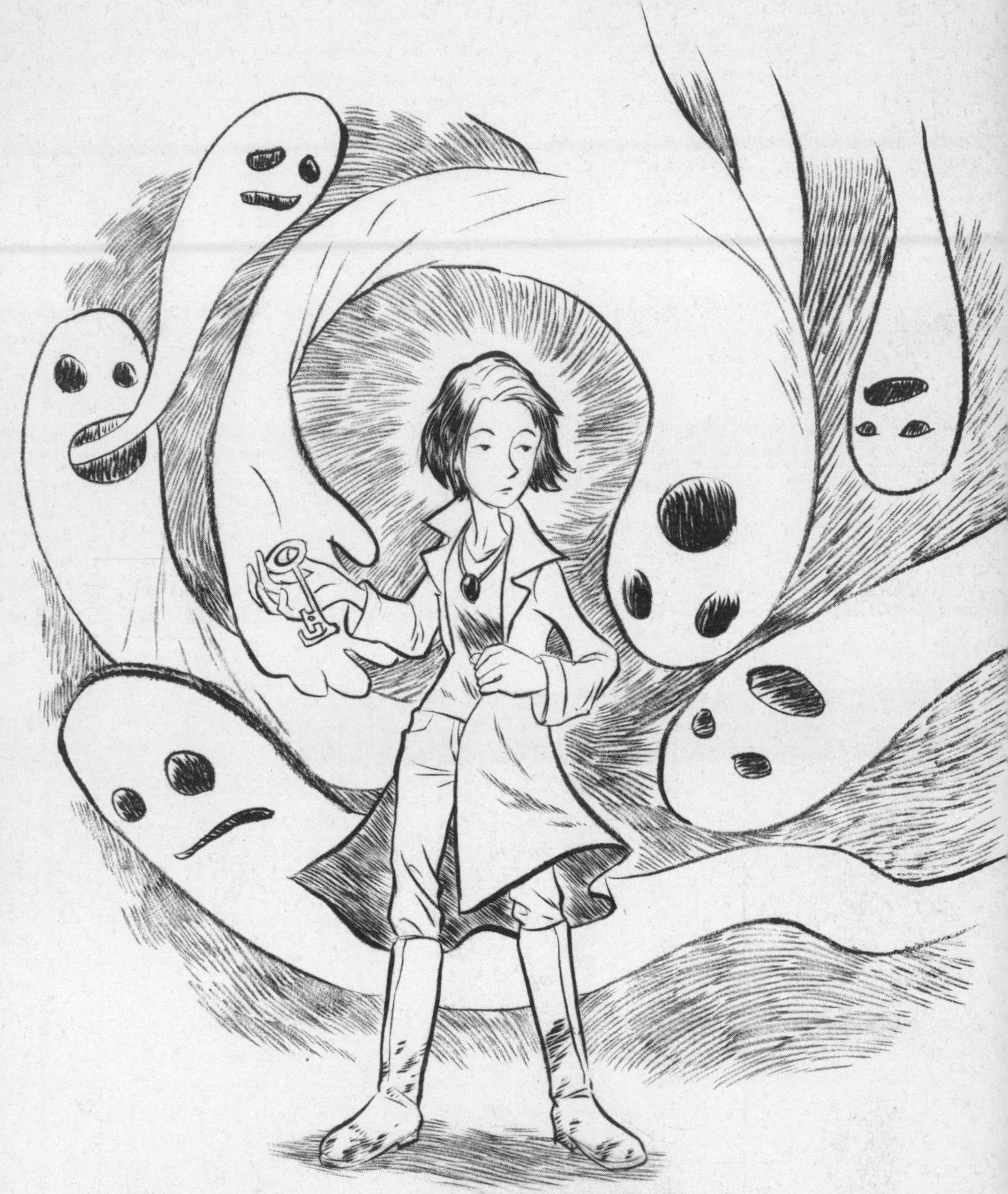

NEIL BABRA

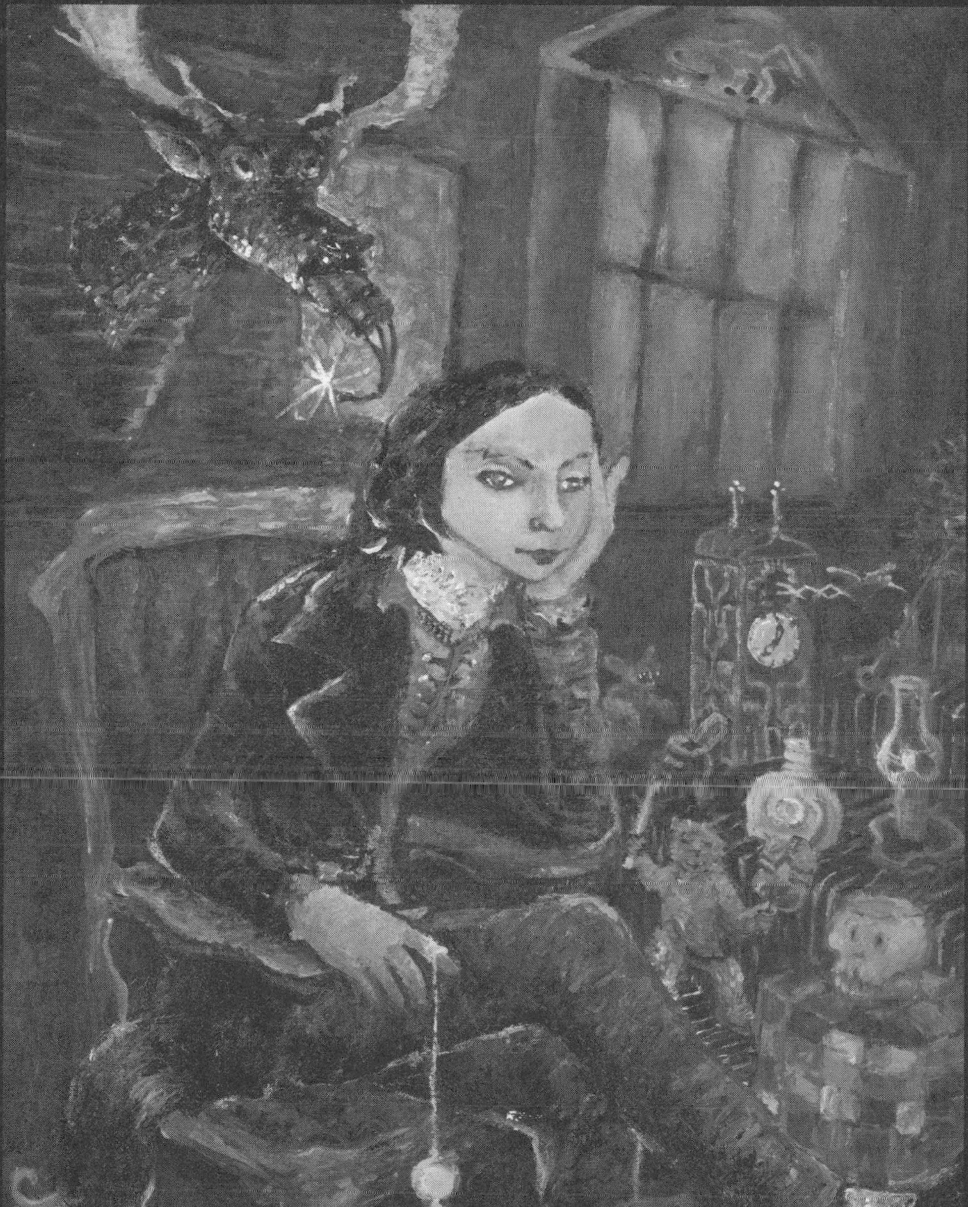

MISS LASKO-GROSS

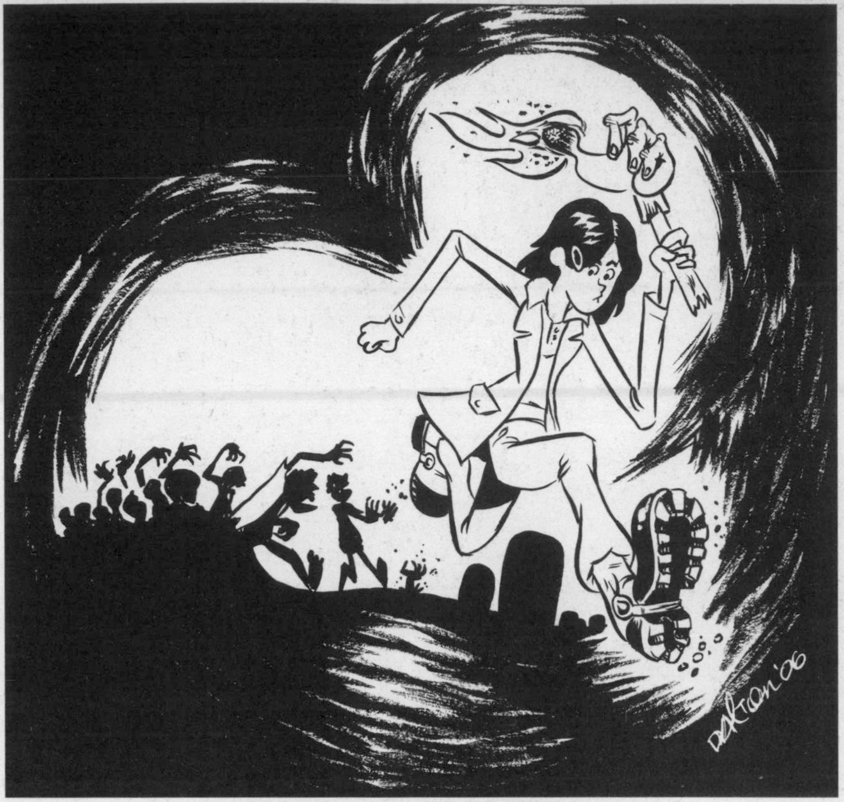
dalton '06

DALTON WEBB

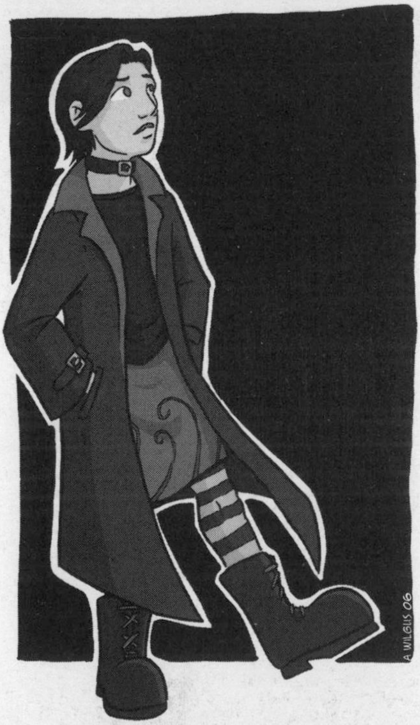
A WILGUS 06

ALISON WILGUS

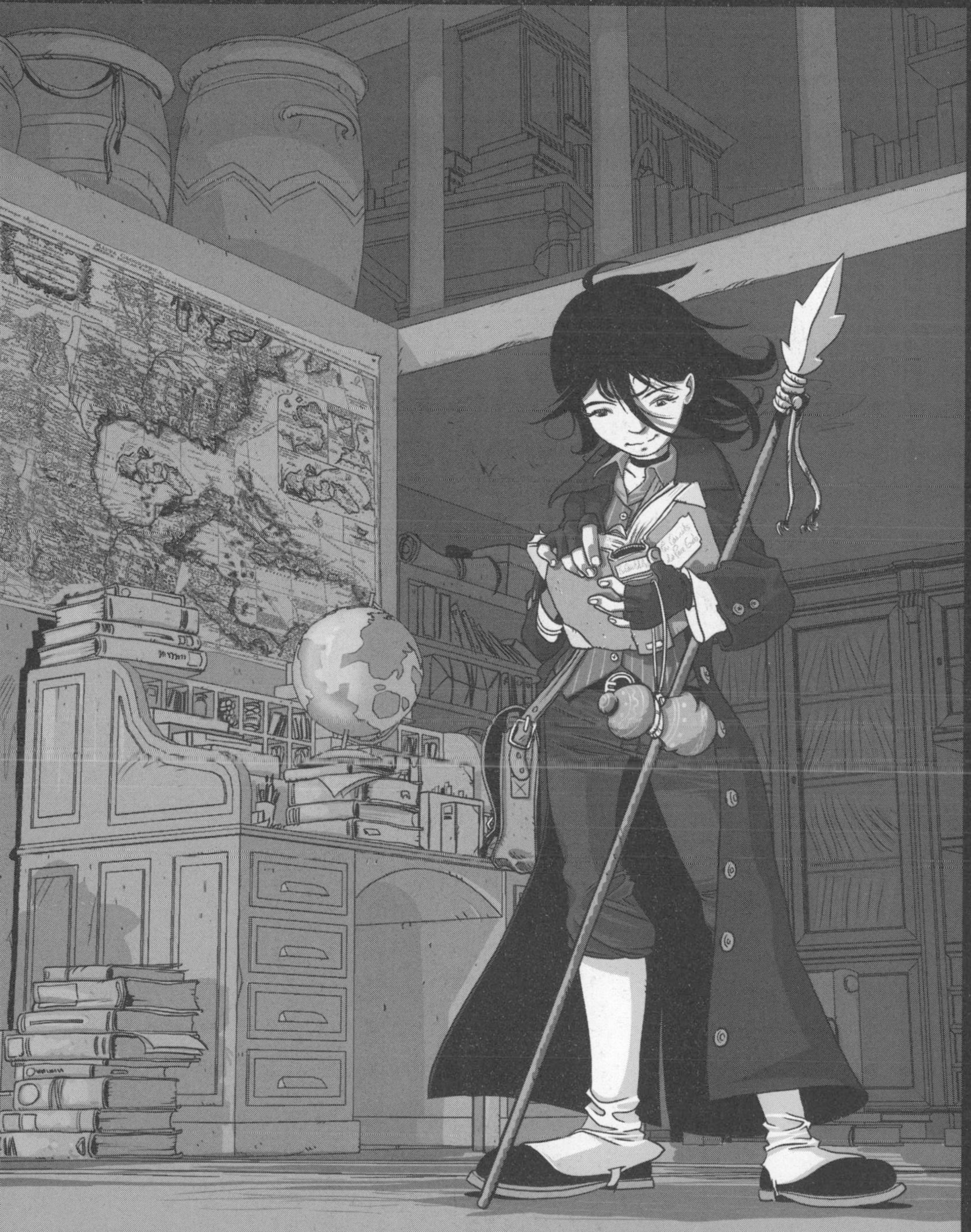
Bannister 06

BANNISTER

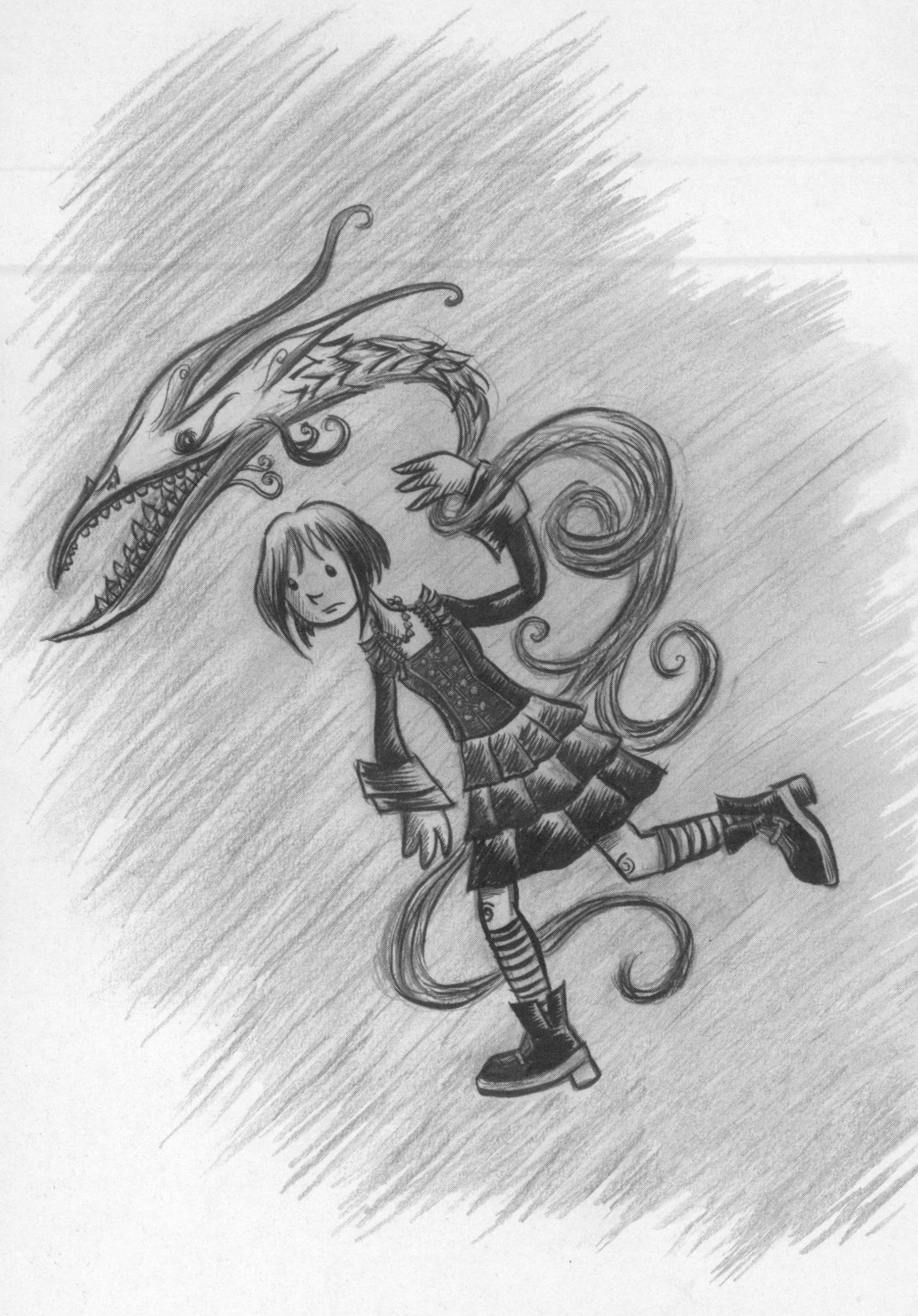

DAVE ROMAN

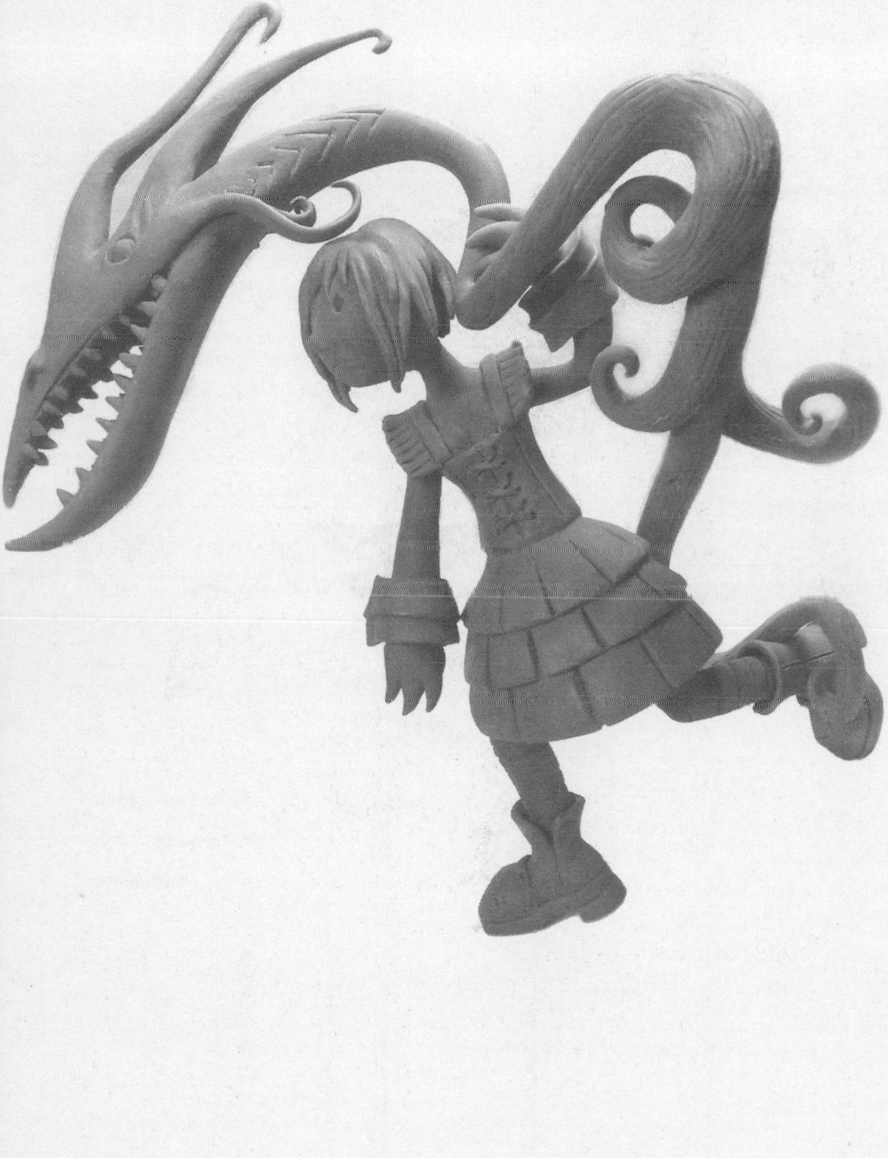

LEA HERNANDEZ

CREATOR PROFILES

This edition is the culmination of work by several accomplished artisans dedicated to the goals of the Data Analysis Keep. Some were subjected to hours of research spent socializing with dead people, getting trapped in crypts, and in one case being buried alive on and off for several days.

Dave Roman

Originating from a Long Island off the coast of the mainland, Dave is known for writing a series of pamphlets called *Jax Epoch and the Quicken Forbidden*, which focus on the exploits of a destructive teenage sorceress. He works in an editorial capacity for the *Nickelodeon* monthly periodical and has been known to independently draw things people have referred to as "cute." These would include *Astronaut Elementary* and a contribution to the third *Flight* anthology. Dave first began writing about Agnes Quill while he was studying at the School of Visual Arts, where he began assembling artists with the hopes of turning her stories into illustrated archives.

www.yaytime.com

Jason Ho

A graduate of the SVA, Jason was the first artist to adapt Agnes Quill into illustrated form. A former laborer in the photography trade, he has spent many hours working in dark rooms being exposed to harsh chemicals. He has done artwork that was used in advertisements for fashionable textile manufacturers such as Babyphat.

www.idrawcartoons.blogspot.com

Jeff Zornow

Originating from a self-proclaimed Motor City, Jeff's line-work has appeared in several places, including comics based on George Romero's cinematic feature, *Day of the Dead*. He's written and illustrated tales of horror for *Cryptic Magazine*, been featured in *Comiculture* and used his art as a means of promotion and packaging for musicians.

www.yourmidnightreader.com

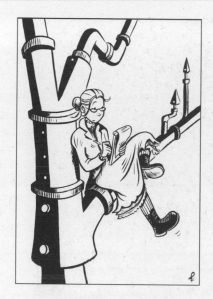

Raina Telgemeier

Born in a Bay Area, Raina has built a reputation for archiving events in her own life into a series of digests under the moniker *Take-Out*. Her work has also appeared in the *Broad Appeal* and *Reflux* anthologies, as well as a computer feed called Smilecomics.com.
She has garnered much acclaim for her works resulting in Eisner and Ignatz Award nominations. Raina is currently working on a series of graphic novels depicting a gang of adolescent entrepreneurs called *The Baby-sitters Club*, two of which novels are currently available in all legitimate bookshops.

www.goraina.com

Jen Wang

A scholar of political and social science by day and master of illustration by night, Jen is known to enjoy big cities, biological mishaps, and stars. She has several ties to the *Flight* anthology and an allegiance to the Pants Press collective.

www.jenwang.net

ENDING NOTE

The stories and archives of Agnes Quill compiled in this printed edition are by no means complete. We hope to continue what we consider a positive and mutually beneficial relationship with the young detective. Further documentation and publishing of her unique activities can only lead to a more comprehensive understanding of the spirit world, and its connection to our own.